DOROTHY DAY

Easton CW Farm, circa 1937.

DOROTHY DAY

*Portraits by
Those Who Knew Her*

Rosalie G. Riegle

ORBIS BOOKS

Maryknoll, New York 10545

Founded in 1970, Orbis Books endeavors to publish works that enlighten the mind, nourish the spirit, and challenge the conscience. The publishing arm of the Maryknoll Fathers & Brothers, Orbis seeks to explore the global dimensions of the Christian faith and mission, to invite dialogue with diverse cultures and religious traditions, and to serve the cause of reconciliation and peace. The books published reflect the views of their authors and do not represent the official position of the Maryknoll Society. To learn more about Maryknoll and Orbis Books, please visit our website at www.maryknoll.org.

Manufactured in the United States of America.
Manuscript editing and typesetting by Joan Weber Laflamme.

Library of Congress Cataloging-in-Publication Data

Riegle, Rosalie G.
  Dorothy Day : portraits by those who knew her / Rosalie G. Riegle.
      p. cm.
Includes bibliographical references and index.
  ISBN 1-57075-467-5
  1. Day, Dorothy, 1897–1980. 2. Catholics—United States—Biography.
3. Catholic Worker Movement—History—20th century. I. Title.
  BX4705.D283 R54 2003
  267'.182'092—dc21

                              2003009844

To my grandchildren,
with hope that their generation
will shock the world into Beatitude living.

Contents

Foreword

Memories of Passion
and Abundant Love

KATE HENNESSY

My mother and I have spent many long, winter evenings in Vermont, gnawing away at the enigma that is Dorothy Day. To have known Dorothy means spending the rest of your life wondering what hit you. On one hand, she has given so many of us a home, physically and spiritually; on the other, she has shaken our very foundations.

She is two people to me—an uneasy marriage of grandmother and public figure. When I was a child, she was one fantastic granny, sending gifts from Africa and postcards from Russia. Much about her was magical, such as her room, stacked with books and papers, possibly in some order, but I doubt it. I never dared touch any of it, not because I thought she would mind, but because I felt I might carelessly disturb the mystery that was her life.

Her briefcase, plain and more battered than most, too, was magical, full of letters from people and places around the world—Uruguayan priests, Californian farm workers, folks from Minnesota, and who knows whom, what, and from where. It also contained instruments of pure magic, her notebook and pen, for to me, the jewel in the crown was the fact that she was a writer.

She was not a comforting grandmother. I never cuddled up to her for hugs and kisses, but she was passionate—for Dostoevski and detective novels, for Italian opera and Russian icons, for her faith and her work. Passion, I believe, stirs the soul and juices up the psyche of a young girl faster than any grandmotherly words.

Recently, I came across a card she sent to me when I was fifteen or so: "You have never written me a letter," she wrote. I was mortified. Was this

Originally published in the *Catholic Worker*, October-November, 1997.

true? Was I shamed into writing her? I don't remember. Perhaps I felt that you just didn't write a chatty, kid's letter to Dorothy Day. I don't know if I understood much of who she was and what she was doing. It was difficult to stop looking through the limited and distorted lens of my own painful experiences growing up poor.

Of course, there is much to be thankful for, first, simply for being raised to believe that writing is an honorable, and, better yet, powerful act. Also, to see a vibrant, female life in action is heady stuff for an adolescent girl. Then, there was the wonderful chaos that is the Catholic Worker.

Clearly, there is much wildness in my feelings for my grandmother—love, admiration, annoyance, inspiration, and a vague sense of bewilderment. Sometimes, I cannot even tell whether her influence is minimal or pervasive.

People have asked me, "Are you going to follow your grandmother's footsteps?" as if I am more qualified, or obligated, than they. Oh, those footsteps with their firm imprint of the Dorothy Day Stomp. They are very difficult to see, never mind follow. I cannot follow another's faith or vision, and without a faith or vision of one's own, actions are suspect and false.

Her power and presence grow stronger as I get older, with all the complexities, I hope and imagine, that might have occurred, if she were still alive. I believe she grows, after her death, in as complex a manner as she lived her life, and I must resist my tendency to tidy up. She does not mold well, in either sense of the word.

When talking or writing about her, we rely much upon vignettes of her life, brief glimpses, words remembered, advice given, admonishments made. She is an intensely personal legend, and everyone has his or her own Dorothy Day, which seems fitting. The trick is to see her as she was, not as our hopes, reactions, and personal experiences interpret her. I believe we must be just in how we remember her and are inspired by her. So often we tend toward extremes and claim she's either a saint or deeply flawed, forgetting that since when has anyone easily lent themselves to such specific categories?

Her call is powerful, and it brings up powerful reactions, both negative and positive. My mother has often been asked, "This is all well and good, but what about you?" by those who, surprised by Dorothy's life, immediately retreat to the personal. They cloak themselves in the respectability of the well-meaning, as if the fearful sight of so much faith and vision is an abyss they would rather not peer into. The role of motherhood, then, becomes the point upon which the full value of Dorothy's life rests. Oh, she must have been a neglectful parent, they say, and breathe a sigh of relief, for they can safely dismiss everything my grandmother has done.

Then there is the impulse to send her off into sainthood, which can be as lethal as complete rejection. Can't quite bring ourselves to dismiss her teachings? Then, place them beyond the pale of us average folk. Can you imagine what she thinks of that? I'm more than a little unclear on the role and definitions of saint and sainthood. I am certainly ignorant of their complexities, but I believe that we run the risk of using them to eliminate neatly and firmly the complexities of Dorothy Day, and, in the process, let ourselves off the hook. And will sainthood make her a better source of inspiration? Easier to pray to? Will it validate her life's work? We are already amazingly blessed. What more do we need?

She is difficult to pigeonhole or place on a favorite pedestal, and she is a dangerous woman to admire. Admiration, in itself, shows that perhaps there is too much time spent in thinking about what should be done and not doing it. Admiration is a comforting distance at which to stand. As she said, "Too much praise makes you feel you must be doing something terribly wrong."

There is clearly something about her story that grabs the imagination. My mother receives many proposals for books, movies, and plays, but I feel we are having difficulty portraying her with the same quality of inspiration she engenders. She is a heroine in ways that are rather inexplicable, acting heroically in ways we don't know how to dramatize. Perhaps we are distancing ourselves and relying upon secondhand or stale views of lives of the poor and feelings of faith, views not held imaginatively but to support convenient beliefs and personal platforms. She turned the life of poverty into something dynamic, full of richly simple moments for those who have nothing. If she was able to imbue poverty with such power, along with a richness of faith and a world view that appreciated the lovely, small details, while keeping a constant eye on the big picture, then can we not do the same with portraying her life?

Memory is fragile, unpredictable, and severely limited. It seems dangerous for memories to be the primary way a person lives on, for they lack wholeness and stability. Dorothy lives on in her writings, but, as any honest writer admits, writing is fragmented, with carefully constructed thoughts and reconstructed autobiography. Her work definitely continues with a life of its own, which shows how on the mark she was. What more is there but to honor her through finding my own path of vision and faith?

There is much my mother and I may not ever discover through our musings, but I have no doubt that my grandmother gives me abundant love and encouragement, along with an increasingly insistent push, a ghostly hand firmly planted on the small of my back, barely there, but never letting up.

Preface

Who was Dorothy Day? She was a writer, an activist, the co-founder of a lay movement that continues to follow her precepts of poverty, pacifism, personalism, and commitment to justice. She was also a devoted mother and grandmother, a faithful reader of the Russian classics, a fascinating and vibrant storyteller, and a person of prayer—perhaps even a mystic, say some of her friends. Her writing was rooted in her own life experience and she wrote always, mostly of her journey to God through the Catholic Worker movement and the many people it touched. She was sometimes impatient and impassioned, sometimes weary and retiring, but most often relaxed and listening deeply to the many who wanted to talk to her. This book recalls some of these conversations and the memories they evoke.

It's easy to mythologize this woman who said, "Don't call me a saint," and yet has been declared a "servant of God," the first step in the official canonization process. "Dorothy stories" abound. She gave a valuable diamond ring to a woman on the streets. She refused a grant from the Ford Foundation. She stuck petitions under a statue of St. Joseph. She never had a social security card. She was jailed for not taking shelter during the air-raid drills of the 1950s and was arrested in support of the United Farm Workers when she was seventy-five. These and other stories, told and retold in person and in print, give cohesiveness to the Catholic Worker movement she founded and ensure her place in the annals of Christian peacemaking. They might also create an unapproachable saint, one whom people could easily dismiss. To keep that from happening is the purpose of this book. In these pages I hope to present a real and believable Dorothy Day, one drawn in portraits from people who knew her personally.

I met Dorothy Day only once—in 1969—but she and the movement she founded "stuck in my craw," as my father would have said. I found that her pacifism helped to ground my work against the Vietnam war, but I made no changes in my day-to-day life. Instead, my attraction to the Catholic Worker was deferred to other tasks—raising four daughters, getting my doctorate, helping my husband to become a probate judge, gaining tenure in English at Saginaw Valley State University. In 1983 I decided to write the Catholic Worker into my life, even if I didn't think I could live it. So I began work on an oral history of the movement, *Voices from the Catholic Worker.* Ten years later the book was published by Temple University Press.

Conducting the 208 interviews for that book didn't diminish my appetite for the Worker, though, and in 1995, after the end of my marriage, I started the Mustard Seed Catholic Worker of Saginaw with Sister Leona Sullivan and Jeannine Coallier. Our community has expanded, and we now have two houses, both offering hospitality to women and children. I live in the original one-hundred-year-old house, now named the Jeannine House after our dear friend, who died in 1999. I find myself very much at home in this small house of resistance and hospitality, not only in the work we do but in the community I've made with Renaye Fewless and Margaret and Thalia Schiesswohl. Finally, after all these years, my insides and my outsides are starting to match.

That's a sketch of who I am, but this book about Dorothy Day inevitably reveals a good deal more about me as well as about the narrators who have shared their memories. I am revealed in the book's arrangement and in the selections from the 134 interviews I conducted, and the narrators are revealed in what they remember and choose to talk about. It is *their* Dorothy they're describing and their relationship with her that made such a difference in their lives.

This is not a biography that sets itself out to construct Dorothy Day's life "as it was," but rather one that describes her as she lives in memories. Just as chronology is often not the organizing principle of our memories, neither is it the scheme that organizes this text. Rather, in the portrait of Dorothy that follows, I have let what the narrators remember determine the structure of both the individual chapters and the book as a whole. The first chapter presents Dorothy and her fellow Catholic Workers, with stories going back to the early years. The second chapter tells how her spirituality nourished an ongoing politics of peace and justice. The third describes this life-giving spirituality, and the fourth gives insights into her relationships with family and friends. A long chapter answers the oft-asked question, "What was she like?" and the final chapter chronicles her last years. The book concludes with narrators musing on her influence and the question of official canonization.

Anyone who has tried to construct a family album knows how many decisions lie behind every selection. This verbal family album is no exception. Because I was working with living memory, I necessarily recorded little about Dorothy's early life, concentrating instead on her life in the Catholic Worker movement. With far more material than could ever fit in a book, I take full responsibility for the hard editing decisions, using the avoidance of repetition and the principle of relevancy as two of my criteria for cutting. In selecting what to include, I've tried not to mediate too much between my ideas and those of the narrators, remembering the blunt honesty I learned from Robert Coles, "to take people at their word." The narrators, of course, were selective as well, and what they told me about Dorothy shows their own core values.

For example, conservative Catholics project her acknowledged liturgical conservatism in later years as proof that she was conservative in other ways. More liberal Catholics pass on the stories that support her anarchism, her wry subversive humor, and her trenchant criticism of both the state and the church she loved. In both cases I was continually struck by the intersections of truth and subjectivity that lie in all our tellings of the world. In that light I often found myself asking, "What is a Dorothy story?"

People who knew and worked with Dorothy are often asked (or volunteer) to speak and write about her. Understandably, they search for vivid stories to illustrate the points they want to make, a technique she herself used to good effect. In fact, some of the stories that most invite factual criticism may have originated with Day herself, as she always taught through stories.

Among the most famous and hard to pin down of the "Dorothy stories" is the one about her giving a diamond ring to a woman from the street who often came into the Catholic Worker. When questioned, she retorted, "Do you suppose God made diamonds only for the rich?" I have not yet found anyone who actually heard Dorothy say those words, but they seem plausible to me, given her sardonic humor and her clear knowledge that people who are poor have the same longings as the rest of us. But did she pose as the model for Duchamps' "Nude Descending a Staircase," a story published at least twice and repeated to me several times in interviews? Decidedly not, as the dates of the picture's composition and when she was in Paris don't match. However, there are tinges of truth here. Before her conversion, Day did serve as an artist's model, she did have the narrow shoulders and wide hips of the Duchamps model, and she lived a bohemian life, both in Chicago and New York, and probably in Paris.

What the Duchamps story tells us about, I think, is how much those who worked and lived with Dorothy wanted to know about her pre-conversion life, wanted to know how she wrestled with the problems they themselves may have been facing. But I cut the artist's model story because, while all tales reveal the teller, this one spoke more of the hunger for myth than to the workings of memory I was interested in preserving.

When I talk to narrators in an oral history session, I'm not a talk-show interrogator, pushing people to reveal embarrassing secrets. But if people are at ease in an interview—and comfortable with themselves in general—what they remember and what they talk about will correspond, and there won't be so much self-editing. I think I was able to provide an easy interview space for most narrators. But even so, some readers may find themselves saying, "That's not the Agnes Bird I know!" Or "Dorothy would never have said *that*!" We all need to remember that there's a gap between how we re-create ourselves and how others see us.

The interview method itself illustrates personalism, a facet of the Catholic Worker movement that Dorothy lived daily. The fact that I didn't know her made me an ideal person to hear the memories of those who did. In the interviews for *Voices from the Catholic Worker*, people wanted to introduce me to *their* Dorothy, wanted to "set me straight" and dispel the myths of "do-gooders" such as myself who knew the movement only from a distance. Many resisted a monolithic telling and wanted to stress her down-to-earth qualities. As Walter Stojanowski said, "I can't explain it, but she was a regular, special person." I noticed in the ninety-four new interviews for this book, however, that although some still wanted to give an unvarnished picture, others—especially older narrators—wanted more varnish. Sometimes, too, I'd get more analysis than actual stories, because people were still, after all these years, trying to come to terms with what Dorothy had meant in their own lives. So what they remember about Dorothy is often part of how they construct their own identity.

Can we know Dorothy Day? Of the thousands of people who worked with Day or knew her, I re-interviewed fourteen of the over two hundred I interviewed originally for *Voices from the Catholic Worker*, used forty from this original collection, and interviewed or corresponded with eighty for the first time.[1] What gives the true picture, the plethora of details in all these interviews or the generalizing we need to do to produce anything readable? If we're too close, the image is blurred, but if we're too far away, the image is indistinct. Donna Sullivan, a perceptive student, gave me an evocative image that may make the distance I've chosen manageable. Think of biography as a bicycle wheel, with the spokes the connections between Dorothy and the narrators. Looking at the wheel from a distance, you see nothing. But as you walk toward it, the spokes and the unifying center begin to take a distinctive shape. Spin the wheel around and you see everything there is to see and also what is not there, so much that it becomes blurred and you can't take it in at one time. Yet you know it's all there and will be available if you slow the wheel down and take

---

[1] While scores of Dorothy's friends had already died, I was blessed to be able to interview many who were still active in their later years. When I stopped interviewing in early 2002, fourteen of the people I had interviewed had died since we talked. All the edited transcripts and the tapes (even the ones of poor quality) are available in the Catholic Worker Archives at Marquette University, a collection ably administered by Phil Runkel.

MARYKNOLL ARCHIVES

time. So I ask you to take time reading this book, to slow the wheel down and concentrate on Dorothy, the shining center.

A few interviews were conducted by phone. While all these interviewees were extremely cooperative, I missed the immediacy and intimacy that a face-to-face meeting brings. Being able to speak with people where they had lived with Dorothy was particularly important. I'll never forget the night I spent with Pat Rusk and Rosemary Morse at the Staten Island beach house. They tucked me in on a sleeping porch, surrounded by pillows and quilts, and the wind and the water counterpointed my dreams as they had Dorothy's. In fact, that night I dreamed of Dorothy. There was no dialogue, just a silent picture of her standing in back of the first cottage, leaning on her cane and staring pensively out at the water. This brief scene, more a vision than a dream, left me with a pale glimmer of what Dorothy means to the people who knew her. As Robert Ellsberg says, when he remembers Dorothy, he is "soaked in memory."

Dorothy's post-conversion life was animated by the life of Christ. As she matured, this identification became deeper and deeper, and Judith Gregory concluded that she lived not by rules but by "deep references." Perhaps for that reason, Dorothy was able to give to her friends a part of herself they could use to grow in holiness and wholeness, as my daughter Kathryn has suggested. I hope the readers of these pages will find a Dorothy Day who helps them to grow in holiness and wholeness, just as the people I interviewed did. Just as she does me as I present these portraits to you.

Acknowledgments

First, I must thank Jim Forest for suggesting that I collect and edit the interviews used to compile this collage of Dorothy Day. Print, sound, and electronic versions of all the interviews, including those I was unable to use in the book, are available in the Catholic Worker Archives at Marquette University, administered with professional grace by Phil Runkel. As always, Phil was immeasurably helpful in my research and unbelievably prompt in responding to my many requests. Jim Loney of the Toronto Catholic Worker recorded several phone interviews for an article on Dorothy Day in *New Times*, the Canadian equivalent to the *National Catholic Reporter*. Jim sent me his tapes and I am most grateful for the insight they provided me. Several selections from his interviews are included in this book.

Other friends who helped in the project include Frank Donovan, Roger O'Neill, and Jane Sammon of the Catholic Worker in New York; Jim Allaire, who manages the Catholic Worker website; Sarah Melici, creator of the Dorothy Day play, *Haunted by God;* Ed Turner, and Johannah Hughes Turner. I am especially grateful for the hours of "email listening" that Ed and Johannah provided as I struggled with "getting it right." Transcribing, formatting, and proofreading services were provided by our most able Saginaw Valley State University secretaries: Elaine Schnepf, Vivian Wressel, Diane Whalen, Patricia Latty, Sharon Opheim, and Saun Strobel. My Saginaw Catholic Worker community—Sr. Leona Sullivan, Maureen Coallier, Renaye Fewless, Margaret Schiesswohl, and countless guests—was most understanding and patient during my days on the road and on the computer. Sister Ardith Platte gave me the words to dedicate the book to my grandchildren. Jack Hart provided valuable editorial advice; Colette McColgan and Morgan Guyton gave timely help in proofreading. Robert Ellsberg, editor-in-chief of Orbis Books, has been a treasure of an editor over the last five years—cheering me up when I was beset by doubts, patiently waiting as I contacted yet another narrator, and shaping the book in ways too numerous to mention.

Most important, I want to thank all the narrators for giving me many interview leads as well as for contributing the heart of this book—their memories. The gift of their "Dorothy stories" is what made my work possible. As someone said of another text, "I didn't so much write this book as receive it." A final gift of gratitude goes to all those I have forgotten to thank—the email friends, the chance acquaintances who helped me with recalcitrant recording equipment, my understanding family, who is so much a part of who I am. All mistakes and misjudgments are, of course, my own.

Prologue

First Impressions

What do I remember about the lovely Dorothy Day? Well, I'll tell you.
I met her when I was six or seven years old. She lived in the apartment
right next door to my grandparents. So I got to see Dorothy almost every day. I was just fascinated! She was so different from the people there
in Little Italy, which was what they called the Lower East Side. I can still
see her sitting there in that room filled with books, sitting in that rocker
and smoking a cigarette.

When I first saw her, I thought she was a foreigner, you know, because
she was dressed in dark colors, except for a white blouse and a kerchief
around her head. She looked like somebody just off the boat. At that time,
in my neighborhood, the Italian women all dressed very modern, so she
stood out like a sore thumb. She really did. She was tall, with no makeup
and stunning eyes. Beautiful! As far as I was concerned, the woman was
a saint because she'd be at Mass every day and always walking around
with her prayer missal, but dressed like a peasant.

—FELICIA CARRANO CARL,
WHOSE GRANDPARENTS LIVED AT 115 MOTT STREET
WHEN DOROTHY DAY MOVED INTO THEIR BUILDING

Meeting Dorothy Day opened my mind to the real world. The average
product of a Catholic school . . . you have sort of a one-dimensional approach to Catholic living. So meeting Dorothy, attending the discussion
groups on Friday—clarification of thought, all the rest of it—was absolutely mind boggling. I spent the entire summer there.

I was most of all impressed with Dorothy's knowledge—her ability to
discuss ideas and respond to criticism. But I also loved her sense of humor! She told us once there were these two nice ladies from the parish
telling her that she surely must be a saint and all this sort of thing. And
she told them, "Bullshit!"

—JUSTINE L'ESPERANCE,
AN EARLY RECRUIT FROM DETROIT

I first met her on Mott Street. She was tall and disheveled, striking in
her austerity—nothing like Fifth Avenue. Really a handsome woman in

her unique way, but rather strict and aloof. Stern, no fun. And the mother of the house, although not dominating, not harsh or cruel in any way. A gentle, refined, loving, and generous woman. And it was a great experience for me to be there, helping a little bit in the office.

Dorothy was strictly business. She paid more attention to the poor than to seminarians and others who came to study with her. There was a procession of people who wanted her to talk with them. She was not brusque with them, but she didn't get caught in many hand-holding, long discussions with people. She knew how to get the work done. She did her duties in the kitchen, preparing for the soup lines and doing the dishes afterward, and she was always busy. I never saw her relaxed, because she was going all the time. That's not where most of us were. As a college student, a seminarian, I was looking for a little fun, a little horse playing, maybe going out to Aqueduct or someplace. Although the rhythm of her life was sort of contagious.

She was at that time a smoker. The custom of most smokers then, especially those without big incomes, was to roll their own. And Dorothy could do that adroitly. For five cents you could buy Bull Durham and roll it in a paper and she knew how to do that very well.

—FATHER HARVEY EGAN OF MINNEAPOLIS WHO,
AS A SEMINARIAN, CAME TO THE WORKER
IN ITS MOTT STREET DAYS

Dorothy was still smoking and using blue language. She was about forty-two years old, and I was captivated! I thought she was—how do I say it—progressive as hell, compared to what I experienced with the Christian Brothers in high school. As a matter of fact, I went back to visit an old teacher and told him what I was up to and this one brother, who was kind of a friend, said, "Well, that's a communist outfit."

I said, "That's news to me! We work with communists but we're not communists; we're Catholic." And he wasn't convinced. Of course, the Worker had that stigma for a long time.

—JOHN THORNTON,
WHO HEARD ABOUT DOROTHY IN PHILADELPHIA
AND LATER MOVED TO NEW YORK

I first heard Dorothy speak in May of '36. Before she'd finished, I had decided to join the Catholic Worker. I was captured by her sense of humor. And by her laugh, which was rather infectious and attractive. I remember saying to myself, "This woman is getting a lot of fun out of life. And I'd like to get some of that for myself, so maybe I'd better try the same kind of life."

The Catholic Worker was then at 115 Mott Street—in Little Italy, just north of Chinatown. A slummy area, with old houses full of bedbugs and rats. Things got pretty sloppy and cruddy. The notion was that, according to personalism, or personal responsibility as it was called, you didn't tell people to do anything. You just set a good example and hoped they'd profit from your good example and begin to do good things. But it didn't work too well. People were sleeping at all hours, and they weren't making their beds. They weren't sweeping up. So I decided I'd post some very simple rules. The first rule was "Everybody out of bed by nine o'clock." Two: "Everybody make their own bed." Three: "Everybody take turns sweeping up."

Well, my roommate (from whom I acquired a very sizeable dose of tuberculosis) was a charming Irish alcoholic from the Bowery, John Griffin. He'd been there for some time and had absorbed more of the [theory] than the others, and he thought these rules were a violation of the sacred principles of personalism. So he appealed to Dorothy and Dorothy agreed with him and told me to take those rules down. So I did. And concluded that what we had there was a form of anarchist dictatorship. There wasn't any democratic, participatory decision-making. Dorothy made all the decisions. She was the abbess, as we called her. She made the rules. Or took down the rules.

She was a strong-willed woman, and it's amazing with the philosophy that she had, that she was able to keep that movement going for so long and so successfully. It says something for personalism and personal responsibility. She was authoritarian, but she seemed to have a sense of when to let people go their own way and when to step in before things got just impossible. When she stepped in, she could step in with a lot of force . . . A lot of force.

Dorothy and I argued a good deal. She used to call me her wayward son. Which is kind of complimentary in one way because I was so argumentative and such a dissenter. But I remember her basically and most essentially as a woman of heroic virtue. There was also this intellectual, not-so-sensible, romantic agrarianism and extreme pacifism, and a little bit of anarchism—all floating up there in her head. She was a complex woman.

—John Cort, a Catholic convert and socialist
who joined the Worker
after graduating from Harvard

We used to say compline every night and go to Mass every morning. Dorothy discovered that some of the men weren't very good about going to daily Mass because they'd stay up late and then want to sleep the next morning. So she wrote them a letter and addressed it as "an epistle to the heathen." When she scolded, she did it very, very well. It was bing, bing, bing, short and sweet! Believe me, nobody missed Mass after that!

—Katherine Mella of Chicago,
one of the early Catholic Workers

Young Dorothy at the time of her arrival in New York.

1.

Dorothy and the Catholic Worker

Whenever you trace the roots of peace and justice activism,
you always come back to The Catholic Worker.
—NANCY ROBERTS

First, some background on Dorothy Day and the movement she co-founded. Born to a newspaper family on November 8, 1897, Dorothy moved often during her childhood and left the University of Illinois after two years for a bohemian life in New York. She became known both for her writing and for her activism, with the first of several arrests for civil disobedience occurring in the cause of women's suffrage. But she was mysteriously drawn to Catholicism and often found herself visiting the immigrant churches that dotted lower Manhattan. For several years she lived happily with Forster Batterham on Staten Island in what she called a "common law marriage," but her decision to become a Roman Catholic after the birth of their daughter, Tamar, severed the relationship and she remained celibate for the rest of her life.

While searching for ways to bring Christian principles to bear on social and economic injustices, she met Peter Maurin, a loquacious and well-schooled French peasant who introduced her to the social teachings of the church. His three-point program called for informed social criticism, houses of hospitality for the homeless, and communal farms where the unemployed could learn a skill. In Union Square on May 1 of 1933, they launched the first issue of the *Catholic Worker* newspaper, and a movement was born. Still distributed to a worldwide readership, the *Catholic Worker* features Christian responses to contemporary social problems and encourages the many houses of hospitality and communal farms that sprang up in response to Day's and Maurin's plans.

In the early years of the movement both Day and Maurin traveled indefatigably, visiting Catholic Worker communities and speaking at colleges and churches—wherever they could find audiences. These audiences diminished, however, as the clouds of World War II shadowed the country. Day's uncompromising pacifism, first articulated in response to the

Spanish Civil War, was hard listening for a nation mobilized in defense against totalitarianism. When war was declared, Day's headline read, "We Continue Our Pacifist Stance." Instead of warfare, Dorothy urged prayer, fasting, almsgiving, and nonparticipation in the business of war, quoting the New Testament as well as the early fathers of the church in support of her stance.

The issue of pacifism caused deep conflict within the movement, the circulation of the paper plummeted, and by the end of the war, the number of houses of hospitality had greatly diminished, from around thirty-five to fewer than ten. Day was saddened and shocked at the destruction of Hiroshima and Nagasaki and wrote forcefully against the jubilation reported by the secular press, urging instead that the United States "destroy the two billion dollars worth of equipment . . . , destroy all the formulas, put on sackcloth and ashes, weep and repent."

Day's commitment to radical nonviolence continued during the Cold War. She wrote in the *Catholic Worker* of December 1948: "Love of brother means voluntary poverty, stripping oneself . . . It also means nonparticipation in those comforts and luxuries which have been manufactured by the exploitation of others . . . If our jobs do not contribute to the common good, we pray God for the grace to give them up." Strong words to a nation gearing up for postwar materialism and a new enemy in Russia.

Tom Cornell, who arrived at the Catholic Worker in the 1950s, says that Day's love of Christ and her depth of commitment to the most vulnerable of the world grew during the isolation of these years, when the Catholic Worker existed on the ragtag fringe of society, along with other small Christian peace groups. It wasn't until the peace movement of the Vietnam War that the Catholic Worker again grew in numbers and influence. During the sixties, Day and other Workers were among the first and most forceful voices against the war, and idealistic young people flocked to the New York house or started houses of their own. There they resisted the draft, fed the hungry, and engaged in acts of nonviolent resistance. Day inspired the founders of the Catholic Peace Fellowship, which was started as an affiliate of the Fellowship of Reconciliation, and she was godmother to the organization that became Pax Christi. Several Catholic Workers were jailed for public draft-card burnings and for destroying draft files. Day supported all of them, even if sometimes expressing misgivings about the nature of their resistance. She also continued to travel frequently, to Australia and Russia and Rome, praying and fasting for a strong peace statement at the last session of the Second Vatican Council. So she was overjoyed to learn that the bishops had validated gospel nonviolence and condemned nuclear warfare in their final document, *Gaudium et spes*. Later, the U.S. bishops' pastoral letter on nuclear weapons was to mention the profound effect of Day's work and to declare peacemaking a requirement of faith for U.S. Roman Catholics.

As the decade drew to a close, Catholic Workers were called increasingly to test the theory of nonviolence with the daily practice of hospitality as they confronted the psychosis, addiction, frustration, and anger of some of their disenfranchised guests, many of them Vietnam War veterans. This day-to-day schooling in the principles of nonviolence continues in most houses as Catholic Workers attempt to practice nonviolence both as a tactic for social and political change and as a total lifestyle. The seventies saw a Dorothy Day dimmed by illness but not diminished. She divided her time between a small beach cottage on Staten Island, the Catholic Worker farm on the Hudson (which everyone called Tivoli), St. Joseph House in the Lower East Side, and the nearby Maryhouse—a large house of hospitality established to care for homeless women. She still traveled occasionally, with her last public speaking appearance at the Eucharistic Congress in 1976. She received the Laetare Medal from the University of Notre Dame in 1972 and several other important awards and thus lived to see public honor for her work.

At the time of her death, eighty houses were listed in the *Catholic Worker*. Many predicted the demise of the movement, but as Peggy Scherer, then editor of the paper said, "We may have lost Dorothy but we still have the gospel." The movement continues to grow. Today there are approximately 180 Catholic Worker houses, including communities in Australia, New Zealand, Germany, and England. In these houses the gospel is lived out in diverse ways, depending on local circumstances. Some houses engage in a specialized ministry to victims of AIDS, some to undocumented immigrants, some to women and children. Some run large soup kitchens, while others exist on isolated farms, trying to live Peter Maurin's green revolution. Despite the differences in style or emphasis, all Catholic Workers are united in their commitment to Christian peacemaking and many resist the payment of federal taxes, either directly or by living below the poverty line.

Dorothy Day's life and work and writing also live on with those who don't call themselves Catholic Workers. I remember the late Michael Harrington telling me that Day might be the most important lay Catholic in the history of the United States, an accolade that echoed an obituary by historian David O'Brien. Ed Marciniak, one of the founders of the original Chicago Catholic Worker, points out that proof of the influence of Dorothy and the movement is not primarily in the small Worker houses that dot our inner cities, but in the fact that its program has been embraced, adopted, and adapted by other groups, including many mainstream churches. As Ed says, "The Catholic Worker is no longer the only game in town." Many lay religious communities and Christian peace groups throughout the world are pointing out the connections between war and poverty and working to eliminate them. They hear the message of Dorothy Day—her faithfulness to God, who lives in the poor and disenfranchised, her radical opposition to the materialism of contemporary life, the clear connections she drew between her spiritual life and her nonviolence. What follows are memories of those who first heard her call.

BEGINNINGS

Being with the Catholic Worker and with Dorothy was always exciting. Never a dull moment.

—Joe Zarrella

Agnes Bird McCormack, who served as Dorothy's secretary from 1938 to 1942, has vivid memories of her years at the early Worker. She recalled fondly reliving "all the wonderful years" in a goodbye visit with Dorothy shortly before her death:

I think Dorothy was as desperate to find Peter as I was to find her. It was 1938, a bitter cold winter, and I just didn't seem to fit anywhere. I was supposedly looking for a job, but instead, I'd spend my days wandering around Manhattan. All I saw were poorly clad people, shivering in doorways. Mostly men, with hunched shoulders and rough, red hands. In spite of the fact that I was rapidly losing my faith, I started praying like crazy and going to daily Mass because I felt if somebody didn't find me, I would go mad.

Then it was June. Dorothy came to speak at our parish, and I went to hear her. I saw this tall, gaunt woman in a long, pongee dress with her straight brown-gray haircut, mopping her brow in the sweltering heat of the hall and speaking in a colorless voice. But, oh! Her words were "a shot of gladness in my heart." She talked about bringing the works of mercy to the men I had seen that winter—the men on the Bowery—and I was totally and completely enamored.

I asked her right away if I could come down to the Catholic Worker, and she said no. Dorothy always said no to young girls. She said they were too much trouble for her. But we all seemed to show up anyway. When I went down that first night, she wasn't there, but Peter was, and I had a wonderful evening, although he was so brilliant and so well read that I only grasped half of what he said. Peter also told me not to come back, that there wasn't anything to do. Luckily, Stanley Vishnewski heard him and told me to come, for there was loads of work.

It wasn't until the following winter that I began to have any contact at all with Dorothy. I was so in awe that I didn't even speak to her at first, but I suspect it was because I typed so well and took shorthand that she began to notice me. So I became her secretary and started on a lovely journey. She was such an enchanting person, with a wonderful sense of fun. She made an adventure out of everything, showed you the color and beauty and warmth in the crowded and dirty city.

Through the years she developed into a terrific looking woman. Heads would turn when she walked into a room, and everyone would ask who she was because they knew she was somebody. She gave up the frivolity of hair cuts and let her hair grow long and braided it and put it up. Also, since she thought skirts were too short, she'd take a dress from the clothing room and get a swatch of dark material and add about a foot-long hem to the dress. It sounds ridiculous and we made fun about it, but she could carry it off.

She was extremely feminine. Neat and clean, which was not easy at the Worker, with its poverty and dirt. She took what she referred to as "a harlot's bath." Just a basin of water, but lots of soap, and wash all over. She liked talcum powder and lightly scented perfume or lavender toilet water. Sometimes Blue Grass. In her earlier years she used face powder. She loved good white linen handkerchiefs with embroidery on them and always carried a clean one. Even living in poverty, she had perfume and nice handkerchiefs because as soon as people knew she liked them, they gave them to her. Of course, she'd give them all away and then people would give her more.

Dorothy *always* gave her possessions away. The second time she was arrested for not abiding by the air-raid drills, I visited her in the Women's House of Detention. Because she had nothing else to give me, she gave me her handkerchief, and when I protested, she laughed and said they didn't lack for toilet paper and it was as good as anything for blowing your nose on. Her laughter . . . I just can't describe it. It was like a young girl's, even when she was eighty! First, her eyes would sparkle and then her smile would come.

You know, I rarely describe Dorothy to anyone because I sound like a sap, so I'll talk about her faults now. Dorothy could be very adamant and firm and even mean in a petty sense when you did not agree with her. Her tongue could be very sharp and she would nag and ferret out what she thought were your weak points and harp on them. She was such a distinct personality, and we all wanted her approval. For me, it wasn't so bad because I had another life, but for the young men who loved her as much as I did, the barbs were sharper and I think she really hurt them.[1]

---

[1] Small portions of this interview were recorded by Bernadette MacCauley in 1983.

Dorothy Day, Peter Maurin, and Joe Zarrella.

Another early recruit was Joe Zarrella; he and his wife, Mary Alice, remain faithful to the Catholic Worker. They met in New York and became one of the first movement marriages, moving to Tell City, Indiana, where Joe organized the workers in a furniture factory. Dorothy was a frequent visitor to their home and godmother to one of their four daughters. Their stories add to the myth, build the tradition.

J OE: You know, a number of books have been written about the early times in the Worker, and as I read them, I recognize the sincerity of those writers. But I find my own recollections quite different in many instances. Well, these are my experiences. I was there.

I wasn't particularly a good Catholic. In fact, I came from a typical Italian family where you were baptized and made your first communion and got married in the church, and that was about the extent of it. My friends were socialists and communists. Interested in social questions. I began to wonder what our church had to say about these things, and somebody gave me a copy of the *Catholic Worker*. Then on May Day in 1935, I took off from work. (Had an upset stomach or something.) On the way home, I suddenly decided to get off at Fourteenth Street for the May Day parade. What possessed me, I will never know. But it was a fortunate decision. When I got down to Union

Square, they were distributing the *Catholic Worker*, and I asked if I could help. That was the beginning—when the bug bit me—and I was captured. Being with the Catholic Worker and with Dorothy was always exciting. *(Pause.)* Always, always exciting. Never a dull moment.

I met her shortly after that, and I was thinking about coming down and joining the Worker, but I said to myself, "God! She's an old woman. How many more years does she have to go?" *(Laughs.)* I was so young . . . so young, and I really idolized her, right from the beginning.

In the very early days, we had very little money. Always up to our eyeballs in debt. That's why Dorothy traveled so much. She was on the road most of the time, but she was lucky sometimes if she got bus fare. At many places the only money she got was for twenty-five-cent subscriptions. She'd say, "Well, I got fifty subscriptions," and send this money back. We lived from day to day. The running of the house was up to us, and people would send in contributions. And every Monday morning, we'd get a dollar from the Lochner girl. Alice Lochner from Indiana. She'd be making six, seven dollars a week and she'd always send us a dollar. Or maybe two. Well, one day she showed up. Came into the office with her big hat.

ALICE: Well, I had the same ideas out here [in Tell City, Indiana,] as they did in New York. And then I found the paper, and I met Dorothy when she came out to Saint Meinrad's Monastery, which is just down the road from us. And then she . . . I have this rare distinction that she asked me to come to New York. I have it in a letter. Dorothy came and visited my family to show them that it was a respectable place.

But after I got there, I was not popular with Dorothy. And I . . . it didn't work out the way Miss Day thought it was going to. I did not become a satellite. The person who was closest to her was the most disrespectful, and that was Mary Johnson, who lived with her husband in the front apartment on Mott Street. They took care of Tamar when Dorothy was on the road, and Mrs. Johnson and Dorothy were great friends and loving enemies. She was older than Dorothy, even, and they were a riot together. Oh, my! She would talk back to her, not like Joe!

JOE: Well, I really, really idolized her. One time she told me, "You could have been my son." I've often thought of that. Most people think . . .

ALICE: He was in love with her.

JOE: Yeah. I really . . . anything that she asked me to do, I did. And, you know, your first great influences mean so much. I really did anything that she wanted. I maybe didn't particularly like it, but I did it. And I'd try to make her life easier. When she'd come home, I'd meet her at the bus or at the train. Have her room ready and maybe some flowers for her. And bring her mail up the next morning and a cup of coffee and toast. Those kinds of things. Once I saved some money and bought her a Victrola [and a record of] Wagner's *Tannhauser*. Because she loved the opera. She loved Wagner, which was something very difficult to understand. So in that way, I did love her. I thought she was absolutely the most wonderful person in the world.

Oh, I always, always think of her. When we went up to the Johnsons with Miss Day, evenings particularly, these were really very intimate moments. There was a quiet intensity about what she had to say. And I think we were very fortunate to have known her in those early days. We were in a formative age in our lives, and Dorothy was growing, too. We watched her grow and we grew with her because she shared the things that became important to her. So you could see her developing spirituality.

She liked to joke and was really very warm when you got to be with her on a one-on-one basis. When we'd be at the Johnsons, she'd talk to us about her friends from the past and about her family. She stayed friendly with those people, and why not? You don't forget people like that. I don't ever remember her saying anything but nice things about them. We used to love to hear her talk about those days. Sometimes we'd even have a glass of wine at the Johnsons, but then she even gave that up. When I get a cold, I always remember her favorite recipe. When we were sick, she'd say, "Take a glass of warm wine. That'll put you to sleep."

Oh, the Johnsons were our salvation! Whenever Miss Day had guests, we'd take them upstairs to the Johnsons. I remember when the abbot from Saint Meinrad came to visit us. All these cockroaches were crawling around while we were having coffee. Now this abbot was a very prestigious person, and you could see him getting so uncomfortable. I got the feeling I'd better move him out, so I took him upstairs. Continued the conversation in a more sanitary atmosphere.

You wonder why the health department didn't come down on us. We violated practically every rule in the book. No hot water. No place to take a bath or anything like that. Primitive cooking facilities. One toilet for a whole floor. No heat except for open fireplaces and a few kerosene heaters. Most of the time we dressed up to go to bed.

And the bedbugs! One time it was so bad that we took the beds up on the roof, soaked the mattresses with kerosene, and blow-torched the bed frames and the springs. But they still came back. Peter seemed to be the only one who was immune.

Even in those days, in my limited way, I was always irritated that Miss Day was not recognized for what she really was. She took such abuse, you know. And knowing her personally and then seeing . . . hearing and reading the things that were said about her, it really hurt. At that particular time, you know, we lived in a very hostile society, particularly for our kind of a group. The church was in a very conservative period, and we were considered communists who were "boring from within." So we weren't acceptable in many places.

But you know, she kind of crowded people, in that sense. You never measure up to her, and that disturbs some people. I think that's why, when you hear these critics of Dorothy, there's a little of that in there.

People always quote her saying, "Don't make me a saint. I don't want to be dismissed so easily." And I think . . . now this is a personal opinion . . . but I think that the reason she said that was not that she was against canonization or saints. Dorothy admired the saints. She was forever quoting the saints and handing out holy cards, like Our Lady of Guadalupe. In my opinion, what she was saying is she didn't want to be considered a saint like people in those days considered them—the Berkeley Street statue, pietistic kind of a person. She had this tremendous admiration for the saints, and she always talked about the kinds of struggles they had. I learned about the real saints from her. And I don't tell this story publicly, but . . .

ALICE: You are. It's going to be on tape.

JOE: Well, Rosalie can do what she wants with it. It's an example of the kind of saint thing I'm talking about. Dorothy did not mingle easily with strangers, and when we had visitors, she didn't particularly care to come down and converse with them. But one day she was in the office when somebody came, and of course this person went up to Miss Day. She asked her, "Miss Day, do you have visions?"

And Miss Day said, "Oh shit!" I figure that's the perfect response to that kind of a thing. She was always talking herself down because people would stand in reverence of her, and she couldn't stand that.

You know, I have never considered us as leaving the Catholic Worker when we got married and moved to Tell City. It never rubs off. If you've ever been under Miss Day's influence, you can't shake it. You're haunted. And you have a guilt complex, in many senses, if you don't do something about a situation. So you're always getting in trouble because when issues come up, you've got to take a stand. And it's usually a minority stand, so you rub your friends the wrong way. But after a while, if you do it right, you learn from people and you earn people's respect.

I think the biggest thing you learn from Dorothy is personal responsibility. Personal responsibility and spirituality. One without the other doesn't go. You know, people always think about her in terms of the social issues, but she was a deeply spiritual person. That's what made her so strong on the social issues. Because in the early days, we were so beleaguered. So battered.

Dorothy was really strong. Never a walk-over. She couldn't be or she wouldn't have accomplished what she did. She got the money, she got people to work, she spread the word. She never hesitated to chide me if my performance wasn't up to standards, but I never found her hard or autocratic, as some have written. You knew where you stood with Dorothy because she was forthright and open, but she was never cruelly judgmental.

I am so grateful that I was touched by Dorothy Day and Peter Maurin. And you know what else? Being at the Catholic Worker I was spoiled. Because at the Catholic Worker I saw the best. The best and most exciting minds in the world. It was always exciting. I've never had a dull moment in my life since I came to the Catholic Worker.

ALICE: I think you said that.

A WRITER ABOVE ALL

She didn't write to depress people into revolution; she wanted to inspire people into revolution.

—JIM FOREST

From her earliest days, Dorothy worked as a journalist, learning her trade at the *Call* and honing editorial skills at the *Masses*. She always defined herself as a writer, both in person and in print, and would list "journalist" as her occupation on passports. In fact, when Dorothy and Peter Maurin founded the *Catholic Worker*, she didn't intend to start a social movement, but wanted a newspaper that would discuss how to live a radical Christian life. Much more followed, for as artist Ade Bethune said, "Peter taught her that you do not just write about hospitality. You do it."

The paper, however, defines the Catholic Worker movement that grew from it. It's still published seven times a year by the New York community, still sells for "a penny a copy," still uses the distinctive Ade Bethune masthead. It's no longer the only periodical that speaks to and for the Christian left, but it is not a house organ for the Catholic Worker movement,

Dorothy reading galleys of the CW, *1962.*

instead treating far-reaching justice issues and continuing an advocacy tradition. While Dorothy was active, the newspaper carried her stamp and always contained her writing, particularly her column, "On Pilgrimage." Reprints continue today, in both the *Catholic Worker* and in the many magazines, newsletters, and newspapers that come from Catholic Worker houses of hospitality around the world.

Dorothy would appoint the best and the brightest of the young Workers as editors, and they often became her close friends. One did not get this position by asking, however, and a friend of the Worker recounts the story of someone writing and asking to be on the editorial board. Dorothy told them to come. "Your work begins at the kitchen sink."

Here Ade Bethune speaks of her first work for the paper:

I wasn't terribly impressed by the masthead. Dorothy had got two little cuts from her printer. One showed a laborer with a maul and the other one had a pick-ax over his shoulder, and they occupied the two opposite corners of the top of the paper. Then an astute reader wrote to Dorothy: "You're really not doing right for all your emphasis on being interracial. Your two workers are white. Where is the black one?" So Dorothy got [a picture of a] black worker [from the printer]. It wasn't quite the same size as the other one, but now at least she had both black and white. [The "astute reader" was Dr. Arthur Falls of Chicago, one of the few African Americans active in the Catholic Worker.]

In 1935, I was going to give Dorothy a surprise. Just rushing in where angels fear to tread, I made a new masthead. I brought the two workers together with a cross in the middle and Christ's arm over them. So there was a black worker and a white worker and they were being unified. Dorothy was really pleased with the masthead.

The masthead still exists, with one change—the white male worker is now a woman agricultural worker, designed by Ade to reflect an increasing awareness of the sexism in society.

Robert Steed was an editor of the newspaper for over five years, and his experiences echo several of the other editors—becoming editor with little experience but learning on the job, and ultimately enjoying it and having great authority, especially when Dorothy would be on the road for speaking engagements. Bob reminisces:

Of course it was her paper, and ultimately, whatever she wanted was done. When she wasn't around, there was no one to argue with me. *(Laughs.)* But when she was home I did whatever she said. Sometimes Dorothy didn't like something in an article, and she'd just cut it out and print the rest, without asking anybody. The author maybe didn't want it published that way, but that didn't mean anything to her. So it wasn't run like an ordinary publication.

Pat Jordan was managing editor in 1973 and 1974. He remembers:

Dorothy was always very self-critical and very, very protective of the paper. Felt a responsibility for every word. Part of this, I think, was in terms of the archdiocese. She'd been called on the carpet for things printed in the paper and had taken the responsibility that she was the editor.

We would have gone over the paper beforehand, but there were always mistakes. She would scrutinize it thoroughly and was usually very negative. She would work herself through that and then begin pointing out all the positive things, but her initial response was always, speaking for herself, "We didn't do well enough." Very self-critical. Toward the end, she got more comfortable with us as editors, and began to say things like, "You can cut whatever you want. You can cut mine." But before that, there was this sort of back and forth.

What impressed us—and she'd stress it so often, too—was that her writing was her vocation. She was a journalist. This gave her a deep freedom even within the Catholic Worker. Something as involving as the Catholic Worker can just zap you of any freedom that you might have. You become burdened by it. But she always had her own ability as a writer to look to, and that gave her an independence from the

Worker and even from the paper itself. This was, you know, a real strength for her. It replenished her.

I remember that the printers would always ask if Dorothy was coming because they just loved her. These were working men and their politics would tend toward the reactionary, but the things she had written had really stood out to them. And how many galleys had they scanned in their lives? She was a remarkable writer. The proof of the pudding was that she could write for that kind of person—for the man in the street, as Peter Maurin would say. Some of the articles by other writers got very long winded and theoretical.

She was always bringing new blood into the paper because she'd meet new people on her travels. That would also keep it much more practically oriented. We'd have somebody who was working with the woodcutters or somebody with the grape strike. Always we'd try to be very practical and personalist in that sense, showing what individuals or small groups of people were doing to create a better place. She often said we should be "proclaimers and acclaimers" rather than "denouncers." We shouldn't just be writing against the government. We should be talking about what was building up the Mystical Body, showing what people were doing, how they were throwing in their lot. So people all across the world could say, "Gee, look at these people! They just opened up their house to people [who need shelter], or they decided to create a small school for mothers who don't have any place to leave their children when they're going to work." Often [Dorothy] would prefer to start the paper with articles like that and then move to the more theoretical things. She also loved to have letter columns because, once again, that was that human voice coming in.

Jim Forest was on the masthead as associate editor from November 1961 to February 1962.

The movement grew out of a journalist's head and her . . . her theory and practice of journalism was quite different from the norm. Even before the *Catholic Worker* got its identity fairly well defined, even in the early issues, you see that Dorothy's journalistic slant is essentially a positive one.

Probably one of the good things about the *Catholic Worker* is that it never wrote a self-portrait of the community. That was never Dorothy's idea. When I was editing the paper, I found Dorothy's slant annoying, in a way. I felt we were perhaps giving people too idealistic a view of the community. But Dorothy had seen so much of the other. She'd come from a family of journalists, grown up with this other idea of journalism, and had been involved in newspapers like the socialist *Call*. Probably the socialist newspapers were much closer to the Catholic Worker press than the mass media, but still they tended to print horror stories, like Dorothy's stories about living on two dollars a week. It was a revolution through fear and anger rather than through love. Dorothy's theory and practice of journalism was quite different. Even in the very early issues of the paper, her slant is essentially a very positive one. She's not writing to depress people into revolution; she wanted to inspire people to revolution, and it's a quite different method.

Ed Turner, who came to the Catholic Worker in the fifties, comments about her style:

It must be said that Dorothy's style is almost inimitable. People would try, but few could do it. Instead, their work would suffer from what one Worker called "the people-and-places disease." Joe Blow's name would pop in, but most of the audience wouldn't know who he was or why he was mentioned. Dorothy could pull this off, though.

It was Dorothy's column that sold the paper, not the theoretical stuff. Also some of the more homey items. Once there was a recipe for making apple butter. A subscriber requested "less apple butter and more on strikes." Dorothy, of course, wrote both, but from then on, we called her column the "Apple Butter Letter." But as I say, it sold the paper.

Nancy Roberts, a professor of journalism who published a book on the newspaper, gave an interview to Jim Loney of the Toronto Catholic Worker. In it, she summarized what was unique about Dorothy Day as a writer:

With a lot of advocates, the cause is what's paramount and communicating it secondary. But she saw them as intertwined, saw journalism as another form of activism. So she put a lot of time and effort into the newspaper and her other publications. Getting the word out was right up there with leafleting, picketing and civil disobedience. Her paper was read by many opinion leaders, so its influences were much more than you would guess by the size of the circulation. Whenever you trace the roots of peace and justice activism, you always come back to the *Catholic Worker*.

I also think of her ability to write literary journalism, journalism that tries to be factual, tries to talk about real people, real events, real things, but deals with the larger issues of human existence as does literature. Literary journalism also uses all the literary techniques that we associate with literature—scene setting and characterization and so forth. Dorothy did that.

One of her strengths was the ability to talk about the everyday—the soup line, the crazy people at the Catholic Worker house, praying to St. Joseph for funds, what they ate for dinner, who stopped in for a visit, her grandchildren, very homespun stuff—talking about the everyday and then getting from that to the ultimate questions. In the same piece. It's an unusual writer that can contemplate the ultimate but still be grounded in real life.

LEADERS AND FOLLOWERS

There's no way out of the Catholic Worker family.
—FATHER JAMES JOYCE, S.J.

Dorothy Day's relationships within the original community she and Peter Maurin founded in New York were markedly different from those she had with other communities across the United States. Even within the New York community, her leadership role changed through the years— because she changed, because of differences in the people who worked with her, and because of cultural events over which she had no control.

To help me learn more about the Dorothy Day who had been so influential in his life, Ed Turner invited me to a party in October of 1998. It was a wonderful evening, with "old timers" sharing theories and insights with me and with second- and third-generation Workers like Bronwyn O'Neil, daughter of lifetime Catholic Worker Roger O'Neil, and Ruby Nichols, granddaughter of Jack Thornton, a Catholic Worker farmer in the forties and fifties.[2] I owe to this party many of the insights in this section.

Dorothy tried several different leadership styles in the fifty years she led the Worker, styles at least partially dependent on who was in the community. Many of the narrators talked about Dorothy's arbitrary leadership, and I'd hear such quips as, "Man proposes but Dorothy disposes," and "Dorothy believed in anarchy, provided she could be the chief anarch."

---

[2] Johannah Hughes Turner's perceptive comment on that evening has stayed with me: "Ro, at that party you had a taste of the magic that Dorothy created, the magic that lives on in all the years since her departure, the bonding of people in the memory of the Catholic Worker experience."

Most agree that her leadership was an innate interior power. Ed Turner pointed out that she "didn't emote, didn't holler, didn't scream" but used finesse and was purposeful and aware of what she was doing all the time. She never had a staff training program but relied on whoever was available. Someone at the party commented, "Most of the time, this worked, but not always."

Ed continues:

D orothy was not a gifted administrator. She was a propagandist, a journalist, and an inspirer of a movement. She ruled the New York house and its attendant farms because she was personally responsible for them. What she said was final. But as for running a national organization, that was not to be. And the one time she tried to lay down the law and bind all the houses together—on the issue of pacifism—she failed and what's more, realized she'd made a mistake.

She encouraged others interested in the CW to go and do likewise. And she would come and speak at their meetings and praise their

MARQUETTE UNIVERSITY ARCHIVES

Dorothy with CW *editors Ed Turner (left), Judith Gregory (right), and Walter Kerrell (far right).*

work. But they were responsible for their own houses. The fact that Dorothy was not an organizer may well be providential. Catholic Worker houses arise where the need is felt and one does not need the permission of the superior.

His observation is echoed by Workers across the United States. Mary Jane Pleasants of South Bend commented that Dorothy "never tried to hold onto people" but was just as pleased if they picked up some of the ideas. "She passed on the spirit, I think, without trying to keep the group as her group at all." Almost everyone I spoke with sees her resistance to founding an institution or to appointing a successor as crucial to the success of the many autonomous Catholic Worker houses today.

She appeared concerned but not frustrated with the problems other houses faced. For instance, when Michael and Annette Cullen, founders of Casa Maria in Milwaukee, wrote her that they were in desperate need of money to say afloat, she wrote back, "Michael, where is your faith?" Michael comments, "She was saying, 'If you think it depends on me, then you're in the wrong place.'"

Sometimes, however, she would be disappointed in the decisions of her Worker friends in other towns. The late Dorothy Gauchat remembered that Dorothy was "very angry" when the Gauchats built Our Lady of the Wayside, a home for abandoned children:

In order to get money, we had to become a non-profit. And the place was going to cost $250,000, and she was very upset with us about that, too. She said, "I just don't believe that. All that money for one building!" And that hurt, because we knew what we were doing and what these kids needed. But once she came to visit, and saw the place and our relationship with the children, she just changed completely and really, really loved us.

Even a casual question from Dorothy might be enough to inspire the direction of a house, as in the story Margaret Garvey tells:

I never thought I'd meet Dorothy. Never even thought of it. Well, the first time I did . . . a funny story. Our house [in Davenport, Iowa] had been running for maybe a year or so. Rachelle [Linner] came to visit. She told us Dorothy Day was speaking at De Paul University in Chicago.

"Well, let's drive to meet her. She's getting old and . . . "

This Rachelle is a very special lady, so I said, "All right. We'll take a day off. We'll drive to Chicago and hear Dorothy and drive back that night." So we did it. Made it for the last two minutes of the talk. I think I heard Dorothy say, "And thank you so much for inviting me and God bless you all."

Rachelle literally pushed me down the aisle and up to Dorothy.

"Oh, Rachelle, it's so good to see you!"

"Dorothy, I want you to meet Margaret Quigley."

Dorothy turns to me. "Oh, so this is who you are!"

And I'm shitting my pants 'cause I thought, "This is Dorothy Day, the saint! My God, she probably knows I threw somebody out the other night."

She said, "Where is your newspaper?"

And I said, "Well, Dorothy, we don't have one."

"Well, what do you do with your time then?" And at this, she was whisked away.

I thought, "You horse's ass!"

I wrote her this just scathing letter and said, "Who do you think you are? I'm sleeping with fifteen men a night. Answering the door all night long, and you're asking me what I'm doing with my time! A newspaper is the last thing I think of." And then, of course, I started a newspaper.

Tom Cornell illustrates the kind of responsibility Dorothy was sometimes called upon to take when she was in New York:

Everybody thought they could bring their complaints to Dorothy, and this was part of her cross. Sometimes she'd dart into the little office right inside the front door on Chrystie Street, close the door, and get on the phone. Other times, she'd walk in and as soon as she was three yards into the place, people would be after her, saying, "You've got to do something about Carol! It's just unbearable. The rest of us just can't stand it."

Then, of course, Carol would be at the table saying, "You don't know what's going on here, Dorothy. Let me tell you."

And so Dorothy would listen to all the tales coming out of our "house of hostility," as Stanley Vishnewski used to call it. Then she'd give admonitions, such as, "No, no, you can't reject a person like this. Someone else will come in her place, and the devil you have is better than the devil you're going to get." Or she'd say something more positive. If it were a woman, a pregnant woman particularly, there was absolutely no question about her staying. She was welcome.

But people would relish her being in New York for reasons other than solving problems. Chuck Matthei explained:

Life at the Worker in its daily details could be quite mundane, even frustrating sometimes. So it was fun to have her there. People enjoyed it. Enjoyed the good conversation over meals or over tea in the late evening. When she was home, she was in many ways very accessible and people looked forward to seeing her. As the foundress and untitled leader, she brought a certain stability and a certain sense of security and order. She also brought stimulation and stories and life and a sense of its larger meaning.

Terry Rogers remembers:

Dorothy lived on the third floor, and I did, too, and it was fun to have her home. She was a very spontaneous person. If she was in the mood to talk, she would. She'd holler out, "Guess who I just heard from?" Or "Sit down and listen to this symphony with me."

Jane Sammon has been with the New York community since before Dorothy died:

She had a magnetic personality. But I'll tell you—Dorothy Day did not encourage a following, at least when I knew her. She really was hardest on herself. In fact, people would ask, "Do you rehabilitate anybody?" She would always say, "We should start with rehabilitating ourselves."

The cult of personality is so dangerous, and Dorothy simply deflected it. I can remember on rare occasions being with her at a Broadway show. People would recognize her because she was often photographed, and they would gasp, "Oh, is that Dorothy Day?" But she didn't encourage that in any way.

Several of those I interviewed commented on Dorothy's relationships with the feminist movement, particularly if they lived with her in the early 1970s. Jean Forest comments:

I wouldn't call her a feminist in didactic terms, but she was a feminist internally. I mean I don't think that anything got in the way of what she wanted to do, so she didn't make choices through imposition.

As Brian Terrell said, "She was a rebel because she wanted to be." But Judith Gregory pointed out that, from her point of view, Dorothy was "very old fashioned" on the subject of feminism:

I got the impression that she had very deep misconceptions about the women's liberation movement, as we called it then, thought it was shrill and full of self and promiscuity. Now she had to see the contradiction in her own life, because she did exactly what she pleased, really, but what she pleased was more or less in an old mold. This is pure speculation, but my sense is that she was very committed internally to the idea that men were the ones who did things. And that women had a supporting role. And I think all of the facts to the contrary—even her own life—just didn't really take with her.

Johannah Hughes Turner noted that people listened to Dorothy Day differently than they do most women, and Dan Delaney noticed a similar innate leadership. "She never thought being a woman was a disadvantage, so feminism wasn't important to her."

No matter how they interpret Dorothy's leadership, all I spoke with who lived and worked with her are grateful for the time they were able to spend with her, for her leadership, however autocratic, and for the Christ-centered community she showed them. Dorothy herself often missed the people she nurtured, as most of them eventually left the Worker. She told Franciscan priest Louis Vitale, "The Catholic Worker is like a sieve. Everybody passes through us. They don't really stick, they just pass through." Another reason for the long loneliness.

LOVE AND FAITHFULNESS

To be faithful to Dorothy's vision is to love.
                                                        —CHRIS MONTESANO

When Dorothy and Peter Maurin began the Catholic Worker movement, Dorothy was thirty-five, hardly old enough to mother the eighteen year olds who came to the work. Conscious of her past and her recent conversion to the Roman Catholic Church, she worried that the women, particularly, would be taken advantage of sexually. And so we see her scolding Eleanor Corrigan Gosselin and holding herself aloof from Mary Alice Zarrella.

Bronwyn O'Neil interviewed Eleanor for a college paper. Here is an excerpt from that paper:

The one gender laden issue that bothered Eleanor at the Worker was that Dorothy had been very worried about a scandal leaking from the house, and she took out her phobia on the women, Eleanor in particular. Dorothy was very suspicious of her beauty and lectured

Eleanor many times on her exposed knees, which showed when she was busy cooking for a bread line of 700 men and a house of 50 people. As far as Eleanor was concerned, Dorothy was afraid of Catholic foreign women. Dorothy simply assumed "that when men and women were in close quarters, they naturally were tempted to jump in the sack. She was wrong. She was going by her own past experience of life in Greenwich Village during the roaring 20s." Eleanor was a very conventional revolutionary and resented the warning because such things were just not done at the Worker.

Mary Alice Zarrella told me in 1988:

The relationship we girls had with Dorothy was one of reverence, really. We loved her, but it was strange and there was a distance. After I learned about Dorothy's early days, I realized she had been worried about us girls because of the things she'd been through. But we were innocent. We were too stupid to be tempted. *(Laughs.)* Of course after Joe and I were married and Dorothy would visit us in Indiana, we became closer, and then I understood our early relationship better.

Nina Polcyn Moore says, "We'd all grown up like the Bobbsey Twins, and she'd led the bohemian life. She was very sensitive to the young people who came, that they would keep their innocence and their purity and not be polluted by their experience there. She had a profound sense of responsibility."

This responsibility remained with her even at the end. Jane Sammon knew Dorothy in the last eight years of her life:

She came out of a generation where you did not hang it all out. For instance, she really drilled into the young women: "Don't you get sentimental about the men that come into this house and think you're going to save them like puppies lost in a storm." Later I thought, "Was this advice based on great experience?"

She lived an examined life, so she wanted to put up the warning signals. "Don't you girls go down there. I don't want to see you dressing in . . . " You know, she could become . . . I wouldn't say obdurate, but *firm*. It revealed another side of her, not one given to sentiment.

When I knew Dorothy, she was probably like a lot of founders—or mothers—aware of the pitfalls the young can fall into. She embraced Catholicism at its great crucible—the guilt factor. So probably, for good or for naught, she blamed herself for a lot of events that maybe didn't go in the way she thought they should go.

I'm not speaking only of the sexual encounters. I'm saying that I felt Dorothy understood sin, understood evil. "Where sin abounds, grace abounds doubly." Dorothy understood that, understood within her flesh what life and death were about.

Dorothy left Forster Batterham, the beloved father of her child, because he would not contract a marriage sanctioned by the Catholic church. So it would appear natural that she would expect the same sacrifice on the part of those who worked with her. And for a time she did. Jim Douglass, who divorced and remarried, was among those hurt by Dorothy's beliefs about marriage:

> Her attitude toward marriage was strict. She felt, I think, that any-one worth his or her salt as a Catholic should be prepared to make the same kind of sacrifice she had with Forster. Jim Forest and I disappointed her in that regard. When Shelley and I were married, that was in essence the end of my seeing Dorothy. I can say that much. And I respected that immensely in Dorothy. She had values that she was not willing to compromise, values that were compromised terribly in the society in which we were living. While I didn't agree with all the applications she made from those principles, I certainly agreed with the nature of the line she was holding. That part of Dorothy was basic to her way of life. She would not say yes to anything for the sake of being agreeable, whether it was a friend's remarriage or something else that was a basic principle.

Toward the end of her life, Dorothy changed, according to Jesuit priest and good friend Dan Berrigan. As he explains in an interview with Jim Loney:

> She was very fervent about the letter of the law for many years, like most new converts. Merton was that way, too, for a while. But the great humanity of these people reasserted itself later on. At one time Dorothy severed her friendships with everyone who had entered into a marriage that was forbidden by church law. But later she changed radically. She told me a couple of years before her death that she had written to apologize to several of these people, including my brother [Phillip Berrigan], and had welcomed them back to write in the paper and be her friends again. So that was marvelous and a tribute to her greatness—her ability to say she had been wrong or not merciful. To say, "I was not compassionate at one point, and now I am sorry about that."

Dorothy knew, even from the beginning, that couples with children in a Catholic Worker setting could be problematic, although many, many couples met and married at the houses of hospitality. "It's just a marriage mart," quipped Australian Angela Jones, who met her husband while at the Los Angeles Catholic Worker. Tina de Aragon is reputed to have said, "Everything comes into the Catholic Worker, including husbands."

Mike Cullen, whose marriage to Annette was one that survived living in a house of hospitality, muses: "She missed human love in her own life and she used to talk about it, although I didn't understand it at the time. She said it had been important for her to give up . . . In other words, she missed the human love but felt we have to sacrifice the human love for the greater love."

Dorothy would be excited about Worker romances, however, because she knew that marriages of like minds had more chance of lasting. Pat and Kathleen Jordan spoke of telling Dorothy they had decided to wed. Pat remembered:

A number of times over the years that Kathleen and I had known each other, she had said, "Don't get married . . . unless it's really compelling." She had seen so many marriages around the Catholic Worker not work out. I think she was trying to discourage romantic notions of both marriage and celibacy. But when we told Dorothy, her response was, "I never thought he'd ask."

Dorothy also believed that marriage and hospitality—at least the kind the Worker practiced on the Bowery—didn't belong together. So she would bid a sad goodbye as the young couples moved away. Dorothy's daughter, Tamar, observes that "Dorothy would have a big depression when people got married, but then when they started having children, she'd fall in love with them all over again, and she'd boast that they met at the Catholic Worker and all this stuff."

Often couples started Catholic Worker houses as part of their marriage and family commitment, following the early leads of the Murphys in Detroit and the Heaneys, who lived for a time at the farm in Easton, Pennsylvania. Chuck Quilty and his wife moved into a house of hospitality from a conventional marriage, a marriage that did not survive the tumult of the sixties. Chuck explains:

When Dorothy came out to visit us, one of the things she really harped on was the fact that I was married, running a Catholic Worker house, and doing resistance. (I'd already been arrested a few times.) She felt it was work single people should be doing, that married couples had responsibilities to each other and to the children and so forth.

I think her concern was certainly legitimate, but I don't think she was right. There's a deeper issue. The most thought provoking writing on this problem is an article by Jim Douglass, "Marriage and Celibacy." The point he was making, I think, is that when most people get married, they're basically into what he calls a "bungalow marriage," raising their kids and getting two cars in the garage and the nice little bungalow. And if somebody within one of those marriages starts taking the gospel seriously, there's going to be a problem. I don't want to reduce everything that happens in every marriage to that, even my own, but I think that's a large part of it.

Dorothy never gave the impression that she thought everyone ought to live a Catholic Worker life. Professor David O'Brien of Holy Cross illustrates:

Far more than I, my wife always kind of had the feeling that if we were really into this, we should live in a Catholic Worker house or move to the inner city and live a Catholic Worker lifestyle, an option I never thought was a particularly good idea.

Well, Dorothy came here to Worcester to the first conference of the New England Catholic Peace Fellowship. Tom Cornell and Jim Forest were speaking, and my wife was sitting in the audience on one side of Dorothy. Mary Pat True, Michael True's wife, was sitting on the other side. One of the speakers said that it was difficult to raise a family in a Catholic Worker setting. Dorothy leaned over to Mary Pat True and said, "It is *impossible*." Here Dorothy was kind of giving us permission, saying that it wasn't absolutely necessary that we live in a Catholic Worker house.

Sexuality of any kind outside the bonds of marriage was another matter all together. Several of Dorothy's friends and co-Workers discussed her generally conservative attitudes toward fornication, adultery, and same-sex liaisons. Yet she clearly loved individual people and was often forgiving, especially as she neared the end of her life. Michael Cullen told me:

[The divorces in the Worker] used to hurt her. They really grieved her, but she had a sense that the ideal of marriage didn't always work out. Another thing that grieved her was when people in the Worker were [engaging] in unfaithful living and in unions that were not marriage. Yet she had this extraordinary gift of compassion and tolerance. She was trying to live the gospel, and she knew that these things don't fit but yet they are being lived out by human beings. So she was always coming down on the side of mercy.

Some people say that her conservative attitude toward sexuality was a consequence of her "waywardness when she was young," as Bob Tavani phrases it. He said he remembered her saying to him once, "God understands us when we try to love."

Most who talked about Dorothy's feelings toward gay and lesbian relationships pointed out that she was homophobic, both because of when she was born and perhaps because of personal experience. Judith Gregory remembers her saying "some very sharp things about lesbians, in a kind of disgust. It made her shudder, I think, but I don't think it was coming from any ideas. It was just personal, very personal." Robert Steed says, "She didn't even want the word mentioned in her presence. She thought it was something your religion would enable you to overcome."

But Dorothy very clearly showed her love to individual people who were gay and lesbian. Tom Cornell illustrates:

I want to tell you a story, a little delicate. There was this guy—let's call him Joseph. He was a very handsome guy and an aspiring actor, who hung out on Chrystie Street and at the farm. And he was homosexual. Well, the courts ordered a young boy to our farm in lieu of some other kind of punishment, I guess. Peter Maurin farm on Staten Island, twenty acres on Bloomingdale Road. He was a working-class kid, kind of an ugly, white-trash kid, but Joseph fell in love with him. Joseph even bought him a horse, but the kid paid no attention to him. He had a girlfriend and just wasn't interested.

So one day Joe is sitting there on a stump of a tree, crying his heart out. "I do everything for him, and he won't give me a break." Dorothy comes along and she holds him in her arms and she comforts him. Dorothy was not a fiendish, puritanical, priggish tyrant. She held herself and all of us to a standard, but she was not hateful. She was not priggish. She held him in her arms and comforted him.[3]

Chris Montesano was in New York during those days:

Historically the real staunch support of the Worker has been gay men and lesbian women. As Catholics, they've had no other community; the Worker was open to them. Dorothy wouldn't talk about the issue of homosexuality directly, but when I was in New York, they started the Good Soup Coop in San Francisco, and we'd gotten a little pamphlet from them. I came into the office and was raving about it. Angry. I

---

[3] Michael Harank says he "never once heard any stories of Dorothy disparaging anyone with a queer sexual orientation."

said, "These gay men are taking advantage of the movement, exploiting it for their own purposes, blah, blah, blah."

Dorothy looked at me very coldly and said in a very stern voice, "*Someone* has to minister to gay people." At that point, I left the room. Now I realize that every other man in that room was gay. Every other man in that room. And Dorothy knew it. She chided me because she'd realized I'd hurt those men deeply.

Dorothy would not open up the issue to discussion because she felt it was too volatile. She was clear that her stand was traditional church. I don't agree with that, but that was clearly her stand. I think Dorothy definitely loved many gay people and loved them very well. In terms of what she did to me, I'm glad she did it. I mean she had to. In a certain sense, she was taking a stand to support them and to love them in a nonpublic way. That's history and it's important and it's a memory I hold dear. I think people who take the conservative stand about gays and lesbians are actually *not* being faithful. To be faithful to Dorothy's vision is to love.

AT HOME ON THE ROAD

She was at home wherever she went.

—Tamar Hennessy

Stanley Vishnewski used to quip: "Dorothy lives on a bus. She created the Catholic Worker, but the rest of us have to live in it." Dorothy was very frequently on the road, traveling to spread the message, to raise money for the work, to see friends and find respite, to nurture the houses of hospitality spread across the country, and finally, because she simply enjoyed the adventure, the friendship, and the paradoxical solitude one finds when traveling.

Dorothy often traveled between the New York communities as well, going back and forth between the city, Staten Island, and one of the several farms the community owned at different times. Ed Turner characterized these changes as follows:

When Dorothy wanted a convent atmosphere, she went to Newburgh; then for her life's blood she came to the city. When she wanted to visit with her literary and radical friends, she would have them at Peter Maurin Farm. There was a luxuriousness to that farm, not that most of the middle class would think of it in those terms. And it was her work, her writing, that financed the whole operation.

Because she was always the one responsible for these communities, this shuttling—and all her travels—afforded others in the community a chance

to exercise leadership in her absence. And Roger O'Neil mused that perhaps Dorothy felt successful when she traveled, in contrast to her time at
the often chaotic New York community:

She stimulated people, started Workers, got good feedback, maybe.
She could feel creative, I think. When she was in New York, the house
was full of permanent problems that she couldn't do anything about.

The late Dorothy Gauchat, founder with her husband, Bill, of Our
Lady of the Wayside in Ohio, says Dorothy used to love the order she
found in the Gauchat home. "We were an oasis where she could relax."
Joe Zarrella, one of the pioneer Workers, remembers Dorothy's early travels, when the movement was young and Dorothy's speaking engagements
in other cities supplied most of the income:

Sometimes she felt guilty, being on the road and not able to take part
in the work here, the food and the dirty scrubbing. She wrote me once
that she missed the poverty while she was on the road, that she felt like
a fish out of water, going from convent to convent and eating all the
fancy food, while we were battling the bedbugs. But it must have been
hard.

Dorothy's schedule was often busy, too busy. Even when she was
younger, the traveling and speaking engagements would exhaust her.
Marge Hughes remembers her coming home tired:

She would get so worn out and visibly need to recover. But she had
a wonderful body for recovering. Give her twenty-four hours in bed
and she would be up and going again.

Often the travels were to lend support to fledgling houses of hospitality
across the country. Mary Farren, a founder of the Rochester Catholic
Worker, tells a story similar to stories of others who hosted Dorothy's
visits to their communities:

When she visited us, she didn't give a real speech, but her sincerity
and her gracious way were tremendously convincing. The second coat
in the closet was given out to the poor—that kind of thing. She could
be very direct, though, and in the questioning period she'd come out
with razor sharp answers, but her self effacement was . . . was as powerful as her response was direct.

An account of a visit to Tennessee in the 1950s shows how resolutely
Dorothy handled a hostile crowd. In *Not without Tears*, Helen Caldwell

Day describes her coming to Blessed Martin House, a racially integrated Catholic Worker house in Memphis. She spoke to a rather large gathering, which included students, priests, brothers, and many volunteers:

> She talked about our unity in God, and of our obligations to each other . . . She talked about the obligations of the rich, and quoted some strong words of Our Lord, beginning: "Woe unto you rich . . . you have had your reward." She quoted Peter Maurin's reminder that we take with us when we die only what we have given away, in Our Lord's name, while we live.
>
> I watched the faces of those who listened. Some were deeply interested and became more and more thoughtful or alive. Some never understood. Some were closed and dead and remained so. Some grew red and angry, and I could see the effort it cost some people not to speak until she had finished. The colored people were awed and unbelieving at all this from a white woman. There was new hope in some of their faces, and . . . for one moment they had been lifted by her out of our little world.
>
> As soon as she had taken her seat, the questions began, some angry and hot.
>
> "Is there something particularly holy about poverty and dirt, or rats and roaches? Does God stop loving a man because he works and saves his money to provide for wants and needs of his family, or is there something sinful about being rich? Doesn't charity begin at home?"
>
> [Dorothy replied:] "No, there is nothing particularly holy about dirt and rats and roaches. But there may be something very unholy about the way we regard those who suffer from these things. The safety of the rich lies in almsgiving. We must give until we become blessed . . . Christ came to make the rich poor and the poor holy . . . Yes, charity begins at home, but we are also our brother's keeper; we talk too much of our own homes, our own children."
>
> "Doesn't the Catholic Worker encourage shiftlessness and laziness by feeding and sheltering people who won't help themselves?" Dorothy denied this. "No. Peter Maurin used to say that we must make the kind of society in which it is easier for people to be good.
>
> "One needs to be happy to be good, and one needs to be good in order to be happy. One needs Christians to make a Christian social order and one needs a Christian social order in order to raise Christians. The paradox again. Such as dying to live. No one pretends it is a simple matter . . . The Christian must live in time and eternity, living with the long view, yet living most intensely at the moment . . . It is necessary to build a society where people are able

by their work to sustain themselves, but also by mutual aid, to bear one anther's burdens when . . . men are unable to work."[4]

California often called to her. Chris and Joan Montesano began Martin de Porres Catholic Worker in San Francisco and later started Sheep Ranch Catholic Worker, high in the Sierra Mountains. Chris recalls:

She came out to us when Martin's was first started. She spoke and we collected all this money—five hundred dollars—and it was really kind of exciting. Anyway, we decided to give it to Dorothy.

She said, "Oh, no, no, no! You're a new house. You need the money."

"No, no, Dorothy! We insist you take it." So she finally took it. The next day somebody walked in and gave us five hundred dollars in cash. "Give and it will be given to you full measure." The early days of Martin's were in that spirit. Just simply . . . I mean we had nothing, only first and last months' rent. I think Dorothy liked that. She was fond of the early times in Worker houses, and she would often come because she felt they were special times of grace and she liked to share in that.

Other California memories were shared by Chris and Dan Delany. Chris says:

Dorothy lived with us for two weeks when we had the L.A. Worker. I was really nervous about her coming. "Oh God! She's the Mother General, and she's going to come and check up on us." But I was just charmed. Dorothy was just an utterly human person. She'd sit at a table and tell stories. Kind of hold court. People would come from all over and talk to her. One interesting thing: I had this thing about murder mysteries. Just loved them. Used to sneak them up to my room and read them like they were pornographic trash because I just . . . you know, everybody at the Worker was so intellectual. (Or pseudo-intellectual.) Well, it came out that I liked murder mysteries, and she began to suggest books I might like, because she was a devotee, too. In fact, she bought me a book by Josephine Tey.

Dan joins in:

Well, one thing that always struck me about her . . . she had a sense of self. Every night, as the evening wore on, she'd start to complain that

---

[4] Helen Caldwell Day, *Not without Tears* (New York: Sheed and Ward, 1954). Reprinted on http://www.catholicworker.com as "Dorothy Day."

she was an old lady. (She was in her early seventies then, and she had a cane.) At about eight o'clock, she'd start talking like that, and then about nine she'd go upstairs. But her light never went out till midnight.

Then in the morning, her light would go on about six, but she didn't come down until nine. So she was putting in three hours at night and three hours in the morning. By herself—doing her correspondence, praying, reading the scripture . . . doing as she damn well pleased! And I thought, "Boy! She really . . . no wonder she's a spiritual power-house!" That impressed me, that she took time for herself . . . had a sense of herself.

Dorothy would always nurture Catholic Worker houses, networking with them and guiding them in their struggles. Tom Cornell explains her visits:

She had a way with her. For instance, she'd go to Detroit or where have you. "Oh, Dorothy we're so glad you came. We're having such a terrible problem. We've been waiting for you."

Dorothy would say, "Let's have a cup of coffee first." So they have a cup of coffee and start chatting and Dorothy starts reminiscing and they tell their stories and Dorothy tells her story and at the end of it, people say, "Isn't it amazing how she solved our problem?"

The next day Dorothy is on a bus somewhere else. She would tell these stories and people heard in those stories what they wanted and needed to hear. Now she was listening, also. I think that she probably developed a technique without any consciousness about it, of listening and responding in an appropriate way, but I don't think she ever thought about it. She never read a book on non-directive therapy or any of that stuff, but she had internalized principles of nonviolence.

Dorothy often traveled out of the country, as well, taking first ships and then planes to Rome, Cuba, England and Ireland, Russia, Australia, and from there around the world.

Dorothy traveled twice to Rome. The first time, she joined women from all over the world who came on pilgrimage in response to the encyclical *Pacem in terris*. Jim Douglass found them lodgings, at Dorothy's request, and later Dorothy stayed with Jim and his first wife, Sally, in their Rome apartment and traveled to the north of Italy with Sally. Jim recounts here Dorothy's second visit:

Then she came back to Rome a second time, at the closing of the [Second Vatican] Council. I had gone back to Rome that fall, too, in order to continue the [peace] lobby with the bishops. It was the most critical session, the final session, and that's when Dorothy came over again to fast with women from Lanza del Vasto's [Community of the] Ark and to appeal to the bishops to support conscientious objection against nuclear war.

I saw her several times while she was there, and I think her fast was the most important element in the bishops' turning from what had been a compromised statement around war and peace to a more direct statement that actually condemned total war and supported conscientious objection.

There were two things going on. One was a lobbying effort to urge the bishops to take that kind of a stand. And Dorothy was involved in that. She put out an issue of the *Catholic Worker* that was totally devoted to that question, and it went to every bishop.

But the deeper part of it was the appeal of the spiritual commitment. As you know, the statement the council finally came out with connected the arms race with hunger, as it very well should have. When Dorothy wrote about the fast, she said that she experienced severe pain, and she felt that she had somehow—she put it "in a small way"—experienced that connection herself during the fast. I believe

Dorothy in Red Square during her visit to the Soviet Union in 1971.

that her presence and the presence of the other women in the fast was the major factor that turned the church from an endorsement of nuclear war, which it came close to doing, to a redirection toward the gospel. A bunch of us did the talking, and Dorothy and the other women did the fasting. That was what was needed; their part was critical at that time.

Eileen Egan accompanied Dorothy and lobbied the bishops while Dorothy fasted:

She told me that the hardest moment of the day came when they were making coffee in the next house, and it wafted across the wall to her cell at the Cenacle. She had pains when she was fasting that she had never had before, pains in her very bones. But she said, "I thought I was fasting with all the poor of the world, and that my gift of fasting was only a widow's mite, my suffering so small compared with the suffering of the people around the world who are hungry every day."

The peace question was raised at the council the same day Pope Paul VI spoke at the United Nations. "No more war" and "War never again." And something happened. The British bishops, who had been sort of favorable to accepting deterrence, had changed. And that was due to the work of Gordon Zahn and Jim Douglass.

All this time Dorothy was fasting and praying. And finally it went to the vote. They did indeed condemn indiscriminate warfare [in *The Church and the Modern World*] and come out in favor of conscientious objection and alternative service. They also said that expenditures on arms are a treacherous trap for the poor. These are things we'd been fighting for.

Vincent Ferrer McAloon, host of the Notre Dame University Hospitality Center in Rome, was also helpful to Dorothy during her stay. He writes in a lighter vein:

During Vatican Council II, it was my grace and privilege to assist Dorothy during her stay in Rome [when] she joined nine other women in a ten-day fast for peace. During the fast, I was to phone Dorothy when mail or telegrams arrived for her. On one occasion she told me that a number of the women had taken to their beds with weakness. When I asked Dorothy about herself, she chuckled and replied that she was a hardened old-timer at fasting. Besides praying, she spent much time reading and currently she was wallowing in Dickens's stories, especially his descriptions of "groaning board" feast-day dinners. Jokingly, I accused her of vicariously breaking her fast!

Her 1962 trip to a Cuba under Castro was criticized and misunderstood by many. William Miller tells us that she visited "seeking concordances" and that she felt she had done the right thing as "the Cuban Catholics to whom [she spoke] welcomed [her] message."[5] Rachel de Aragon, daughter of one of her pre-conversion friends, has a more intimate view:

It was personally very important for Dorothy to see dismantled the decadent and sexually degrading arena of Havana night clubs. This had been, unfortunately, one of her father's stomping grounds, and its exploitative basis was something she felt very acutely. Further, it was a great joy to her to see a socialist country that was not anti-church and where the issues for both church and state could be resolved without enmity. When she came home, she gave me a religious-political medal from Cuba, a Virgin with a dove of peace.

In fact, Dorothy came back bubbling with stories of people she'd met and things she's seen. Personally, I have never known her to be more effervescent and genuinely happy about a trip or experience. Common things and ordinary people were as much a part of her stories as the issues of church and state. I think, looking back, that it was a very confirming visit, an experience which validated her own vision of Catholicism and communalism . . . and the road she had taken to get there.

Dorothy had traveled to Rome and to Cuba by boat, because she was afraid of air travel. Eileen Egan recounts a trip to England and Dorothy's first flight:

In 1963, Dorothy and I were invited to speak at the Pax annual meeting, which is called the Spode House Conference. You remember, she was scared to death to fly. But we wanted to go from Italy to this Pax meeting in England, and an Italian priest had . . . oh, it was a relic or a medal from Our Lady of Good Counsel. He gave Dorothy this relic, said it would give her the courage to go on a plane. She said she'd try it, so we went to the airport, and she took her first plane ride. To England and then back to the United States. So I guess the relic worked, because from then on we traveled by plane all the time. Even all the way around the world! We went to several Spode House Conferences together and once she gave a long talk on reconciliation. Tremendous! They were just delighted to have Dorothy.

---

[5] William D. Miller, *Dorothy Day: A Biography* (San Francisco: Harper & Row, 1982).

I remember once Lord Peckingham, who was one of the few Catholic peers in the House of Lords, asked us to have lunch with him in the House of Lords. Dorothy said, "Why not?" So we had a wonderful lunch. And while we were waiting for him, sitting in this little study, there was all this House of Lords stationery. Dorothy took some and began to write to a young man. She said he was very depressed, so she wrote to him on the House of Lords stationery. She said something like, "You see what this paper is. These are all high and dignified people." Then she said, "Remember that you are the brother of Jesus and the son of a King. Never forget that."

She was always thinking of others, and she always remembered what the poor would do in difficult situations. One day we took a boat down to Greenwich from London, and it was a rotten day, damp and windy. Dorothy bought a newspaper and she tied it around her, like a . . . like a lifesaver, back and front. The newspaper kept her from feeling the cold, wet wind. She said, "You can always learn something from the poor."

St. John of the Cross has written, "The loss of the home has as its corollary the love of the world."[6] Dorothy so loved the world in all its variety that even when she was failing in health, she continued to travel. In 1970 she went with Eileen Egan to Australia and from there around the world. Eileen recalled:

An Australian peace group invited us to come and gave us round-the-world tickets. Because of my travel experience with the Catholic Relief Services, I took care of the details. Dorothy accepted the vicissitudes of travel, though, and she was not a complainer, which was nice. What bothered her on that world trip, though, was that she didn't have the energy to go out much. For instance, in Calcutta, there was a flood, and I went out with Mother Teresa to the flooded areas. Dorothy never complained, but once she said, "How I wish I could do what you're doing."

That visit was the first time she met Mother Teresa. At the end of our time together, Mother Teresa took the black cross with the corpus of Christ, as worn by the Missionaries of Charity on their saris, and pinned it on Dorothy's left shoulder. She said, "Now you're one of us."

Another of Dorothy's longest flights was to Russia with Nina Polcyn Moore:

Dorothy asked me to go to Russia with her. We'd talked of going together for years, so when she got a scholarship, she called me up and

---

[6] Thanks to Jack Hart for alerting me to this apt quotation.

asked if I could go.[7] We had a delightful three weeks. This was in 1971. Dr. Jerome Davis was the leader. He was a Methodist minister from Yale and was in his eighties and had been to Russia twenty-five times or something. Had an autographed picture of Lenin, spoke Russian fluently.

We went to Moscow, Leningrad, Warsaw, and let's see . . . to Hungary, Romania, Czechoslovakia. Every place we went there were discussions with local people on the peace movement. Dr. Davis had the contacts, and that was important. We saw a great deal of the Hermitage and Leningrad and just had a marvelous time with the people. They were all trying to build bridges between ordinary people who wanted peace. Dorothy was great in that sense of bridge-building and seeing what we could agree on. That was the joy of the whole thing.

Chuck Matthei, a Catholic Worker who worked on community development before his death in 2002, had in common with Dorothy this love of travel. He recalled:

Hers was very much a life of the road. And we'd talk about that. Sometimes she'd tell interesting and inspiring tales of places and people and projects all across the country, the kinds of things that she reported in her column "On Pilgrimage." And some were just the personal feelings, you know, the sense of joy and excitement and liberation as you travel as well as the times of loneliness and weariness.

The life of the road is a vocation unto itself. And when you travel as much as Dorothy did, it's a lifestyle, not a trip. If you're on a trip, you expect to come home. But if you travel as much as she did, you'll never have an ordinary home life. It's not without reason that she called her book *The Long Loneliness*.

TIVOLI

Tivoli was overwhelming!

—Tamar Hennessy

Many of the people I interviewed talked of the mansion and outbuildings on the Hudson that Dorothy purchased in 1964 and sold in 1980. A haven for wandering hippies, men from the road, idealists seeking utopian community, and Dorothy's aging friends, Tivoli ultimately became "her

---

[7] Her trip was paid for by Corliss Lamont, whom William Miller identifies as "the wealthy publicizer of a humanistic philosophy based on science and not religion."

hubris," according to a friend of the Worker, being too large and too unwieldy in its decrepit condition and in the diversity of needs it attempted to fulfill. But for several years Dorothy was able both to achieve a modicum of privacy and to provide community for individuals and groups. Tivoli remains a symbol of both the best and worst of those turbulent years.

Marge Hughes, a mainstay at Tivoli, gives us the flavor of the community:

We had a wonderful mix—students, professors, artists, musicians, invalids, gardeners, carpenters, idlers, drunks, bakers, the depressed and the euphoric, the young and the old. And they were taking care of each other. People like Helen Iswolsky gave classes in things that we wanted. (She was a living, walking example of *noblesse oblige*.) Other scholars would come, too, and people like Mary Lou Williams, the stride pianist. She used to bring a side man up and sometimes a vocalist. They'd play once a year in our living room. And oh, could she play!

Christmas was celebrated religiously. And joyfully, mostly. There was always a tree and millions of little presents and a really good meal and peace and quiet until the drinking started. But on Christmas, even the drunks were peaceful. Even the worst alcoholics would hold off until after Midnight Mass and mostly, if they really had to drink, they'd go up to their room alone. Most people took Christmas very seriously.

One Christmas I will never forget. Allen Ginsberg came over for the Mass, which was in the living room. Everybody was standing up the whole time. Allen followed along and at one point—I think, it must have been after the Gloria—he did a few "ommmms." *(Laughs.)* And then afterward, he and some of the young people played music and sang and skipped around the room.

The times were different. Extreme. Those young people in the sixties and early seventies were moving in streams all over the country. Some would just sleep the night in their sleeping bag and have some homemade toast and coffee in the morning, say thank you, and go on their way. I made bread and so did a lot of others because it took a lot to keep us going. Most of the young people tried to be considerate about noise and loud music, and they took on various tasks, but you know how those things go.

We always had the rosary at Tivoli. People like Helen [Iswolsky], Arthur [Sullivan], Stanley [Vishnewski], and various others kept it going. They understood the value, the great value, of these rituals of prayer. We had a nice little chapel, too, with the Eucharist. That was a privilege. Sometimes we had priests living with us. I think it was to let them have a place where they could perform the sacraments but not be a source of scandal if they fell off the wagon.

How did Dorothy relate to this diversity? The late Pat Rusk told me that for a time Dorothy had a community of her peers at Tivoli:

There was Deane [Mowrer], a poet and professor who regularly wrote the farm column. Helen Iswolsky, who was also a professor. Peggy [Baird] Conklin, her friend from the old days, who started the Staten Island connection by urging Dorothy to buy a bungalow there. These women were not around all at the same time, but most of them were around enough so that Dorothy would not feel so overwhelmed by the presence of draft resisters and their young women followers.

Not everything at Tivoli was fun for Dorothy or for those close to her. Johannah Hughes Turner, daughter of Marge Hughes, describes the intense conflicts that erupted in this community, and how these conflicts affected Dorothy:

When Dorothy was at Tivoli in the sixties—and this was before she became weak and sick and begged people to take responsibility—she encountered something she'd never had before. There was a young crowd there that didn't accept her authority, and didn't obey her orders, for good or for ill. I mean some of them were brats. She would tell them to leave, and they'd say, "No, we like it here. We're staying." And they counted on the fact that she wouldn't call the police and she couldn't force them to leave, and no one else would, either.

So that was something new. It wasn't something good. And it wasn't like the conflicts that I understand happened years ago when the community would think that it would be wise to do something on the [Newburgh] farm, for example, and Dorothy would just nix it and say, "We don't agree." The Tivoli conflict wasn't over respectable issues, at all. They were misbehaving and taking drugs and she said, "I don't think you belong here. Hit the road." And instead of leaving, they would stay. So she lost some of her power in that sense. But not her influence, if you know what I mean.

There was this sort of hippie ideology. Everything belongs to everybody and nobody can tell us what to do, even Dorothy. Lots of people who came to Tivoli in the seventies had no idea what the Catholic Worker was or what the farm was, and were just taking advantage of a place to crash. But through all that mess, there was a core group, and the Catholic Worker was still going on, even with all this other extraneous stuff. Dorothy never really changed. She was still kind and still contradictory, still cranky sometimes.

And then she began to lose her strength. At times she suffered memory losses. (She didn't have enough oxygen or something. It was off again, on again.) She had heart trouble. People would still look to her to make all the world's decisions and solve all the world's problems and all the little fights [within the community], and she would beg people to please grow up and take some responsibility. She found it hard to let go of the power to make the final decision, but she was also asking people to take some authority, whether they wanted to or not. Unfortunately, I think a lot of people failed in that.

Pat Murray has an outsider view of this trying time:

She was pretty tired out by that time. And pretty distressed with what was going on there. The old people—Hans and John Filliger and all the others—were working their tails off trying to keep that place going and the young people were lying on the grass smoking dope. Dorothy didn't like that. That was pretty painful for her. And then there were so many people. Every nook and cranny was filled with young people, just "crashing."

It must have been difficult for her, as her quip to Franciscan priest Louis Vitale attests. He recalls Dorothy coming to Chicago to accept the Franciscan Superior Award. He said to her, "My gosh! You came all the way out here on the bus!" She replied, "I'd go anywhere to get away from that crazy farm."

2.

Politics and Protest

PACIFISM

Before Dorothy Day there was no Catholic pacifist theology.

—ED TURNER

During her lifetime Dorothy Day's staunch, courageous, and unswerving pacifism was perhaps the least understood of her virtues, and one that, until after World War II, caused deep division within the Catholic Worker movement itself.[1] This division is relatively absent today, with Christian pacifism increasingly the mark of a Catholic Worker, in fact the mark of a number of thoughtful citizens of all persuasions. This was not so in the early years of the Worker. Dorothy opposed the Spanish Civil War on pacifist grounds, thereby confusing both her fellow Roman Catholics—who almost unanimously supported the Franco forces—and her old leftist friends, who were staunch Republicans. She dedicated the *Catholic Worker* to pacifism at the advent of World War II, writing, "Our manifesto is the Sermon on the Mount." As there was little theological support for pacifism at the time, with most theologians still hewing to the just-war theory, Dorothy built her position strictly from the gospel. Her friend Eileen Egan explains:

Even in the early days, Dorothy was very bold in using [the word] "pacifism." She didn't mind at all what people said, even if they called it a heresy. Whereas I for years would use [the term] "gospel nonviolence."

Peter wasn't overt in his pacifism, but his cardinal principle was "the daily practice of the works of mercy." War turns every one of those works of mercy around. Instead of feeding the hungry, you blockade

---

[1] Father Harvey Egan calls the factions the "200% pacifists" and the "yes-but pacifists.'"

43

countries, see that the hungry don't get fed, and so on. So while Peter never used the term, I think he was [a pacifist] in effect, because he taught a way of life that excluded violence and war. Now, how did Dorothy come by her pure pacifism? I think she got it right out of the Sermon on the Mount.

When WWII was declared, she wrote, "We will not help the war effort; we will help all those who refuse to take part in the war effort." Which they did. If deserters or conscientious objectors came to the Catholic Worker, they were given refuge. Dorothy herself went to Washington with Joe Zarrella when the draft law of 1941 was being discussed and asked the Congressional Committee to give exceptions to Catholics who wouldn't join the war effort. A cleric was also giving testimony. First of all, he asked her what right she had to speak. "We've already spoken for the right of priests and especially brothers and seminarians not to be drafted." She replied, "I'm speaking for the lay people." Here she was already speaking up for lay Catholics. That took an enormous amount of courage.

The federal government did decide to allow conscientious objection for Roman Catholics and authorized a Civilian Public Service camp where Catholic CO's could do the required alternative service. The CO camps of the traditional peace churches were supported by the governance of their respective churches; all the Catholic camp had was the struggling pacifist Catholic Worker. Gordon Zahn, who later became one of the early leaders of Pax Christi, first met Dorothy at the camp:[2]

I'd never even heard of the Worker until I registered as a CO. And the first time I met Dorothy was when she visited us at Camp Simon, outside of Warner, New Hampshire. We were funded by the Catholic Worker. Can you imagine them having enough money to really support a camp? So there were always problems.

It never got to the point that we were antagonistic toward Dorothy, because we felt that she was doing the best she could. No one could really blame her for the Worker not financially supporting the camp very well, but we felt she probably could have been protesting more to the powers in Washington. It must have been something of a personal trial for her to be in that position, not only feeling powerless but being connected with the federal government in this way.

---

[2] For a complete story of the Catholic CPS camp, see Gordon Zahn, *Another Part of the War: The Camp Simon Story* (Amherst, Mass.: University of Massachusetts Press, 1979).

Dorothy seemed sort of a mythical character, especially when you heard the men from the Catholic Worker talk, and her coming was like a visit from above. We had been fed the Catholic Worker line about her, and it was true—the sacrifice and all she represented. She also was a total pacifist, and that came through when she talked. That was pretty inspiring because I was, too. So I was prepared to be impressed and I was.

Years later, in Pax Christi, we chose her as what I call a luminous figure because she was the best known of the Catholic peacekeepers. I like that word *luminous* because that's largely what she was at this point. The mother. Not in the group as much as shining on it. She had a tremendous influence on the peace movement. The males around her were influential, but they got their influence, I think, from her. I still think she *was* the Worker and the Worker was the crystallization and the genesis of the Catholic peace movement.

Sometimes Dorothy tried to organize and lead the movement in the direction of pacifism, working—it seems—against her natural proclivities for freedom of thought. In the summer of 1940 she sent a letter to all the Catholic Worker houses, saying they should dissociate themselves from the movement if they would not distribute the paper with its pacifist articles. Many houses canceled their bulk subscriptions and some closed their doors, partly because their young leaders had volunteered for the armed forces and partly because they were unnecessary in a war economy that provided jobs for workers. According to some, this letter caused much angst to Workers around the country; to others, it didn't seem so much an issue, at least in retrospect. Marge Hughes remembers the retreat where the issue of pacifism was much discussed:

At the end of the retreat there was an important discussion about pacifism. It had rained all week, but on the last day of the retreat the sun came out and it was just gorgeous. Everything dried up fast, and in the afternoon we discussed a letter that she had sent around to all the houses.

I can still see everyone sitting around the hillside, arguing and talking. People from each house jumping up and having their say. Some people thought the letter said we are all going to be pacifists and if you don't want to, get out. People who didn't know her very well interpreted that as saying, "My way or no way." What she was trying to do was warn them. They didn't know what was going to happen to them personally if they opposed the war, so they had to decide whether they wanted to be vulnerable to that or not. That was what she really was doing. But there were all kinds of theological arguments and the whole country was popping with the war issue. I mean we had people every night on soap boxes.

We would be invited around to talk about our stand against the war because [the ideas were] very controversial. The people that picked up on it first were mostly priests and nuns. They realized Dorothy was speaking true values. But she was accused of being a communist and the *Brooklyn Tablet* made a big campaign against her.

Julian Pleasants, one of the founders of the first Catholic Worker house in South Bend, Indiana, discusses what he perceived Dorothy's attitude was toward her friends who were less adamant about pacifism than she was:

The South Bend house never espoused total pacifism and when she talked at Notre Dame in 1940, she didn't press on it. We hadn't really thought that it was an integral part of what we were joining, and I don't think we even knew about the letter that so upset the Chicago house and others who were not pacifists. I signed up for noncombatant service. But the other fellow with me didn't even sign up for that. We'd get big bundles of the paper to distribute, and if it had something in it we didn't agree with, we just didn't send them out that month. The strange thing is that she rather put up with this. She never was hard on us. Years later, I wrote a piece saying that I felt the Catholic Worker had so much to offer people who were only against particular wars, people who were not total pacifists. She printed that in the paper.

Jim Forest gives details and a contemporary perspective:

It certainly wasn't that she didn't sympathize! She was not naive about either the communists or the fascists. She hadn't the slightest doubt about the evil of the Nazi movement! But however passionate she was about Christian pacifism, it never broke relationships.

Dorothy took a huge beating over both the Spanish Civil War and World War II, though. I think if I remember what she said correctly, the *Catholic Worker* was expelled from the Catholic Press Association over [her neutrality in the Spanish War]. Dorothy never would rejoin, as I remember. Once I proposed it to her and she said no. She hadn't forgiven them. She was very . . . that had hurt. But pacifism was nothing new for her. The [other Catholic Workers] had just never taken [her views on this] too seriously. And precisely because she was a matriarch, she wasn't ashamed to be out of step with practically everybody in the movement. She did the right thing, but it was a very peculiar idea at the time.

Again, I would just say that sanctity makes it possible to be free. She was free to do anything, and she never felt that she was out of step with the tradition by doing it. She knew that she was out of step with most people. But she felt they were out of step with the biblical tradition, whether they were bishops or running a Catholic Worker community.

Dorothy was both politically a pacifist and committed to nonviolence as a way of life. As Franciscan Sister Rosemary Lynch says:

Dorothy always understood the connections between the power of nonviolence within the [Catholic Worker houses] and the power of nonviolence in bringing political peace to the whole world.

During the Vietnam War, the issue of nonviolence came to a head again, this time not over whether being against war was itself morally good, but on how to make one's resistance known. Opinions differ on whether and when Dorothy supported the draft-board raids, such as those of the Catonsville Nine and Milwaukee Fourteen, which operated in secrecy and included violence to property. Janet Kalven of Grailville remembers that Dorothy "was really upset with Dan [Berrigan] and thought it was exaggeration and kind of a self-indulgent, theatrical gesture [burning Selective Service files in Catonsville, Maryland, in 1968]. Yes, they had very different styles, but they were great friends and had great respect for each other."

Dan Berrigan himself told Jim Loney of Toronto:

I think she had reservations, going back to Gandhi and the Bible, about this kind of pro-active resistance and I think she was a little— or maybe even more than a little—uneasy about where it might go in the wrong hands. I don't think that any of it ever has fallen into the wrong hands, the hands of people who would escalate into violence, but that was part of her fear.

Tom Lewis-Borbely was one of the Catonsville Nine defendants:

I remember we were sitting up in front of the courtroom, and Willa [Bickham] tapped me on the shoulder and said, "Someone is here to see you." And there was this beautiful face, almost like it was surrounded by sunshine . . . the white hair and great smiling face of Dorothy in the courtroom. To me that was very much Dorothy supporting the draft board protests.

Michael Cullen, founder of Casa Maria Catholic Worker, was arrested as a member of the Milwaukee Fourteen, a group that burned draft-board files in the late stages of the Vietnam War. Michael remembers that Dorothy told him:

"**Y**our suffering is what redeems the action. The action in itself—its secret nature—is not in line . . . it breaks the line of nonviolence."

I felt that Dorothy's influence was very, very important. Once I had made the decision [to do the] action, there was a tension in me about the danger of violence becoming a part of it. There was the woman who was cleaning in the building, and she had the keys . . . the keys in the end had to be snatched [from her]. That would not have been something I would be in favor of [doing] again. Then we had to pay for this thing. It wasn't easy, huh? But Dorothy was saying, "The suffering is what will redeem it."[3]

Jim Forest was another member of the Milwaukee Fourteen:

Her first thoughts about the Catonsville Nine were very approving. She expressed them in a talk at the National Liturgical Conference in Washington, the summer or fall of 1968. I was there to hear it, and her opinion meant a great deal to me. I was connected to the people who participated in the Catonsville Nine, and approving of it, but it had never occurred to me to do anything like that. But Dorothy's opinion had a lot . . . pushed me a lot. And I was, of course, passionate to do something about the war in Vietnam. Then when she turned around and had a second thought, I was quite let down. By that time I was in jail.

Dorothy finally didn't agree with what we had done. But she treasured us and supported us, wrote about us, published our things in the newspaper. *(Pause.)* She also made it clear that this was not her idea of the best way to bring about the change that we wanted.

Tom Cornell adds:

About the draft file raids, Dorothy said, "These actions are not ours." And why aren't they ours? It's not that they are unjust or immoral. It's because they don't fit our idea of what nonviolence is. The Catholic Worker's definition of nonviolence includes the idea of openness. We do not enter into conspiracies that are exclusive and secretive. That's primary. And another is . . . well, the War Resisters League office was raided, and its subscription list was confiscated by people who believed they were doing the right thing. They were right wingers. Fascists, perhaps. Who knows? But they were sincere. Sincerity is not enough. What's the difference between raiding draft files and taking the subscription

---

[3] Michael was deported to his native Ireland, along with his young family. It wasn't until the 1990s that they were allowed to reenter the country.

list out of the War Resisters League office? Well, the comparison isn't exact. Nobody in the War Resisters League files is liable to be put into a position to kill or be killed. But there was enough truth, even in a limping analogy, to persuade Dorothy. She said, "Do not do to others what you don't want to have done to yourself. If you don't want to invite people to ransack these offices, don't ransack theirs."

Chuck Matthei discusses other problems Dorothy had with those who practiced different approaches to nonviolence:

She was always warm and supportive when we'd have conversations about dealing with courts and jails. I was inclined to practice noncooperation. I was always courteous, always communicative with authorities when that communication was possible, but I typically would politely refuse to play by the book. So I would refuse to participate in any way in the process, wouldn't walk when arrested or stand up when the judge came into the courtroom, and so forth. My feeling was that I had acted on the basis of my own conscience, and the law had nothing to do with that decision. I didn't act in order to break a law, but I wasn't willing to act simply in order to obey it, either.

Dorothy was quite sympathetic to the philosophy and spirit, but also, I think, often personally uncomfortable with the practice. She wasn't someone who enjoyed being carried or dragged around by the police, and I think she was also self-conscious about the inconvenience or the risk that it posed to them. Would they strain their back? Would they get aggravated or irritated? Would the occasion be the cause of tension or conflict? So she was ambivalent about it. She was both respectful and appreciative but also a little conflicted about it, so we had some interesting conversations about that.

She certainly understood defensive violence, just as Gandhi did. You know Gandhi used to say, "It is better to fight than to do nothing at all, but it is better to respond with an active nonviolence than to fight." Again, this was not the nonviolence of retreat, of isolation, of withdrawal into a personal security. This was an engaged practice—bringing a certain faith and spirit into the very difficult and conflicted events of the world.

Dorothy's pacifism grew and matured over the years. Although, as many point out, she was essentially an American, personally and politically, in her strong and consistent pacifism she differed from the assimilationist American Catholic community she had joined and instead proved to be a harbinger of the global Christianity that may well be the hope of the twenty-first century.

CIVIL DEFENSE DRILLS

Everyone went underground for the civil defense drills,
but Dorothy said, "I will not go."
                                                    —JUDITH MALINA

The end of World War II found the Catholic Worker movement diminished in both numbers and influence. Those who persevered, however,
report that the fifties were times of deepening intellectual and spiritual
commitment. Terry McKiernan from South Bend, Indiana, spent time at
the Worker in 1949 and calls them "the glory days." Thinking and writing about the intellectual roots of radicalism occupied a small and some
would say elite band of Workers when they weren't feeding and housing
the men on the Bowery. Activism was not the order of the day, but Dorothy Day, Ammon Hennacy, and their friends challenged the government
and were arrested several times for resisting Operation Alert, the air-raid
drills concocted by the Federal Civil Defense Administration to allay citizens' fears of the atomic bomb.

Civil Defense drill protest, Washington Square Park, 1956. Dorothy is
on the end.

Nina Polcyn Moore, co-founder of the Milwaukee Worker and one of Dorothy's lifelong friends, told me that when Dorothy was arrested with twenty-nine other pacifists in 1955, Nina wanted to pay her bail. But Bayard Rustin told her, "Don't do it. She's been in jail before and she'll be okay. We'll get more money if people know she's in jail." Nina paid the bail anyway.

Father James Joyce was only in grammar school at the time, and the publicity surrounding Dorothy's arrest is his first memory of the Worker:

I remember this picture in one of the afternoon papers. She's [sitting] on the ground, looking up at a police officer, all radiant and smiling. He's in his brass buttons and blue coat and smiling back at her, taking her by the arm. The headline was something like "Peaceniks Picnic in Park, Crazies Circumvent CD [Civil Defense]." Well, "circumvent" might have been too big a word for that paper, but I remember seeing the word "crazies."

Karl Meyer was young and idealistic when he met Dorothy. Now at Greenlands Catholic Worker in Nashville, he's still idealistic and often jailed for protesting against war and injustice:

Well, there isn't too much before I met Dorothy, because I met Dorothy before I was twenty years old. I was already a pacifist and interested in the ideals of voluntary poverty. Had a scholarship to the University of Chicago but dropped out after a year. Where was I going to go? Well, people head for the big cities, so I headed for New York City. Got a job at Barnes and Noble.

I had read about the civil defense protests in the *Catholic Worker*, where Dorothy and Ammon and a small group of Catholic Worker people . . . it was the third year that they had refused to take shelter during the compulsory air-raid drills. After going back and forth about the whole thing, I decided at the last minute to join them. Ran out and hailed a cab and told him, "Step on it, buddy!" Walked upstairs at the Catholic Worker on Chrystie Street. Dorothy and Ammon Hennacy were sitting there and some others. Judith Malina and Julian Beck, the anarchists of the Living Theater. About a dozen people. It was a very relaxed and friendly kind of atmosphere, with everybody just chatting and talking, preparing to go out at the appointed time and sit on the benches in the sunlight, sit in the park across the street. As I recall, Dorothy was even knitting. It was that kind of a . . . and Dorothy was . . . both Dorothy and Ammon were tremendously warm conversationalists. I introduced myself and said, "I would like to go with you in refusing to take shelter in the air raid."

Dorothy said to me, "Well, that's fine. But there's a couple things you should know. One is we plead guilty, and two, we don't take bail." (They didn't want to get involved in the legal process, just wanted to do civil disobedience.) "Now, you don't have to do it that way. But if you go with our group, we prefer that you do it that way." Right then, I would say, I crossed over from being a careful moderate to becoming a radical. I said I'd go along with it. Dorothy didn't ask me anything else, my age or anything. There was that acceptance—you were a responsible person. You had made your choice.

So I went out and sat with them on the bench and we were arrested. That night I slept on the floor of the cell with Ammon and Julian Beck of the Living Theater. It was one of those tanks. And Ammon gave me the whole story. The next day we went to court, and we pleaded guilty, and we got thirty days in jail. I was the only juvenile in the group, so I was sent to Rikers Island. And the rest of them were sent to the other prisons. Well, I guess Dorothy and Ammon worried about me that whole thirty days. I was separated from them and all alone. But I got along fine. Wasn't scared and didn't have any problems. We served the whole thirty days. When I got out, I immediately went down to the Catholic Worker, and from that time on, I was in with Dorothy and Ammon.

Arrested in 1957 with Dorothy were actress Judith Malina and her husband Julian Beck of the anarchist-inspired Living Theater. Judith tells a moving story of being in jail with Dorothy:

We shared a cell. She asked to be put in the cell with me in order to protect me. You see, I was being set upon by some tough, young women with clearly sexual implications. I was much tinier then than I am now, even, and young and was wearing a little white lace dress and my hair was long. One young woman asked in a loud way to have me put in her cell because she was interested in me. And Dorothy, seeing this as a danger to me, said in a voice . . . it was extraordinary. She merely spoke an irrefutable statement: "She belongs in my cell." Now this was exceptional for her. She generally was quiet and humble in the prison situation. But firm. Oh, as firm as a rock!

Now here's a kind of theologically interesting story. Dorothy had asked that I be put into her cell because of this aggressive woman. Shortly after that, this woman (let's call her Maria) was freed. And a few days later, her picture was in the paper because she had shot herself in the stomach. She had gone back on heroin, and didn't want to face it, and had shot herself.

Dorothy immediately initiated prayers for her. And she said that she felt that she should not have interfered, that if I had been put in this

Arrest following noncompliance with Civil Defense drill, 1956.

Under arrest.

woman's cell, it's perfectly possible that I might have helped her. (This was Dorothy's point of view. I'm not sure of it at all.) Dorothy felt this was a lesson in not interfering. She very much felt it was her fault and said she should have let me go into Maria's cell.

In political activism, there's a seeming contradiction. (Although in the saints, all seeming contradictions are resolved in love.) We sense a contradiction between the activists who take the step—make the decision—and those who possess a certain quietism of allowing God to do the work. Of stepping aside and looking at the suffering and saying, "Where I can, I will prevent it. On the other hand, this is the way of the world."

Dorothy was an anarchist. My affinity to her was as an activist, anarchist comrade. My theater [the Living Theater] is about a hope that we can organize our lives in an anarchist way, in a more humane way. And I had in common with her this spirit. All the time we were in jail, she tried to teach me that anarchism is holiness, which I had never understood. I had thought there was much contradiction between anarchism and holiness. But now we come to the contradiction between activism and holiness and activism and anarchism.

Anarchism is activist. Dorothy walked out on the street to make that civil defense protest in order to make what anyone would call trouble. That is, she wanted people to notice the contradiction, so she sat out in the street in the sunlight. Saying, "This is my street and I'm not going to fall in a hole because I'm afraid my fellow man is going to kill me. I'm not going to support that structure."

This was an active decision, challenging the whole society. And also a tension-building decision. Everyone went underground for the civil defense drills, but Dorothy said, "I will not go." A very strong act of will, an act of will in which she contradicts what everybody wants her to do, including the church. It was a great privilege and marvel to be secluded with a woman like that, to come close to such a soul. A beautiful experience. But a contradiction, too, because it was also the most horrible place I'd ever been in. Surrounded with . . . with ugliness. Architectural ugliness and more. Nine hundred women, and I think eight hundred were prostitutes and about seven hundred were drug addicts. Whole layers of suffering and misery. So it was incredible to be exposed, at the same time, to both the highest that the human spirit is capable of and the most incredible expressions of suffering.

Dorothy became very quickly a legend in the prison. There was a lot of press at the time and a picket line outside. Everybody was aware of it, and we were certainly celebrities of a sort inside the prison. Most of the guards were Catholic, and they came to her and had their Bibles blessed and their rosaries kissed. Priests came. And the wealthy came on pilgrimage. She was always sort of annoyed about this, at how people were outwardly . . . When she would hear, "Nineteen Philippine priests would like to see you," she would make an angry face. But then I'm sure she was absolutely heavenly when she confronted them, because she was . . . because she responded to any human being. She responded the same way to these terrified, struggling, suffering women in jail, these women who couldn't speak without uttering the Oedipal adjective, who felt themselves compelled to say as many negative things as they could.

There was unbelievable fear in the prison. Most of the women had that dreadful word "incorrigible" stamped on their record, which means that they had to go to jail for a certain period of time every year. They were in that field of repeated suffering . . . like a wheel of suffering. Like their mothers and their grandmothers and their great-grandmothers, all without really steady men in the family. But a succession of women falling back into prostitution or drugs, going through the same suffering and misery. And feeling really indicted by fate. Angry and victimized. Angry and struggling. Somehow Dorothy managed to bring a certain light.

But like everyone else, we were strip-searched. It was extremely humiliating and the jokes that were made were unpleasant, but I have a tough skin. But Dorothy . . . Dorothy had been chaste for many, many years. When a chaste woman is poked like that and subjected to really thoughtless handling in which someone searches the inside of her body, without any consideration for the dignity of the person they're searching . . . Dorothy bled for several days after that and was in considerable pain. When it happened, I was standing in the outer part of the office and I heard her cry out in pain.

The two young women who searched us were not medical or paramedical people. They made obscene jokes during the whole procedure. I think Dorothy could forgive the obscene jokes. (She used to say she has a deaf ear which she turns on in such moments.) But it was really horrible to see the lack of dignity. Everybody who came into that prison was subjected to the same kind of treatment, probably on the basis that they were all rotten and deserved it.

And everyone's nerves are raw, if only because they can't go down to the drugstore and have a malted milk or because they can't call their brother or get to sleep on a metal plate that serves as a bed. The noise is terrible and the heat is . . . when I was in with Dorothy, we were in the middle of a heat wave.

It was unbelievably cramped in those narrow quarters. The Women's House of Detention was built to hold about three or four hundred people and there were nine hundred there. Dorothy and I were in a cell which was about four and a half feet wide with that tiny space taken up mostly by a bed that had another little metal bed that pulled out under it. In which Dorothy slept, not I. Because you can't deal with a saint. You've got to take the more comfortable bed because she won't.

You can't say, "Look you're older and more decrepit." Not to a saint. She wouldn't hear of it. This is one of the troubles with dealing with that kind of person. But most of what was different was just better. The same as with other people, only better. I think the only difficulty one might point to is that a saint is, as it were, a living reproach. One wants to live up to the good example, but as my friend Steve Ben Israel says, "We've all been swimming in dirty water." If we all feel our own "dirty waterness," and we feel the world and its greed and its fears and its anger . . . when you confront someone who approaches these things from a higher level, you have to take their example and start to work very hard on yourself. I had to, as it were, try to become a saint myself. Dorothy was very careful about that, though. She was not sanctimonious. She was not irreproachable.

For instance, when we met the warden . . . The warden arranged a meeting with us in the most clumsy and unpleasant way—in the middle of the dining hall with the prisoners all standing around listening to us. And he told us immediately that he didn't regard us as being in the same class as the other prisoners. They are all hearing this. Now, can you imagine!

Dorothy immediately . . . she was knitting something. She said to me right away, "Don't argue." She didn't want to continue on that level, but I couldn't help myself. I argued with the man. (I argue with everybody. And I try to make everybody understand what I think are some very basic fundamental principles. I do this all the time. I think you might have noticed it.) *(Laughs.)* Identifying the ground on which we differ and then trying to unify it. The more I talked, the more Dorothy muttered, "Don't answer him. Don't argue."

Later she talked to me about it, and I think in a way she's right. Although I have my character to deal with here. One has to know when to enter the arena and when to remain outside, when it's wise not to meddle, and when one must take an active step. I think she was particularly wise in this knowledge, in this sensitivity to what is useful to human suffering and what, in spite of our good intentions, can only increase it.

Oh, here's a strange tale. I don't know what would have happened if it had actually come to something. As I said, it was unbelievably hot. There were just six little panes of glass for windows. There was a little screen behind them, but it was completely clogged. Just no air at all. Sweltering! In the middle of the window, there was one little pane of clear glass, the only one we could look out of.

And I said, "Oh, God, if only there was some air coming in!"

Dorothy made a little prayer to Vincent Ferrer, whose story we were studying. (The same St. Vincent Ferrer who put all the Jews into synagogues and set fire to them. But he also had some noble aspects.) And she made up a little jingle. "St. Vincent Ferrer, give us some air." We were both sweating terribly and really suffering from the heat. It was unbelievable—close and damp and hot.

I said, "I'd like to break that little window!"

Dorothy said, "Go ahead! Break it! Break it!!"

And I took off my shoe and tapped the pane with the heel, and it cracked. I thought surely this would mean the end. They would put me in seclusion, in the tank or whatever. I was absolutely terrified! I had broken a prison window.

Dorothy said, "What are you frightened of? I told you to do it."

"Look. You told me, but I did it."

"I'm going to say that I stirred you up to it."

"And I'll say that you had nothing to do with it. I broke it of my own free will!"

We argued about this question, and then it was decided . . . I don't remember if Dorothy suggested it or I did. It was decided (using the passive voice) that when I was swabbing the cell, I broke the window with the handle of the mop.

That was a lie born of fear, as all lies are. Fortunately we didn't have to use it. No one ever saw the broken window. But we lived in twenty-five days of fear. Every single time the guard walked by, we lived in fear of that broken window. My guess is that if we had been questioned, that neither Dorothy nor I would have talked about that ridiculous mop handle. I think we would have told the truth, in spite of this madness of deciding we were going to lie.

Our whole experience there . . . I must say that my relationship with Dorothy for those thirty days was like . . . was very girlish, in a way. Somehow we were determined to have fun, too. In spite of the tragedy around us. In spite of the seriousness of our cause. Certainly, either of us was willing to break into highly serious rhetoric at any moment. She could do it on a high level, and I certainly could do it all the time. To a fault. But I think that there was a certain spirit of fun, a certain spirit of even joyousness that Dorothy exuded. Always did.

Oh, she was a great storyteller. She talked about Mike Gold, Eugene O'Neill—all those people she knew before the Worker. She also talked a lot about Forster. Forster joined the pickets outside the prison, and that touched her tremendously.

We talked a lot about sexuality and woman's life. We talked about children, all those things. Very deeply . . . very deeply. We also laughed a lot and giggled after lights out, telling funny stories. She would read me something from the *Lives of the Saints*, and I would read something from our [Jewish] liturgy, and we'd talk about holy things. Then after a while, we'd start telling funny stories and laughing a lot, too. It was wonderful that we had both.

I think she unified the concepts of idea and practice better than anyone . . . better than anyone. Her ideas extended all the way to the pacifist idea, all the way to the anarchist idea, all the way to the poverty. Dorothy's human generosity could include the most pitiful person and the finest in the same embrace, and so I finally learned what she had been trying to teach me, that anarchism is holiness. It's a holiness here and now that consists of treating every person as a holy being. No dividing into good ones and bad ones.

PIETY AND POLITICS

Michael Harrington may be the most widely known of those influenced by Dorothy Day. Two of his books, The Other America *and his autobiography,* The Long Distance Runner, *show how his "politics on the left*

*wing of the possible" were influenced by the two years he spent with the
Catholic Worker. He left the Worker when he left the Catholic church in
1953 and then began his career as a writer and activist, defining himself
as a democratic socialist and working in both traditional and alternative
politics. He is most frequently cited for* The Other America, *often credited for inspiring the Democratic administration's* War on Poverty. *In
1984, Harrington learned that he had cancer. Through surgery and che-
motherapy, he continued the work of advancing his ideals. I spent an afternoon with him in July of 1988, when he was in remission; he died one
year later.*

When I was at the Worker in the early fifties—which was, in some
ways, a low point in terms of influence for Dorothy, when she was least
popular with anybody—we appeared as a small band of nuts. Catholic
puritans. Totally marginal radicals. Who would have predicted, at that
point, that the bishops of the United States would write a pastoral letter
on nuclear weapons and quote Dorothy Day? It turns out the Dorothy
Day in 1952 was closer to what became the official position of the hierarchy than [Cardinal] Spellman. Spellman is nowhere in there, 'cause he was
simply a cold warrior. I don't think Dorothy ever understood how enormously influential she was. Once at a party, I said to Bill Buckley, "When
the history of America and Catholicism in the 1950s is written, Francis
Cardinal Spellman will be a footnote and Dorothy Day will be a chapter."

The Worker is . . . well, it's hard to say because the Worker was so
many different things, so many different strands. Certainly, Dorothy kept
a pacifist witness at a time when practically nobody else was doing it. And
that was very important. The anarchist theory isn't worth the powder to
blow it to hell. The decentralism is important if you don't take it too literally—the message that there was an enormous danger in socialist and
left-wing statism, that the left had been much too uncritical of bureaucracy, much too impersonalist, much too authoritarian, too much in favor of social engineering. Communitarianism. Decentralization. Personalism . . . I think if you don't get too literal-minded about them, they're
profoundly true.

Dorothy's criticism of socialism was in terms of the notion of sub-
sidiarity, the principle that, wherever possible, things should be done on
the most decentralized and intra-personal level, should be done by the
family, the neighborhood, the community, rather than the state. And I
think most socialists now understand that.

Dorothy was basically not political at all. She called it anarchism, but
what she wanted was for everybody to perform the works of mercy. To
transform their lives in a Christian way. Dorothy was for community. She

was for charity. She was for the works of mercy. That's what Dorothy cared about. And if everybody did that, you wouldn't need a welfare state. Where she was wrong is, don't hold your breath until everybody starts to lead that kind of a life. In the meantime, people are hungry and, by God, somebody has got to give them food stamps! And thank God they've got food stamps! It's better than nothing.

Even at the Worker, I was a bit of a heretic. Because I was . . . even though I would not go as far as to vote Democrat, I actually believed that political action could change things. I remember Dorothy was very upset when I joined the Socialist Party. Dorothy didn't vote and just couldn't understand why I'd embraced Holy Mother the State. I remember saying at the time—it was true then and it's true now—that I certainly rejected any kind of a centralized, bureaucratic socialism. And that no, I was not embracing Holy Mother the State, but that I did believe in political action.

I used to have big arguments with Dorothy. I said that if you really wanted to go back to organic farming to grow the food of the world, you'd better have some plan for the several billion people who were going to starve to death. Because without our current agricultural productivity, we can't begin to feed the world. We would have endless discussions about these things. About why there should be traffic lights, et cetera.

That was something about the radical movement in general during that period: There was time to think. The one good consequence of Joe McCarthy was that we didn't have to spend our time organizing demonstrations. There were no left-wing mass movements of any kind—no antiwar movement, no anti-intervention in Central America movement.

Well, there were some exceptions. I remember I helped organize in the campaign for clemency for the Rosenbergs while I was at the Worker. Wrote the articles in the newspaper and did some of the communicating with people in Europe. But we . . . the difference between that period and, let's say, the period of the Vietnam War is enormous. During the Vietnam War, the Worker was a center for people seriously involved in mass mobilization, draft resistance, and all that sort of thing.

I was at the Worker during the Korean War. We were opposed to it and in favor of some form of resistance, but there was no mass movement. We would regularly picket on behalf of the workers in Barcelona. Or go to May Day meetings at the Labor Temple where you would have only a handful of people. The whole non-communist left in New York City would fit into a pretty small auditorium at that stage of the game.

I got on quite well with Dorothy. I think some of it was that I'd been brought up in a very middle-class way. Taught that I was to stand up whenever a woman entered the room and so forth. So when I went to the

Worker, I still had these very middle-class habits, and I think Dorothy liked that old-fashioned aspect of me. She loved the fact that I held the door open for her and pulled her chair out, even if it was sort of ridiculous in the dining room at the Catholic Worker, where we had rats and roaches.

Dorothy was very feminine, which was strange for a woman whose first arrest was as a feminist. In the period when she first came to New York, Dorothy led a liberated life, certainly. For a young girl, moving in with Forster, having a baby without benefit of clergy . . . yet there was this very feminine, very old-fashioned aspect.

At the Worker, people would give us books. I remember I was interested in something by the psychiatrist Steckel on auto-eroticism. Dorothy got terribly upset. "Michael! We do not even talk about such things!"

When Dorothy talked about her own girlhood in the Village, she made it sound much more innocent than it was, as it turns out. I mean you would have thought that Forster was the only man Dorothy ever had anything to do with, which was not the case. And of course we didn't know what we know now from the [William Miller] biography—that she had had an abortion.

Yes, she was very puritanical. I remember when Dwight McDonald was interviewing her for the *New Yorker*. Like so many people, Dwight fell in love with Dorothy. Not in the passionate sense, but in admiration. So he did something that . . . if the magazine had known about it at the time, it would've blown a gasket! He gave Dorothy his manuscript before he turned it in. I was right there when Dorothy was sanitizing her life. Dwight had come across the quotation in Malcolm Cowley's book, *Exile's Return*, that said Dorothy could drink all the Italian gangsters under the table in the Sixth Avenue speak-easies. And to hear Dorothy tell it, when she was in these speak-easies, she was drinking sarsaparilla or something.

There used to be endless speculation at the Worker about her Village days. Who were her lovers? Did she have an affair with Eugene O'Neill? To this day, I don't have any idea whether . . . I mean to hear Dorothy talk, she and Eugene O'Neill were simply good friends. My impression of O'Neill was that if he were good friends with a woman, it tended to go beyond friendship. But we never knew. That was a very funny thing about Dorothy. For all of her radicalism politically, Dorothy had a profoundly conservative streak in her makeup. She was a very conservative Catholic, theologically. Had some real trouble, I think, with some of Vatican II.

For instance, here's a story: I arrived at the Worker shortly after Cardinal Spellman had sent [John Francis] McIntyre down to read the riot act. What was apparently bugging Spellman was that the paper was called the *Catholic* Worker. What he was angling for, and didn't get, was for her to drop the word *Catholic*. He believed [the name] was an attempt to in-dicate that this was a *Catholic* position, and he didn't want anybody else speaking for the church. This was the famous occasion when McIntyre said to her, "What would you do if the Cardinal told you to shut down the Catholic Worker?"

She said, "If our dear, sweet cardinal, who is the vicar of Christ in New York City, told me to shut down the Catholic Worker, I would close it down immediately." She was dead serious. That's what drove me crazy. Dorothy really did go around referring to Spellman as "our dear, sweet cardinal" and "the vicar of Christ."

This was the Pius XII church. Women were supposed to keep their heads covered and their mouths shut. The man was the Christ figure, and the woman was the helpmate. Very explicit male chauvinism. Now that was strange, because we were living in a community where, whenever we made a decision, we all had a completely democratic, anarchist discussion, and then Dorothy made up her mind. The place was run on a führer con-cept, and Dorothy was the führer. So you had a house totally dominated by a woman, but it was male chauvinist in its ideology.

When I interviewed him, Michael had a print of Fritz Eichenberg's "The Last Supper" hanging in his office, a print that hangs on the wall of almost every Catholic Worker house. Michael swears that he's in it, that the young man standing in the doorway, with the long nose and the book in his pocket, is him. I asked him if he were coming in or going out. He didn't answer.

The Worker was not an unhappy place. There were tensions, though, and I think there were tensions about me. I started playing a fairly sig-nificant role very quickly. I got along with Dorothy and I spoke well and very quickly began to do a lot of writing for the paper. As time went on, I did a lot of speaking. Dorothy was wonderful. She'd get invitations, invitations sent to Dorothy Day, but she'd treat them as if they were in-vitations to the movement. And she would answer: "Thank you for the invitation. Michael Harrington will come." To someone who had never heard of Michael Harrington. I'm not sure how happy they were. Here they are trying to get this famous Catholic woman and instead they get a twenty-three year old.

One of my happiest periods at the Worker was when I was the night watchman. I forget how long it lasted, maybe six months. I would make a tour of the house every hour and press one of those security things to show that I'd been to a check station. It would take all of five minutes. I'd listen to good music and write poetry and read books. All night long.

You see, I had come back to the church, not on a Jesuit basis but on a Pascalian, or Kierkegaardian, basis. Not with a sense that I could prove the truth of the church, not with a rationalist "it's all in Thomas Aquinas" Catholicism, but with a rather heterodox and existentialist variety. So I lived with a tension, an ambiguity, for the entire two years I was at the Worker.

We used to talk about two St. Teresa's, known around the house as the "big T" and the "little T." Lisieux and Avila. St. John of the Cross was very fashionable. We thought Cardinal Spellman wasn't a very good Catholic, that he was much too lax. We felt that the pope should give away the Vatican and that sort of stuff. There was a standard Catholic Worker statement in my time: "What are you here for?" And the proper answer was, "To be a saint." We were gung-ho. Dorothy was always talking about being fools for Christ. A heavy dose of existentialism in Dorothy.

You know, I never was a dogmatic Catholic Worker. There was a dimension, a scrupulous Jansenist dimension, that at times became a denigration of material comfort, period. I remember very well saying to myself, at the time, that "good food is better than rotten food." We ate rotten food at the Worker. We bought the cheapest cuts of meat or begged for the meat the butchers were about to throw out. We usually ate stale bread. And I said to myself, "This is not good." If you didn't conform to this line, you know, [they said you] were not radical. The ultimate insult.

I used to try to go to Mass daily. Many of us recited the Hours privately, and then we had monastic compline together, so there was a lot of liturgical prayer. But in that entire period, I was carrying on a dialogue with myself. I finally came to the conclusion, "No. Much as I still admire this institution, much as I still love this institution, I don't believe in it."

I thought the decision would be terribly wrenching, would be a psychologically horrible moment for me. And instead, it was just okay. I left the Worker when I left the church. It was rather hard to be at the Worker and not be a Catholic, so I took off. Dorothy called me up, which was unusual. Asked me to go to lunch, which was super-unusual. She'd heard I had left the church, and she wanted to know why.

"Was it a woman?"

And I said, "No, Dorothy. It's theology."

And Dorothy sort of said, "Oh, I'm so happy to hear that."

Dorothy was a real Pius XII Catholic. Quite puritanical, but I suspect she was a very passionate woman herself. Even though she drove Francis Spellman bananas with her politics, she shared that Spellman sense that the real sins were the sins of the flesh. And [my leaving the church] was only intellectual, something you could get over, whereas the sins of the flesh really grew on you.

GOD AND MAMMON

One time I said to Dorothy, "My heavens! With all these
people, do you ever figure you can't feed them?" And she
said, "Well, it hasn't happened yet."
—Sister Teresa Murray

Dorothy's attitude about money and property was both faith-filled and pragmatic. After the initial years of renting, Dorothy purchased the house at 223 Chrystie Street, and later a simple corporation purchased two buildings within a few blocks of each other, buildings that remain the home of the Catholic Worker in Manhattan—St. Joseph House on First Street between First and Second Avenue, and Maryhouse nearby on Third Street.

When the Catholic Worker needed money, Workers would confidently ask God for it, sometimes by fasting or setting up continuous prayer vigils at the local church. Another way of asking was through St. Joseph, who was a powerful intercessor in matters concerning real estate, according to the Italian neighbors of the Lower East Side. So Workers would tuck petitions under the statue of St. Joseph that always resided in the office. Mary Durnin remembers the financial miracles and the touch-and-go situation of the early days in New York:

A virtue at the Catholic Worker was "precarity," something we usually fear. One time Con Edison came by, threatening to turn off the electricity unless we paid the bill. Well, Dorothy had just opened a letter and a check in it contained the exact amount of the bill. So we were saved! And we practiced precarity, too, on the farm in Easton. Hail would flatten a crop, but we carried on anyway, just like my people back in Wisconsin. Hope is eternal.

Dorothy's distrust of the state always influenced her financial transactions. Sister Teresa Murray recalls:

Remember when she sold the [Chrystie Street] property to the city, and they wanted to give her an additional amount of money because it had accrued interest or something? She wouldn't take it. I asked her about that, and she said she wanted to let them know that money was not a commodity, but just a medium of exchange. She really lived that. The money came into the Worker, and the money went out. When they felt they needed to make a plea to the readers, they did.

I asked her one time if she'd ever take money from the government. And she said, "Well, I took my public school education." She didn't want to be beholden to "Holy Mother the State," as she called it. I remember once we were shown through the Municipal House, the men's place there on Third Street. She didn't have any criticism of their taking in people, but she herself wouldn't take any money [from the government]. Or from foundations, either.

Dorothy felt big government violated the principles of personalism by which she lived. As a consequence, conservatives often try to claim Dorothy as their own, to say that because she was against centralized government, she would not support government aid to the poor and needy. While she was no fan of Washington, Dorothy was a radical, not a reactionary. Ed Turner elaborates this distinction:

As for being opposed to centralized government, yes she was. But to apply to her the cliches of reactionaries to "the welfare state" is a damnable lie. She worked all her life and supported not only herself and her daughter's family but also the CW family in New York and its various "farms." And, of course, the Catholic Worker has always encouraged those who needed help to apply for any welfare they were entitled to. What was more significant was the help individual members of the staff would give when the bureaucracy snafued. They would go to the welfare office with the "client" and straighten out whatever needed straightening out. If it meant getting documentation, they would see that it was done. On the other hand, Dorothy understood that "what the state has given the state can take away." Once the paper had a headline: "Holy Mother the State."

Dorothy saw clearly that if people were really helping people, whether through the offices of the state or one-on-one as Christianity asks of us, there would be no need for soup lines. Bill Griffin explains that "she thought that society should act as a kind of family." Tom Cornell remembers a tough financial time for the Worker:

It was a very, very difficult time, one of the real low points in the Catholic Worker history. The Chrystie Street house had been confiscated by the city. Couldn't find a house to rent and no one was going to give her a house. We rented the storefront at 175 Chrystie Street but had to hire apartments around. Depressing beyond belief. It looked as if the Catholic Worker might even die. Money just wasn't coming in. The subscriptions had not gone up much from the post–World War II period. Couldn't pay the grocer, the printing bills.

Now the annual budget then was less than $70,000 for printing and all of it. The Ford Foundation offered Dorothy a grant of $65,000. Money for a year's budget. Dorothy turned it down.

I said "Why, Dorothy?" Now, I wasn't defending the idea that she should have accepted it. I just wanted to hear why she turned it down.

She said, "I knew a guy who worked for Ford out in Detroit, worked on these concrete floors for how many years, and he got arthritis. And they wouldn't put a carpet on it and wouldn't put a wood floor down, either."

I didn't believe it. I knew that Dorothy always gave the answer she felt like giving at the time. Ask her ten minutes later, and she'd give you another. They could both be true, though. But from piecing it all together and knowing her, I figured it out.

She was shrewd. A lot shrewder than she appeared to be. If she accepted $65,000, she would feel constrained in conscience to tell people. If you've got a year's budget in the bank, why should nickel and dimers send . . . why should my father-in-law send his ten dollars every three months? That's what you really need—a lot of people giving small sums of money. That way people feel an investment in the Worker, an identification with the Worker . . . It may be only a little bit, but it's real, and it means something to them.

And another thing about the Worker that I think is very admirable—as long as Dorothy had money in the bank, she'd never put out an appeal. It's not like some joints that have three million dollars in the bank and are still making the same solicitation.

Robert Ellsberg reminds us:

She never really tried to be successful. Or wanted to be. She never compromised in ways that would have brought more security to the Worker, or made it more "professional," or put it in touch with influential people—whether bishops or politicians. She always felt those concerns were irrelevant. She just stayed close to her vocation, which was the Little Way of St. Thérèse.

THE LONG VIEW

Tom Cornell came to the Worker permanently in 1962, serving as editor of the newspaper for the first two years of his association with the movement. In 1964 he married Monica Ribar, whose parents were Catholic Workers in Cleveland. Tom and Monica's two children are active in the movement today. Tom was a founder of the Catholic Peace Fellowship, a specifically pacifist organization affiliated both with the Worker and with the Fellowship of Reconciliation. In the eighties he and Monica ran a Catholic Worker house in Waterbury, Connecticut, and in 1993 they

moved to the Catholic Worker farm in Marlboro, New York. From there,
Tom continues his long association with the New York houses, acting now
in the role of senior statesman. His memories span the last fifty years and
include stories of Dorothy's relationship with the newspaper.

I knew Dorothy Day. I first met her through *The Long Loneliness*. It was
the fall of 1952 or very early in 1953, and her autobiography had just
been published. I was a freshman at Fairfield University. [The book] spoke
to my condition. Answered some of the questions and raised still others.

Finally I said, "I've gotta go down to the Worker and see for myself."
So I took the train into the city, I walked down the Bowery, I walked
around the corner, and before I knew it I was at the Worker and up the
stairs and into the library, where the Friday night meeting had already
started. All the chairs were taken, and people were sitting on the floor and
standing up along the walls. In the corner was a woman sitting cross-
legged and knitting. I don't remember who was talking; I don't remember the topic. All I remember is that the knitting needles clacked when she
didn't like what she heard. When she liked what she heard, there was a
nice steady, quiet, sound of knitting needles touching. She had large bones.
She had almond eyes. She had gray hair, braided and twisted into a crown.
Someone nudged me and said, "That's Dorothy Day."

COURTESY TOM AND MONICA CORNELL

Dorothy with Tom and Monica Cornell on their wedding day.

In the question-and-answer period, somebody got up and talked about people having a natural right to basic security. But Dorothy said, "Security. Why talk about security? The young people here tonight don't need to hear about security. Great things need to be done and who's going to do them but the young people? And how are they going to do them if all they're thinking about is their own security? Laying aside treasure for the morrow? Let the morrow take care of itself. Consider the lilies of the field, how they grow."

Well, I was breathless. She had me right then and there. If I had been introduced to Peter Maurin and not to Dorothy Day, it probably wouldn't have taken. After that, whenever I had any free time, I came into the Worker from college.

I knew Dorothy. She opened me to the world—the really most important currents, a mystical current. This was the most important thing in the universe, and she put me in contact with it. I was able to participate in it. What more can you ask? *(Pause.)* How grateful you are. That's why you cry. *(Long pause.)*

It was a couple of years later before I came to the Worker full time. In my heart of hearts, I wanted to be the editor of the paper. I had written to her to tell her I was coming. She calls me and says, "I want you to come in on Monday morning." She didn't ask if it was possible. Or convenient. She didn't say, "Would you like to?" She said, "I want you to come in on Monday morning; I'm taking a freighter to Havana on the next night, so will you be here?"

So I took up my sleeping bag and hightailed it to New York. She put me at a desk at 175 Chrystie Street, third floor, right by the front window. The front wall was about to fall right down on the street, by the way. It was horrible. A dilapidated, decrepit building. Leaked like a sieve. Then she gives me a sheaf of galleys and a booklet with the proofreaders signs—the little squiggles: delete this, transpose this, lower case, italics, stuff like that.

"Read this. It will tell you all you have to know. You're going to put out the paper." I hadn't done anything like this since I was in high school.

"I don't know how to do this kind of stuff!"

She says, "Oh, don't worry. The printers will teach you."

Suddenly here I was, working directly with Dorothy! It was marvelous. Because what she would do . . . see, she lived in the same building. And I would stop by her apartment in the morning, and we'd have a cup of coffee and talk about manuscripts. Actually, in the two years that I was putting out the paper, Dorothy participated in the production of only three issues out of twenty-two. She was very rarely there, so she left me in charge [of selecting] the manuscripts. Of course, if I received something from her, it was understood that it was to be printed as is. Well, sometimes I had to make linking sentences; sometimes I had to repair a run on; sometimes I would have to change Rochester to Syracuse.

Did I ever leave stuff out? Never! *(Laughs.)* You had a hard enough time explaining why you had to change Syracuse to Rochester. She would say that she was having coffee with Professor X at this school in Syracuse, and then in the next paragraph she's in Rochester. If you can't get her on the phone, you just throw a dart. What's it going to be? Rochester or Syracuse? But when she worked at it . . . and in even her most casual stuff there would be at least one paragraph that was a gem. One paragraph that would just really shine right off the page.

I mean there aren't that many people who can write that well. She was a craftsman. Her craft was writing and she practiced it and when she wrote her very best, it was terrific. It was riveting and it stays. I don't know how many times I've read *The Long Loneliness* from 1952 until the present. And it's going to stand up. They tell me that all of her columns will be available on the Internet before long.

I did what I thought I should do for Dorothy. I tried to understand her mind and to translate that into . . . uh, policy for the paper and policy for the movement in its relationship to the larger peace and justice movements. How did I do this? Well, basically reading what she wrote, listening to what she said. She was not at all hesitant to give people correction. If she thought that a person was too far over on . . . say, a Marxist orientation, she would give them a corrective in that way. But if she thought the person was too bourgeois, she'd push them the opposite direction, in the direction of understanding things from a class perspective.

We did fight a lot. The first time she upbraided me was for the second issue I put out. It was October of '62, and I had three priests in one issue. She said, "This is a layman's paper." (She didn't say lay paper.) "One or two priests are okay. Three is one too many!" She was not anticlerical, but she did have an idea from Peter, and I think it's valid—that lay people, not priests, should be the leaders in the social area. If I made a mistake—for instance, I let an anniversary of Peter Maurin's death go by without putting any "Easy Essays" in the paper—if I made a mistake, Dorothy was incensed at first, but she'd always make it up.

I was the liaison between the Worker and the larger peace movement during much of the sixties. She was interested in the other groups, especially the people in them. For instance, she became very fond of people at the War Resisters League. She was very respectful, especially of Dave Dellinger, but it was I who went out. Dorothy really . . . she was an intelligent, educated woman, politically sophisticated. But she was not . . . she could not deal with some things on her own without the advice of others whom she trusted. There are areas of political and philosophical thought where she just was out of her element. I'm not saying out of her depth, but out of her element.

I had proved to her my loyalty and my ability to understand her mind and to speak it. People said to me, "Tom, how can you do this? I mean, you're just a mouthpiece for Dorothy Day. You're not a person in your own right."

I said, "This is the person I want to be. I want to be Dorothy's mouth at this time. Let me grow more, let me experience more, let me understand better, let me get anywhere near to Dorothy's spiritual depth, and then we'll talk about something else." I didn't realize she was coming to depend upon me.

Those were the days. (Pause.) We all miss her a great deal. We loved her. She was ordinary, and she always said the things she did were what anyone could do. But she was extraordinary, too. You see, in spite of everything I have a faith that we are going to move forward. I believe that the human experiment is basically a comedy and not a tragedy in the classic sense, that we can go forward and we will go forward. It's because there were people like Dorothy Day to give a model of action. That's what it's about. (Long pause.) I thank you.

THE SIXTIES

All Dorothy's children are here.
                    —BETTY BARTELME, AT AN ANTIWAR PROTEST

It wasn't until the time of the Vietnam War that the Catholic Worker began to grow again in numbers and influence. Catholic Workers were among the first and most forceful voices against the war, with several jailed for public draft card burnings or other forms of resistance. It was in the sixties that I discovered the Worker through my involvement with the Saginaw Valley Peace Watch and the two short-lived Catholic Worker houses in Saginaw during that decade.

Tom Cornell gives an overview of Dorothy's influence during the sixties:

The Catholic Worker would do a lot in coalition with other groups, and Dorothy would take my advice on these actions, whether it was the War Resisters League, the CNVA [The Committee for Non-Violent Action], or the FOR [Fellowship of Reconciliation] where I was on the staff. Perhaps we had some success in restraining the government. We didn't end the war. It lasted twelve years. (Pauses.) The longer it went on, the more desperate our young people became. By 1968, you found that people were questioning their commitment to nonviolence. We'd done everything. Petitioned en masse. Written letters and articles. We'd had demonstrations, we had educated people, we had fasted, and we had prayed. And it only got worse.

Kathe McKenna with her husband, John, founded Haley House in Boston in 1966. Her views reflect the more militant members of the movement:

The times they were the most ferocious. The realities of the draft permeated everyone and everything. So debilitating! You felt you weren't accomplishing anything, that all of your energy was not stopping the war. Half or two-thirds of the people we were seeing [at Haley House] were veterans. Thank you, Uncle Sam! All of our friends were going off to jail, but we weren't seeing anything change and we were impatient—one of the terrible afflictions of youth. And just drowning in anger.

But Dorothy was always present, always supportive. There was no one saying all Catholic Workers needed to make the same decisions about these complex issues, but just a total respect and understanding that these were decisions of conscience. In contrast, we were young and very fired up. There was among us—and maybe she was aware of it—a tendency to grade people. You know, to think you're more radical than someone else. Whether it came to Catholicism, or your antiwar stance, or your decisions around nonviolence. But one never felt that with Dorothy.

I remember when Dorothy came to Boston to give a talk to some sisters. John and I were on the same program, representing local people who were doing the work. I was trembling in my boots. Here was the matriarch!

Now John and I were not pacifists at the time. And we were going to talk about that, about our anger and our . . . even if she was there. We were prepared for the worst, because we knew that she tended to be rather adamant about pacifism. Well we did, in fact, share how we felt, and I remember when we broke loose and told the nuns. It was rather emotional. Intense. We were saying things they didn't expect. And Dorothy didn't expect it, either.

After it was all over, we were drinking coffee and Dorothy came up to us and said in her wonderfully stiff, warm way: "You must feel very strongly about what you believe." And she just smiled and left it at that.

What she identified with was not our beliefs as such, which clearly clashed with hers, but with our struggle. Psychologists are always trying to teach people how to do this. She simply said, "I understand."

And that's exactly what happens when we're in the soup kitchen and listening to somebody tell about their . . . their nastiness. They're full of venom and bile and you can talk to them about it by simply saying, "I understand how deeply hurt you feel or how angry you are." And they relax and then you can go on to something else. Once you recognize and honor their feelings. That's what Dorothy did for us.

Tom Cornell continues, describing some of the feeling in the New York house at that time:

It's 1969 and the war is still going on. People storm into her room, using every foul word in the book. Why hadn't she stopped that war? "You're a fake. You're a phony. All you do is go flying around to see the fucking pope. The world is burning down, and you're not even scraping a carrot!" Some very nice people were really unnerved. And their hatred for the authority of the church was coming out, as well. When she began to sense this hatred, it shook her very, very deeply.

They would have mock Masses, even down on Chrystie Street. Dorothy was furious. You do that kind of stuff and you're out. That's all there is to it. There's no court of appeal, you're out. I asked Dorothy once . . . it seemed to me that there were a lot more crazies around then than before. She said, "No, no, no, no. It's always the same." But then toward the end of her life, she admitted that it had been terrible.

One of the worst times was Roger's death. Roger LaPorte.[4] I found out from a reporter at 5:30 in the morning. I figured I'd call Dorothy around 8:30. She'd already heard about it. Chris [Kearns] just shooed all the reporters away. Let everybody at the house know that if they talked to reporters, that would be against Dorothy's will, which is tantamount to saying goodbye. But we realized we had to say something to the press. By about 10:30, I had something written. Read it to Dorothy and she said, "You can release that." They came with cameras and heavy equipment and all the cables they had to have then. It was just one interview after another all day long.

What would have happened if we had a rash of suicides, of self immolations? We make this moral judgement: "This is the wrong thing to do." What do we tell our constituencies—the younger and less stable people, or any people, any people at all— so no one else will do it? And still respect the sacrifice of Roger LaPorte? Very delicately, that's how.

---

[4] In 1965 Roger LaPorte, a young volunteer at the Catholic Worker, immolated himself in front of the United Nations in an action similar to that of the Vietnam monks who were burning themselves in protest of the war.

COURTESY TOM CORNELL

Dorothy and A. J. Muste at draft-card burning, 1965.

I was also very much concerned what the Catholic Worker was going to look like.

Jim Wilson also had memories of that tragic day:

What occurred with Roger was pretty life-changing. I don't remember us being in such awful shape that anybody needed to be concerned about how it was going to affect us or whether there were going to be people following in Roger's footsteps or anything like that. There was a basic response that anybody would have to losing a friend, especially in that way. And it was probably more concerned about what Roger was thinking, how terrible it was for him. But we knew that people were talking about what other people would do, and I didn't get it. I don't think Dorothy worried, either, but I can't tell you that for a fact.

Dan Berrigan came down and did a liturgy, and there was a statement from Dorothy, but she didn't write it. But the amazing thing . . . you see, Roger didn't die right away, and while he was in the hospital, the lights went out all over New York. Now you can read all kinds of things into that, but the time the lights went out in New York was very close to the time of his death.

What I remember most about that time was staying up all night. A group of us walked the streets, and I was just amazed at the way people were taking care of everything. Pedestrians were helping cars get through traffic, things like that. The whole infrastructure was gone, but people were making things work. It was very symbolic and sort of solemn.

Anne Perkins remembers a letter that Dorothy received from Thomas Merton after Roger's death:

She was cross and upset, annoyed with Thomas Merton. She told me, "Well, he wrote me a letter saying, 'I wouldn't let your people do these things if I were you.'" As if she had told any of her people . . . She thought that was quite unnecessary.

Tom Cornell concludes:

Well, that was 1965; 1968 was no easier. There was despair and frustration, leading to ultimate acts. What if a Catholic Worker house blew up? I pride myself on having participated with others in trying to talk sense to people. Trying to offer alternatives. Fasting and prayer. The Tiger Cage project. Meal of Reconciliation. The political prisoner issue. Holding up [as models] the Buddhists in Vietnam. Addressing things that we could address. And building the mass demonstrations. We were in on every single stage, all of those demonstrations. When the bishops wrote the peace pastoral in '83, I was one of only three pacifist consultants. I think that the recognition that Dorothy was given in their letter was important, and it probably wouldn't have happened if we hadn't kept a steady keel during the sixties.

Chuck Matthei grew up in the north suburbs of Chicago and got to know Dorothy through his antiwar work in the sixties. Here is his analysis of Dorothy's feeling for the decade:

Dorothy was formed in the twenties and thirties. Yes, the sixties were different, but I think the decade had more in common with the thirties, when the Catholic Worker began, than either period did with the intervening years. Sure there were changes, you know, changes of demeanor, changes of lifestyle. She was troubled by the culture of sex, drugs, and rock n' roll, as the media called it. But for me, and I think sometimes for Dorothy, the sixties was a period of idealism and of social mobilization.

In some places, like the Worker, that period was defined by a religious commitment and idealism, and even in many cases by sacrifice and an overriding concern for the well-being of others. And by a sense of both possibility and personal responsibility. Dorothy had a conservative streak in her upbringing, and she also had that unusual mixture of traditionalism and conservatism on the one hand, and radical, political perspective on the other. That mix spoke to many in my generation, including me.

I remember when Dorothy was very concerned about the number of young Catholic Workers around the country who were relinquishing their commitment to nonviolence and were drawn to support the NLF [National Liberation Front in Vietnam] or to believe that armed struggle was a necessity. She even made some trips to different houses and issued a sort of informal pastoral letter to try to address this tendency. She understood where it was coming from. She certainly knew the frustration—the despair, the anger, the sense of urgency, the urgent need for change. But she had a historical perspective and years of experience and wanted to share those.

I also remember the concerns that she would express [about the] personal behaviors among this one or that one in the household. But I think to say Dorothy was uncomfortable with the sixties, that she was sort of out of her element and couldn't understand what was happening and was defensive and resistant—to me, that doesn't capture it.

Sure there were times when she would say, "This is wrong. Get out of the house." But she also, I think, was profoundly moved and energized by this other dimension of events.

Dorothy was not on the sidelines. She wasn't somebody who had grown old and was watching the young set forth. This woman was your friend. She was your ally. She was your coworker, and that's the spirit that she conveyed. And loyalty. That's the word that comes to mind when I think of how she supported us.

Jim Wilson also felt that respect and loyalty. He was one of

WNET-TV/HARRIET NORRIS, 1972
COURTESY OF MARQUETTE UNIVERSITY ARCHIVES

the first to burn his draft card, at the organized demonstration at Union Square on November 6, 1965.

If you look back at the headlines throughout that whole period, the presence of young Catholics in the movement was pretty awesome. Dorothy knew this was creating confusion within the church. She would chuckle about it, because she understood the paradox. This was the message she'd been preaching for a long time, finally getting to a much larger audience.

I sensed a real crossing of generations and a mutual respect with Dorothy. She related to a number of people like this and would spend time with them and ask them questions, not about the operations of the house, but in terms of protests and demonstrations. What did people think and why? I think she was struggling, along with the rest of us, trying to figure out the politics of everything that was going on.

The first draft card burning was a very organized effort, but I didn't want to be part of the political planning process. Dorothy and A. J. Muste were both on the platform and the crowd was yelling "Moscow Mary" and "Burn yourselves, not your cards." That sort of thing. While the four or five of us who were burning our cards were lighting them, someone out of the crowd shot a fire extinguisher. The first thought that I had—and I think other people had this, too—was that it was gasoline or something, and that we were all going to blow up.

Dorothy was an elder and a strong leader and extremely supportive of me. I know that. She had seen my written statement about my spirituality and belief in Gandhian pacifism and was extremely supportive of that. She spoke that day, and she didn't show any fear. I think she had a great deal of respect for the people who were doing these things.

Jim wasn't arrested at the time, and when he was, he learned that he had been the only one on the stage at Union Square with an active A-1 draft card.[5] He represented himself at the trial and pled guilty "in the Catholic Worker tradition," with Dorothy's full cooperation, but surprisingly got only three years' probation. His draft board, however, called him up for induction, and when he refused, he was sentenced to three years in prison, a confinement hard for him and hard for his wife and son, who was born shortly after Jim was sent to Lewisburg Penitentiary. Long-time

---

[5] He told me, "Years ago I asked for my file as part of the Freedom of Information Act, and it very clearly indicates that there was someone involved in the movement who was an FBI agent. Participating in all the planning."

Worker Pat Murray told me that Dorothy grieved for the young men who had such a hard time in jail and for the friends and family whom they had left behind.

Dan Shay tells a lighthearted story about Dorothy paying his bail for an arrest in Washington.

On the tenth day, word came that Dorothy was outside and asking if anybody needed bail paid. I had a house of hospitality back in Detroit, and I was nervous about a couple of men there who were ill and elderly. I decided I'd made my statement, so I said I would like bail, and she paid it. When I got out she gave me a hug and kiss. I got a kiss from Dorothy!! Then she looked at me and said, "You could have stayed longer!"

Bill Griffin came to the Worker after fleeing to Canada to avoid the draft and then serving as a medic in stateside hospitals. He remains on the masthead of the paper.

I remember one of Dorothy's columns where she wrote of her grandson's returning from Vietnam safe and sound. (We heard later that he's had problems with Agent Orange.) She could be thankful for his safety and also write about that horrible, vicious war. So she could be part of American society—love it and still criticize it. The people at the Worker were resisting the war, but they hadn't become as violent as the people they were opposing. In a certain sense, during the sixties, the Catholic Worker redeemed the honor of the country.

3.

Love Is the Measure

If I have accomplished anything in my life, it is because I wasn't embarrassed to talk about God.
—Dorothy Day to Jim Forest

SAVED BY BEAUTY

She loved the richness of the world.
—Judith Gregory

Dorothy's spirituality was truly immanent and incarnational, a love of God as seen in creation, especially in those the world has forgotten. Jim Forest would often quote her as saying that "the real test of our love for God is the love we have for the most repulsive human being we know." Yet she saw the goodness or "God-ness" in everything, whether it was in the haggard faces of women waiting in line for food, a fine linen handkerchief, or the scraggly beauty of an ailanthus tree struggling against city cement. Frequently she repeated the line from Dostoevski that reminds us that "the world will be saved by beauty."

Pat and Kathleen Jordan, who met at the Catholic Worker in the early 1970s, remained close to Dorothy after their marriage—especially when they lived next door to the Catholic Worker retreat on Staten Island. Pat recounts some of what they learned from Dorothy:

She kept a sense for femininity. She was a very beautiful person with a real reserve about her, almost Victorian. When we were at the Worker, we heard a story about this from a college student who came for the summer. She had gone up to see Dorothy one morning. Dorothy opened up her purse and took out some perfume and put it on a handkerchief and gave it to the young woman. "Just always remember that you're a woman." To make sure that even in a very poor situation, you remembered what a gift it was of who you were. And she was also saying to her, "You have to maintain your dignity in an environment that's pretty rough."

I remember once I was down at the front door of the Worker, working off my anxieties or something by cleaning. Sometimes we'd get loads of white shirts that nobody on the clothing line wanted because they'd get dirty so quickly. So we had stores of white shirts, and I was just about to rip up this perfectly fine white shirt as a rag for cleaning. Dorothy stopped me. She said, "You can't do that with that perfectly good shirt. Everything is sacramental." It stopped . . . me . . . short. That you really have to pay attention to everything.

She didn't separate the natural and the supernatural. Judith Gregory explains:

When I think of Dorothy, what first comes into my mind is her love of the world and her sorrow that there is so much suffering. She had a sense that the world is good because it's made by God. So she thought each one of us, with our particular gifts and interests, was good. It's not that we need to change to be holy; we need to live what we are in the consciousness of God.

She loved the richness of the world. Anything that was positive in the world—do it. If you like to collect old books, by all means, do it. She loved it when people took initiative and would be impatient with people wanting to be told what to do because there was *so* much [that needed to be done].

One of the riches of the world for Dorothy was music. Whenever she was in the city, she would listen to the Metropolitan Opera's radio broadcasts on Saturday afternoon. Pat Jordan recalls seeing her listen "almost in ecstasy" and said it taught him "a great deal about what prayer meant to her."

Ade Bethune's art has been a trademark of the *Catholic Worker* almost from the beginning. She told me:

Once, some people complained that my drawings were not angry enough, not critical, too easy. So I asked Dorothy, "What do you want me to do?"

"Oh, no! Please," she replied. "We have too much trouble and bitterness in the world. I want you to do beautiful things, vines and grapes, and mothers and children, and works of mercy. Good things."

The late Rosemary Morse says Dorothy would remind her friends of the source of the beauty by telling the following story about one of her young granddaughters. Seems the little girl was talking to her about how beautiful the day was, and Dorothy said, "God made it beautiful." And the little girl looked up right into Dorothy's face and said, "I like God."

When we read her autobiography, *The Long Loneliness,* we see that Dorothy's incarnational spirituality was always present, and that she recognized its stirrings even as a young girl. Eileen Egan and Michael Harank place her spirituality in chronological perspective. Eileen observed that she was hounded by God even in her high school days:

Now this didn't come from her home. Her mother was Episcopalian and her father didn't practice anything. So the mystery of it all is where her initial interest came from. She started reading the Bible when she was only in high school. Said she wanted to be perfect, and that the scriptures told her she could be. And she read the Bible for her whole life, even though the practice wasn't really adopted by other Catholics until after Vatican II. So in that she was quite Protestant.

When Dorothy came into the church, being religious meant saying the Rosary, making novenas, going to daily Mass, and reading the prayers in our daily missals. But besides all that, Dorothy had straight scripture, and it *does* affect you.

Michael Harank, who knew Dorothy in her final years, feels that her "most profound conversion may have occurred during her first prison experience, when she became aware of all the ways people can be dehumanized and hurt in this world." When Dorothy was thrown into solitary confinement, "all she wanted to read was the Bible."

Besides the reading of scripture, Dorothy's spiritual practices were quite traditionally Catholic—daily Mass whenever possible, compline with any who wished to join her, the Rosary, intercessory prayer, the Jesus prayer, and private silent prayer. She would instruct her friends, "When you are left alone, pray."

Jim Douglass underscores the importance of prayer life to Dorothy:

I think her spirituality is the key—Mass, prayer, and taking the time to go back so often to Dostoevski and the Russian literature that she loved. If she had just totally lost herself in the Worker, it wouldn't have been Dorothy Day at all. She obviously resisted being overwhelmed by the work and took her time to be private and to read and pray. This was a woman of silences as well as intense activity, and you felt it when you were with her.

Jean Walsh had several warm stories of Dorothy's absolute faith in the power of prayer. She remembers when a child who was visiting Dorothy on Staten Island drank something and Dorothy thought it might be poison:

It wasn't anything really serious, but Dorothy put her in the car and rushed her to the hospital. She told us later that the only prayer she could think of was "Bless us, O Lord, and these thy gifts . . . " She was so nervous her prayer didn't come out right, but she prayed just the same.

One day she came in from chapel at the Peter Maurin Farm. She was absolutely radiant, and she said to us, "Rejoice, rejoice! All of you, rejoice. We're all going to heaven because I have asked our Lord every single day of my life that everyone who comes to the Peter Maurin Farm will be saved."

Another day when we were driving, she said she didn't care if Forster died in a little room all by himself, because she asked God every day to save Forster and God was going to honor her prayer. That's the type of faith she had.

Jim Forest describes Dorothy at prayer:

When I think of Dorothy, I think of her first and foremost as a woman at prayer. I can picture her in the chapel at the Catholic Worker farm, first on Staten Island and later up at Tivoli. If she was at the farm, there was a good chance you'd find her in the chapel, kneeling by herself. She would be there for a long time. On those old knees with those thick, dark stockings and those bulky shoes.

I can remember—nosy, snooping around person that I was and still am, I suppose—going up to look into the missal she had left on the pew, and seeing all these lists of people that she was praying about. In that unmistakable handwriting.

Dorothy realized there was no time with God, only eternity, and was quite convinced that you could pray at any time for something that had happened in the past. In fact, one of the most important parts of her intercession was praying for people who had committed suicide. She had a great deal of sympathy for them. You couldn't reverse the fact that they were dead. You couldn't change history in that way. But you could perhaps change something about that person's death or something that happened in that person's thoughts. I'm not sure what she thought she was doing, but she knew that she could pray for them and that God's eternity is different from time.

Dorothy was absolutely . . . I mean if Dorothy did one thing in her life, it was pray for people. And pray for them year after year after year.

She had this huge network, and not even God could convince her to stop interceding for them.

And she'd remind me that if someone "doesn't pay attention to our prayings"—she used it in the plural—"and what that means, then he'll miss the whole point." Late in her life, she said, "If I have accomplished anything in my life, it is because I wasn't embarrassed to talk about God."

We live in a post-Christian world. Christian activity and Christian belief are not normal, even among Christians. Most of us are constantly trying to conform ourselves to the people at the front of the crowd, so that our religious activities aren't too ridiculous and too embarrassing and too isolating. Dorothy Day was able to work through that and to find the place where she would be free to be a believer. And when you are with one of those people, it hits you pretty hard.

Dorothy Day at 223 Chrystie St., circa 1957.

Dorothy Gauchat, who joined the Catholic Worker in the early years, was one of the women who was hit pretty hard. She remembered going to Mass with Dorothy once when things were really pressuring her:

She said to me, "You know, sometimes when I was so discouraged, I'd feel a hand on my shoulder and it would be Jesus' hand." Jesus' hand was on her shoulder! It was wonderful that she would share that with me. She was a mystic. Yes, she was. (Now she was a very private person so that wasn't something she made public.) There would be no way that she could have gone on, especially during the [Second World] War, when she was so alone and so torn in so many ways, unless the Lord was pouring in this wellspring of spirituality.

Dorothy felt both the communion of saints and communion *with* saints and was particularly devoted to some of them—St. Thérèse of Lisieux, St. Teresa of Avila, and St. Francis of Assisi come to mind—all saints to whom she has been compared. Her devotion to the saints gives us an unusual story. Jim Forest remembers how startled he was to find, next to Dorothy's bed, a tiny statue of Joan of Arc, wearing armor.

It didn't fit at all in my idea of what . . . I thought maybe St. Francis of Assisi with some birds. But Joan of Arc? I asked her about it. And Dorothy said . . . it was with a kind of mixture of irritation and defensiveness. She said, "Well, she wasn't canonized for being a soldier. She was canonized because she followed her conscience."

The more I think about it, the more I think that Dorothy admired St. Joan's armor as much as her conscience. And thought all of us should be willing to put our lives on the line, to fight for what we think is right. Use every resource at our disposal to do what needs to be done. Dorothy wasn't embarrassed to admire this young warrior, dead before she was out of her teens. For her, it wasn't inconsistent at all.

The late Father Richard McSorley of Washington, D.C., recalled Dorothy's deep love for St. Thérèse and the Little Way:

I've also been very impressed by her deep knowledge of the lives of the saints and her use of those in her writings. Her commitment to the saints, and her willingness to learn new things all the time. That story of the time when she had her daughter and the woman in the bed next to her said, "Why don't you call her Theresa?" And she didn't know anything about Theresa then. When she found out, she was turned off by the life of this contemplative nun who prayed a lot. But she [continued to] look into it, and the more she did, the more she found that it was not what she [originally] thought. She finally said, "I don't know any one of my radical friends who could live one day on the routine that Sister Theresa of the Child Jesus lived." And at that point she decided to write the book [about St. Thérèse] from the point of view of the radical.

Her justly famous autobiography, *The Long Loneliness,* is a classic conversion narrative. People who joined with her in the Catholic Worker movement speak about what many call her second conversion, which added depth to her spiritual life. A major factor was the influence of Father John Hugo and what Dorothy called "the Great Retreat."

The retreats that guided the deepening of Dorothy's spirituality were loosely based on the Ignatian *Spiritual Exercises* and developed by a Jesuit priest, Father Onesimus Lacouture of Montreal. Dorothy first received the retreat notes from her friend, Sister Peter Claver, the woman who gave Dorothy a dollar to print the first issue of the newspaper. At Sister Peter's suggestion, Dorothy went to Oakmont, Pennsylvania, in 1941, made the retreat with Father Hugo, and returned "exuberant and filled with joy," as Sister Peter tells us. From then on, Dorothy made it often and encouraged everyone connected to the Catholic Worker to attend, also. Father Hugo endured much controversy for the retreat and was later enjoined from giving it for many years.

A member of the Catholic Worker family explains the retreat's attraction this way:

Father Hugo spoke in terms of samples. Samples are perfectly legitimate things God has given us that we can use without fault. But given our fallen nature it is better for us to give up these samples to live the perfect life. Any step that is not upward is a step downward.

For Dorothy, who was an active person, who wished to emulate Peter Maurin's detachment, a spirituality that put everything in the hands of God was a godsend. She could listen to the opera and have the merit of grace by intending it as the will of God that she have this respite in her heavily responsible life. But accepting insults as the will of God and not responding verbally in retaliation must have been a very serious penance for her.

Ade Bethune has a more pragmatic view: "Dorothy loved going to the retreats largely because during a week's retreat, she would have a moment of peace, when she could read, pray, and meditate."

Father Harvey Egan is a priest from Minneapolis who lived at the Worker while he was a seminarian and remained in contact with Dorothy through letters and visits:

Sister Peter Claver first gave me the retreat notes. Then I myself made the retreat many times, and it's just been a great joy in my life, as it was for Dorothy. I can't imagine what I'd be like without the retreat. Maybe playing the horses. Or maybe I wouldn't have stayed a priest. But by no means were those who were pro-retreat a majority in the movement. The retreat was a dispute and people had very strong feelings. But thank goodness I made what Dorothy would call "THE retreat." For "THE family." And those who made it became another kind of family, within the larger Worker family.

Now this was not a quicky evening of recollection; it was an eight-day silent retreat. A full charge of liberal Christianity, liberal not so much in the sense of the social issues, but in the personal issues of one's own prayer life and penitential life and service to the church.

You see, Dorothy really had two conversions. Her second conversion, after she started making the retreat, added the interior life to her exterior life, I guess you'd say. She had been in her first conversion from 1933, when the Worker was established, until she made the retreat. What she was doing was the works of mercy, the exterior life. After she made the retreat, she continued with that. She did not diminish, didn't become the solitary or live aloof from the house. But she began to read the scriptures every day. She loved the word of God. She went to Mass, read the lives of the saints, really latched onto the traditional religious experiences.

Julian Pleasants of the South Bend Catholic Worker made the retreat in 1941:

Dorothy said [the Catholic Workers] had to make a retreat. Said if we didn't make a retreat, we'd fall by the wayside. She didn't say that we were out of the movement if we didn't go, but she said it was essential. And so . . . golly! I had just gotten out of the hospital, but we hitchhiked to that little place . . . Oakmont, Pennsylvania. We had an eight-day closed retreat—very impressive.

The most important thing I got out of it was the necessity of daily meditation. We had been going to Mass every day, but meditation seemed an awful thing to do when there was so much to be done at the house. Father Hugo convinced me it was essential, and I think he was right. It wasn't meditation in the usual sense of contemplating something very abstract or spiritual. It was often just saying to myself, "How will I deal with what I have to do today?" "What would Jesus have done and what can be expected of somebody like me?"

I didn't agree with the giving up things at all. Father Hugo said that the best thing to do with good things was to give them up. And I just didn't think that was Dorothy's attitude at all. She didn't want to give them up. She wanted to give them *away*—a totally different approach. Dorothy liked her good literature, her good music, and she never really felt obligated not to enjoy them. I think she got out of the retreat only the notion that you had to be *ready* to give them up. She took what worked for her [from the retreat] and hoped other people would take what worked for them.

But some took it all. Father Hugo became their spiritual guide, and they followed him implicitly without any questioning. I remember once she wrote me about a woman who had made the retreat. Dorothy felt that she had gone overboard on the value of obedience, and she asked me to write something for the paper about it.

Dorothy and Bill Gauchat had a Catholic Worker house in Cleveland and were strong supporters of the retreats. Shortly before her sudden death, Dorothy Gauchat gave me her memories of the retreat:

It was all St. John of the Cross, and he was one tough guy. Now Dorothy was a terrible chain smoker—used to roll her own, like a lot of people did during the Great Depression. But she gave herself completely to all the ideas and ideals that Father Hugo presented to us. And right then and there, cold turkey, she stopped smoking. Smoking was one of those small consolations in a life that was so busy, so overwhelming. For her to just say, "This is it! That's what I can give up. I'm too attached." It was amazing!

At that retreat . . . we'd gather in the dining room, and these nuns made such beautiful meals. But people would sit down and not eat that food. To sacrifice it. And I still can see [Father Hugo] at the table saying, "Hey! That's not the message. If somebody puts a good steak in front of you, you don't say you can't eat it, you thank God. On the other hand, if having steaks every day and having all the extras and niceties in your life is your consuming drive, then you're on the wrong track." One of the quotations Dorothy left with me . . . Dorothy said, "You must receive as humbly as you give."

Betty Doyle from Minnesota is trying here to understand the retreat's attraction:

Dorothy really went all out for the whole Father Hugo idea, but I thought his whole attitude was too strict. Too cold and not human enough, really. I couldn't understand how Dorothy could cotton to it, with all her warmth and . . . Of course, she knew him very well and talked with him a lot.

There used to be a lot of dissension about the whole thing with the Catholic Worker people, and I'm trying to think of the word that we'd use. Oh, yes! *Detachers*. People were detachers. He was very much a detacher and a lot of us didn't think we should be detached from the world in that way, giving up all these beautiful things and living such a strict, bare kind of life. But I suppose Dorothy saw so much . . . so much need and such poverty always that the idea of people living luxuriously was very difficult for her to accept. That was earlier, though. When she'd come out here years later, she was a much more comfy kind of person. Comfortable to be around, you know.

The retreat wasn't for everybody. As a friend pointed out to me, it could be a disaster for the scrupulous as well as for the procrastinator. But for Dorothy Day it provided a spiritual armor that allowed her to persevere when the euphoria of the early years had disappeared. Father Hugo was exactly what Dorothy had been looking for all her life. She had become a Catholic partly, I think, to find an identity she could live with, to solidify her feeling from birth that she was not meant to march with the crowd. And in meeting Peter and founding the movement, she forged that identity, but it was not with joy and not with the surety of faith and righteousness, in the best sense, that she needed to carry on through a long and productive life. The retreat solidified her identity and gave her spiritual practices that delineated her relationship to a Christianity she deeply loved but whose compromises with the world she could not condone.

Nevertheless, people would sometimes tell stories that hint at a certain scrupulosity, perhaps coming from the Hugo retreats, but also from a discerning conscience. Beth Rogers recalls:

Late one night, when everybody was tired, including Dorothy, a seminarian was asking her some questions, and I guess she answered rather abruptly. Early the next morning we were walking up to Mass and she said she felt so badly about what she'd said, and she said she was going to pray that it . . . uh, wouldn't be offensive. And she said, "You know, with God, there is no time, so you can pray after you've done something."

Dorothy saw what we would call personality traits not as faults that could be mitigated but as sins that demanded confession and penance and that "firm purpose of amendment." She went to confession weekly and was under spiritual direction, which might account for at least some of her day-to-day inconsistencies.[1] She was very humble about her quick tongue and would ask people for forgiveness when she hurt them.

---

[1] Ed Turner told me the archbishop "required" her to be under spiritual direction as the leader of a group of Catholic lay people.

© VIVIAN CHERRY

**THIS EIGHT-PAGE SEQUENCE OF PHOTOGRAPHS WAS TAKEN
BY VIVIAN CHERRY IN 1955 AND 1959.**

WHY SHOULD THE RESOURCES OF HUMAN GENIUS AND THE RICHES OF THE PEOPLE TURN MORE OFTEN TO PREPARING ARMS... THAN TO INCREAS- ING THE WELFARE OF ALL CLASSES OF CITIZENS AND PARTICULARLY OF THE POOR?

POPE JOHN XXIII

ACT FOR PEACE

Judith Malina joins Dorothy in antiwar protest.

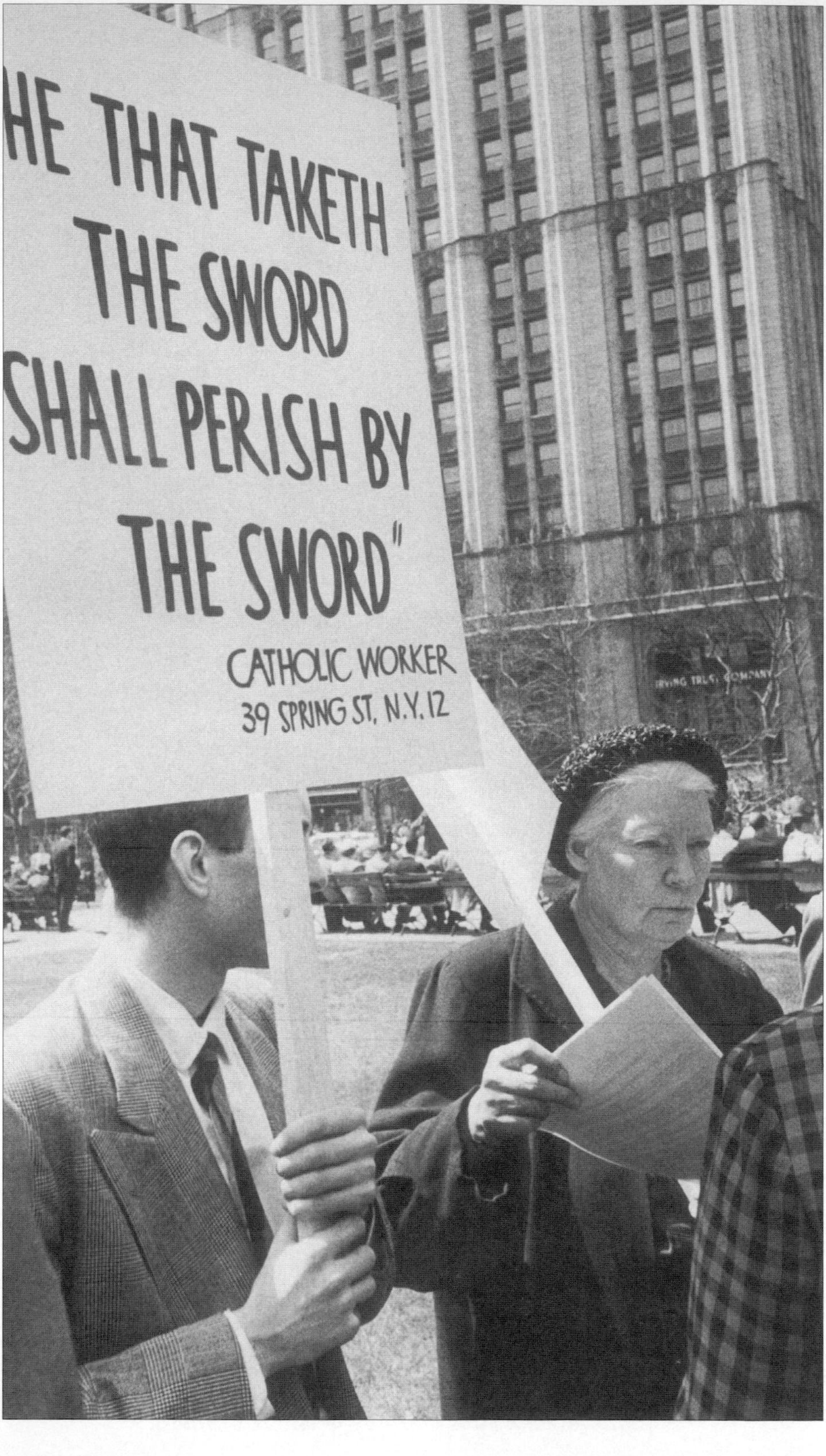

© Vivian Cherry

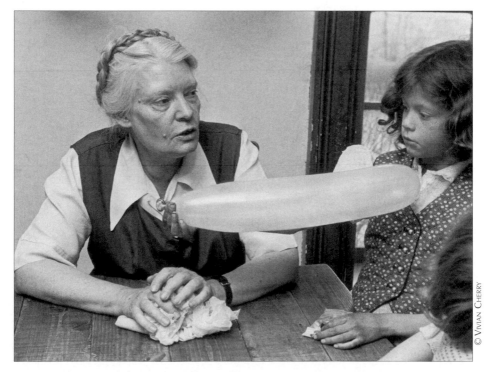

Dorothy at a birthday party for one of her grandchildren

Pat Jordan remembers that she used to pray, "O Lord, cleanse me from my hidden faults." And she told Jean Walsh: "You know, St. Teresa of Avila says that God hid her faults from her nuns. It's just the opposite with me. He's showing my faults to everybody."

But these fine tunings of conscience should be seen in the light of her trust in God's help. Joe Zarrella read me a holy card Dorothy had written on and given him. He carries it in his billfold, all these years later: "We should not be discouraged at our own lapses . . . but continue. If we are discouraged, it shows vanity and pride. Trusting too much to ourselves. It takes a lifetime of endurance of patience, of learning through mistakes. We all are on the way."

As a guide to being "on the way" and following the Benedictine values Peter Maurin preached of hospitality, farming communes, and prayer, Dorothy became a Benedictine oblate. She chose St. Procopius Abbey of Lisle, Illinois, because of its special work toward the reunion of Rome and the Eastern church. As Ade Bethune and Joe Zarrella point out, in addition to the "bread for the strong" of the Hugo retreats, Dorothy was drawn to the balanced view of the Benedictines and enjoyed the worldwide fellowship that oblation provided.

Russian spirituality added yet another dimension to her faith. She got much of her theology from Tolstoy and Dostoevski and always felt an affinity for Russian culture and spirituality. Jim Forest recalls a time when she spoke at New York University at the height of the Cold War:

We went into this really smoke-filled room and somebody asked her, with great venom, "Miss Day, you talk about loving your enemy. Well, what would you do if the Russians invaded?"

Without any trouble at all, not annoyed or incensed or ready to cross swords, Dorothy just said, "I would open my arms and embrace them, like anyone else." Which was a staggering response at the time.

Dorothy would sometimes go to Russian Orthodox liturgies, and we went to Third Hour meetings, too. (That was one of the first ecumenical groups involving Catholics. They were called Third Hour because that was when the Holy Spirit descended on the apostles, the hour of the Spirit's descent to bring the community of belief into being.)

Dorothy's good friend Nina Polcyn Moore summarizes Dorothy's spiritual influence:

When you came to her, you wanted to present your best self. You wanted to just peel away like an onion and be the purest kind of person you could be because she had that purifying effect. She did that without knowing that she did it, and I'm sure it was because of her life of prayer. Now I don't know what a mystic is, but she must have been one. There was just this . . . this staggering fidelity.

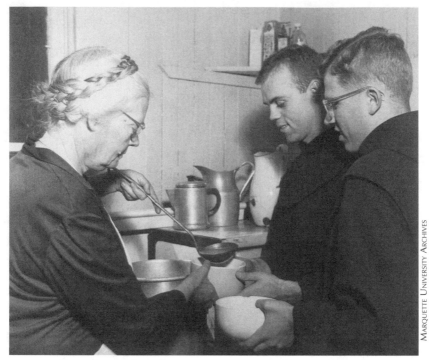

Dorothy serving soup to Franciscans at Detroit CW, 1955.

HOSPITALITY OF THE HEART

*Ultimately the most astonishing thing about Dorothy
is that she stayed.*

—JUDITH GREGORY

Hospitality is the heart of the Catholic Worker, hospitality both to those who come with physical needs—often called guests—and those who come with spiritual needs, called Workers. Although Catholic Worker theory makes no distinctions, in common parlance the ones who come to help in the work are called staff and the others are called guests. But as Kassie Temple told me in 1988, "The people who come [to the New York house] because of Catholic Worker philosophy tend to spend shorter times and some of the people called guests have lived here in Maryhouse for twelve years or so. So who's the host?"

Changes in the kinds of guests over the years have made the distinctions more pronounced. During the Depression, it was often only bad luck that separated the men on the soup line from the men who served the soup. Anne Perkins, an editor for Harper and Row, met Dorothy when Dorothy was in her mid-sixties. She remembers Dorothy telling her about the changes in the kinds of people the Worker served:

"We have very difficult times because people who come in really have problems. A man came in the other day with a snake around his neck." Well, we had all read her column in the paper, so we knew the people who came into the Catholic Worker weren't exactly well-heeled, or well-fed, but I wasn't . . . I hadn't really any idea there were so many people who were . . . uh, not well knit. And one of the observations she made to me some years later is that in the 1930s, many people who came were simply jobless or poor, but that in later years, so many people were also mentally ill.

At the Worker, one didn't have to work in order to get food. It was hospitality given freely and without restriction. Hospitality was the essence of Dorothy's Christianity. Jim Wilson explains:

The Catholic Worker was a place where anybody could come, no matter what baggage the person was bringing. Dorothy was not a judgmental person. (Well, she was judgmental about Cardinal Spellman, and about generals in the Pentagon, but she could work that out, too.) In terms of someone who was just trying to make it on this planet, she was not judgmental, whether it had to do with abortion, people mutilating themselves, or people having problems with alcohol or sexuality.

Betty Bartelme adds:

The soup line was everything! Without the works of mercy, the place wouldn't exist. But Dorothy was thoughtful and generous in other ways, also. For instance, one of the volunteers there had a beautiful voice, really a beautiful voice. And Dorothy paid for her training. She was able to take voice lessons from a very fine teacher and to have a concert at Town Hall. So Dorothy's mercy extended to more than just the Bowery men.

It extended to old friends as well as strangers from the streets. Cleveland Catholic Worker Dorothy Gauchat tells a poignant story:

I was going through my own trial because [my husband] Bill was an alcoholic and it was really, really rough. Her telling me to keep praying is what helped me to get through it all and not wind up in despair. What she was telling me was what she was doing herself.

Once I remember becoming absolutely exhausted and getting on a train and going to New York. And there was Dorothy, welcoming me with open arms. She could see how tired I was. She took me up to one of the bedrooms and she put clean linen on the bed—I think it was on Chrystie Street—and she said, "We're running a bath for you and I want you to just take a long sit in the water and relax." A very tender person.

Often she came across as being severe, because she was such a strong looking woman, so I suspect some people might have been afraid of her. But I wasn't. Dorothy was so sensitive to everybody's suffering. Everybody's.

At her wake, you saw Frank Sheed and all these famous people. And then a street person would come and stand by the casket and weep. A raggedy, pitiful man. One of them kept saying over and over, "She loved us, she listened to us, she loved us." Then he bent over to kiss her.

Father Richard McSorley said, "I've often used her quote that the real test of our love for God is the love we have for the most repulsive human being we know." And Jim Forest remembers a social worker asking Dorothy how long people were permitted to stay:

"We let them stay forever," Dorothy answered. "They live with us, they die with us, and we give them a Christian burial. We pray for them after they are dead. Once they are taken in, they become members of the family. Or rather, they always were members of the family. They are our brothers and sisters in Christ."

In fact, she had a most amazing tolerance for everyone. Tom Cornell recalls a conventionally unlovable man who made the Worker his home:

Remember Paul Bruno? Some people called him Mad Paul. Dorothy would write about how Franciscan in spirit Brother Paul is, how he loves the birds and the animals and how he feeds them, how they wait for him to show up with scraps. Well, what he'd really do is take this wet garbage out of the Catholic Worker—foul, foul stuff—and dump it on Second Avenue, and these horrifying pigeons would come, defecating all over. And she would see St. Francis in this. She saw something that I couldn't see, but that may be my deficiency, not hers. That's one of the things that I loved her for. She truly saw the beauty and the dignity and the warmth and value in the lives of poor people.

Dorothy's hospitality also went out to priests, sometimes the priests no one else wanted. Because of her love for the Eucharist, she was always eager to have a priest living in the houses. And of course many, many priests visited the Worker over the years, both while they were in seminary and after ordination, and the number influenced by Dorothy Day is countless. Jesuit James Joyce said that her telling him that "people need priests" was the reason he stayed with the priesthood. And the late Pat Rusk said that "Dorothy had a heart for priests." A former Worker explains:

In terms of the "natural man," she appreciated the burden they carried in their promise of celibacy. And she was aware of the fate of diocesan priests who in their old age were on their own. A few older priests were too proud to beg from a bishop who had opposed them, especially those who supported unions, because many a bishop was beholden to the charity of capitalist employers who opposed unions. One of these union priests was Father Faley, who had supported the West Coast International Longshoremen's Association, whose leader accepted support from the Communist Party. There was the usual violence, especially instigated by the owners and by red baiting. So Father Faley became persona non grata in the local diocese. In his retirement, Dorothy invited him to be resident chaplain at Maryfarm and in a clash with a young Worker, Dorothy took the side of Father Faley and sent the young man to the city.

Then there was Father Elias, an Eastern European alcoholic who had suffered under both the Nazis and the Communists. He saw Dorothy as a Communist and when he tied one on, he'd stand outside the Catholic Worker house and go on for hours, hurling invectives up to Dorothy. She wouldn't call the police.

Pat Jordan explains this combination of compassion and common sense:

When Kathleen and I were at the Worker, the most remarkable thing was the sense of forgiveness within the community. You would see people do terrible things to one another and yet, because of this unwritten sense of Christian forgiveness, people were able to come back and start again. We saw this happen again and again and again. Dorothy kept repeating "seventy times seven." You have to forgive seventy times seven.

Dorothy not only taught hospitality and forgiveness, she modeled it in her own graciousness. Johannah Hughes Turner says:

Dorothy had the knack for making a place where you felt just absolutely comfortable and protected. She had lots of books and comforters and things like that, and if you weren't feeling well, she knew how to put you into a rocker or a bed and give you just the right pillows to make you feel cozy and protected. Just the right music, the right books . . . the right food.

Wherever she was living, she created what Nina Polcyn Moore called "a propitious atmosphere." Sheila Dugan called her "the perfect bed and breakfast hostess," one who sensed how to put the people together who needed to be with each other.

Dorothy's daughter learned from her mother that "a good Catholic Worker warms you up, gets everybody smiling. That's the essence, the essential ingredient of hospitality—loving kindness. The people do the healing themselves. You just have to stand aside and let it happen."

But this loving kindness can't happen if the hospitality isn't thoughtfully given. Brian Terrell reminds us that Dorothy knew how to set limits and tried to teach that to the young people who came to the Worker:

When you're a young person first at a Worker house, your tolerance for all kinds of insanity and chaos is very, very high. At first I couldn't understand the logic of setting limits and shutting the door. "As long as we've got soup on, I'll keep serving no matter how late it is." But then the next day, people would break windows because yesterday they came at that time and got soup.

Dorothy would say to me, "Why do you let all these people in? This is crazy!" In effect she was telling me, "You're young and agile. You can duck. Well, other people can't. They have no other place to go. They should be able to sit quietly and have a cup of tea without somebody coming in and shouting all kinds of racial garbage and having schizophrenic episodes and throwing soup against the wall and things like that. Maybe you're young and idealistic and romantic and you think that's cool. But this is somebody's home and we have to keep it that way."

Eileen Egan told a story that shows Dorothy's sensitivity to the people from the streets:

We'd always say grace before meals, usually the one that included, "May the Lord provide for the wants of others, and be the eternal food of our souls." One day I said to Dorothy, "You know, sometimes people want what they shouldn't have. Let's say instead, 'May the Lord provide for the *needs* of others and be the eternal food of our souls.'" And Dorothy said okay. So for two weeks we said, "May the Lord provide for the needs of others." Then one day Dorothy said, "Eileen, let's go back to our old way. Let them have what they want."

Eileen concludes, "Sure, people want a lot of things that we might not approve of or might not want for ourselves. But we should let them have what they want, not what we want for them."

Jim Forest calls the kind of hospitality Dorothy practiced and taught "hospitality of the heart" and says "it transforms the way we see and respond. When we 'get it,' when we finally understand what she was teaching, we see that we're in the presence of something sacred whenever we meet another person."

LOYAL DAUGHTER OF THE CHURCH

Dorothy was through and through a Catholic.
—MICHAEL AND MARGARET GARVEY

Dorothy's relationship to the church of her conversion was steady, loyal, and intense. The late Ade Bethune commented that Dorothy thought it so important to become a Catholic that she was even willing to sacrifice what meant most to her—her love of social justice and the poor. "She thought she had to make that sacrifice. And then, through Peter Maurin, she discovered the social encyclicals. She gave up everything, and God instantly rewarded her!"

When she became a Roman Catholic, Dorothy accepted the entire church—doctrine, devotional practices, ecclesiastical structure. From the beginning, however, she went beyond the conventional passivity most clerics expected and received from the laity. Dorothy acted out of her own conscience, studying scripture, the papal encyclicals, and the writings of the saints to discover how to live her newfound faith. While the American church as a whole sometimes ignored her and sometimes worried her by its questions, the institution finally gave widespread approval and belated honor, including the greatest honor of all—adoption and institutionalization of much of the Catholic Worker program. Dorothy anticipated many of the social justice issues now adopted by segments of the institutional church: a preferential concern for those in poverty, active involvement in peace issues, opposition to racism and anti-Semitism, ecumenism, lay involvement in the liturgy, and a scripture-based spirituality.

She may have both accepted the Catholicism she found and anticipated themes a late twentieth-century church embraced, but she was also critical of the institution. Her intense relationship to the church she loved gives new meaning to the term "loyal daughter of the church," a descriptive sometimes used divisively by those who see her loyalties to the poor more clearly than her other gospel consistencies.

In private, Dorothy would frequently quote Romano Guardini: "The church is the cross upon which Christ is crucified." She was not blind to its faults, and she frequently called it to task for its participation in the culture of materialism. Michael True, professor emeritus from Assumption College in Worcester, says:

I don't think the hierarchy quite knew what to do with her. She was like having a time bomb in your diocese because she might tell all. She could see the scandal, see all the rich properties owned by the church. So she's one of those people who's much easier to applaud now that's she's dead.

Several people told of her criticizing religious orders for their standard of living. Margaret Quigley Garvey recalls someone telling her about Dorothy talking to seminarians and then lining them up at the window overlooking their cars in the parking lot. "For a first step," Dorothy said, "get rid of all that."

Dorothy didn't go to the bishops demanding attention or support but instead went to them only when asked to do so. She also didn't ask their permission before she made decisions. Supporters point out that this attitude of respectful distance didn't give the bishops a chance to say no and probably muted criticism in the Catholic press. Her gracious middle-class manners also helped, and she related very well with bishops and cardinals, including Cardinal Spellman, who frequently was at odds with her consistent pacifism.

Betty Bartelme remembers her being called down to the Chancery office one day and coming back with a box of candy from the cardinal's lawyer. Betty commented, "I guess she just charmed him." Jim Forest said to me once that she "was about as naive as a cardinal." Her faith and forthrightness and perhaps also an innate sense of grace helped her to negotiate what could sometimes be touchy situations. He elaborates:

I don't think any of us knew how nip and tuck it had been sometimes with Dorothy and the Chancery, how hard it had been for her to keep the paper going as an up-front Catholic publication called the *Catholic Worker*. Not *Christian Worker* or *Jesus Says*, but *Catholic Worker*.[2]

But Dorothy didn't compromise. I can remember opening a check from Cardinal McIntyre in Los Angeles. "This is to thicken the soup." Well, we didn't have a "thicken the soup" fund at the Catholic Worker. It was just one bank account, and Cardinal McIntyre knew that. Dorothy never made any pretense to the contrary. If you sent fifty dollars to the Catholic Worker, it got used. Period. The Cardinal sent the money anyway.

---

[2] According to Ed Turner, adversaries such as the *Wanderer*, convinced of her heresies, would routinely denounce her to the Vatican.

But here's another interesting thing about her relationship with the hierarchy. People at the Worker would be very critical of the hierarchy, especially Cardinal Spellman. Dorothy could be very critical of him, too, but if anyone spoke against him, she'd always stand up for him. And it wouldn't be in generalities. She told me once that Spellman had priests who didn't like to receive calls to go down to the Bowery to administer the last rites, so he'd go down there personally. Dorothy knew things like that about people, and she would tell them to show their good side. She was quite different from most of us. If we decide we don't like somebody, we make it a kind of hobby to collect reasons not to like that person. We develop quite a number of reasons to justify our irritation. Dorothy had a lot of reasons to dislike Cardinal Spellman, but it was more her hobby to find out things to admire about him.

Peter Lumsden of London has an interesting insight into Dorothy's relationship to the hierarchy:

Women are not taken seriously in the church, and that gave Dorothy an enormous advantage. She could say things and do things that weren't taken seriously in some ways and therefore didn't arouse the antagonism that a man would have done.

She had the naive enthusiasm of the convert, as well, which was very appealing to Spellman and McIntyre and so forth. I think she was able to . . . she had a capacity for diplomacy that enabled the movement to flourish in spite of these dreadful reactionaries.

But she evidenced more than charm or diplomacy in her final speaking engagement. Richard McSorley, S.J., told me:

Dorothy was always reliable for doing the best thing. Like at the Eucharistic Congress in Philadelphia in 1976. They had scheduled a military Mass as part of the Congress—and on Hiroshima Day, August 6.

A committee of us went to see the priest who was running it, and he said he didn't know it was Hiroshima Day, which was even worse. We asked all the main speakers to say something, and the only one who did was Dorothy Day. She did it in her own unique way, however, without criticizing the archdiocese. She just said that this was the day that commemorated Hiroshima and that if we went to Mass on this day, we should certainly do it in repentance.

Robert Ellsberg, who was at the Worker at the time, remembers that the responsibility really weighed on her:

She wanted to express both her love for the church and . . . her sadness. It was hard for her to be critical of the bishops to their faces. She felt it was a great honor to be invited, and she worried that she was not worthy. But who else in the American church had greater moral authority? Here she was, seventy-nine years old, and this was the only time that she had been invited to do [something like] that. For so long she had been kept at arms' length as a radical.

It was the last talk she gave, and they had given her the title—"Bread for the Hungry." She begins by saying that she assumes she was invited because she is associated in people's minds with bread lines and all the hungry men and women in our cities. But then she talks about her devotion to the Eucharist and says, "My conversion began many years ago, at a time when the material world around me began to speak in my heart of the love of God . . . My love and gratitude to the church have grown through the years. She was my mother and nourished me and taught me."

Then she goes on to say that the church also taught her the need for penance, and this idea of repentance leads her into her challenging words about Hiroshima. Dorothy brought these two dimensions of the political and the mystical together. There is a passage in *The Long Loneliness* where she talks about how her deep love of the church is inseparable from her dissatisfaction. So different from the people who are zealously orthodox and very insistent on their love for the church, yet intolerant of any criticism.

Because she spoke from her heart, she was able to express both her love for the Eucharist and her deep dissatisfaction with the church's compromises toward the world. She saw the necessary connections, perhaps better than most of the bishops in her audience. As Tom Cornell points out, "Her radicalism was rooted in faithfulness to the church. She called on the church to practice its own doctrines." Father McSorley also saw other unifying aspects of her life as a Roman Catholic:

Since Dorothy's time there has been an increasing division in the church between what you what might call the right and the left, in gospel terms. The right are those who see religion as personal, without any social aspect to it. Then there are Catholics on the left who work for justice and peace and very often don't do much personal prayer. That division is widening by misinformation from one group against the other. Dorothy and the Catholic Worker bring it together.

The hierarchy didn't see it that way, however, especially during the early years of the Worker, when Dorothy's neutrality during the Spanish

Dorothy with César Chávez and Corretta Scott King.

Civil War, her pacifism during World War II, and her consistent support of the growing labor movement all put her at odds with a financially and politically conservative clergy.

As she neared the end of her life, however, these disagreements became muted. Father McSorley visited her a year before she died, and she spoke with him about her early relations with the hierarchy. He says he asked her all kinds of "controversial" questions:

She was very serene in answering them. For instance, she had been on record as saying that she wasn't in favor of women priests. But this time she said, "Well, I don't think that it will go on [the same way] forever. We will have women priests, but I think that the culture of the Catholic church in the United States right now is not ready for it. Probably the first step will be married priests. And then, when women are closer to the altar by being associated with priests, married to them, then the culture will be ready for women priests." She seemed very peaceful and calm about it.

I asked her if there was any time that she had conflict with the diocese. And she said, "No, I don't recall any."

I said, "How about the time when you helped support the strike of the gravediggers, and the archbishop had the seminarians out digging the graves?"

She just kind of parried that question by saying, "Well, I was called into the Chancery office once in New York, and I passed rows of desks with secretaries and important people at them. Finally I got to this monsignor's desk, and he stood up and he said, 'Thank you, Miss Day, for coming. Now would you please be seated.' And so we sat down and he said, 'We got some complaints in our office about what you're doing. But we know what you're doing. We don't need to be instructed by other people. We told them that we would talk to you. Now we have seen you, and that's enough. Thank you for coming.'"

She smiled and said, "That was the way we got along with the archdiocese." Looking at it from the point of view of a bishop's Chancery office, she had identified herself with the gospel and with the poor in such a clear way that any criticism would tend to make the Chancery look as though it was against the gospel.

Oftentimes she was asked, "What would you do if the archbishop told you to close the Catholic Worker?" She always said, "Well, I'd close it. Because if it's God's work, it will be taken up by somebody else." Now the archbishop knew he would get that obedience. So there was no point at which it could be tested and still make the diocese look as though it was on the side of the gospel. I don't think she maneuvered that. It was just a fact.

The archbishop was representing what the Catholic church taught and should be representing, even when it wasn't. So that . . . for example in that gravediggers' strike against the church that hired them, I'm sure the diocese didn't want any publicity about the fact that the strike was being broken by the diocese while the church was saying that gravediggers have a right to picket for a living wage.

She said once that the miracle of the loaves and fishes would go on in the Catholic Worker every day in her life. With no foundation support, only the providence of God. And the fact is that for all these years [she had] not been stopped by any bishop's office or in any way interfered with. That's a miracle in itself, I think, considering the way the church has been in history.

Some saw evidence, however, that she had at times an exaggerated respect for the hierarchy. In 1975 David O'Brien, professor of history at Holy Cross, was helping the bishops to organize the first Call to Action conference:

In preparation for that conference, we held hearings, and one was held in Newark, New Jersey. Twenty or twenty-five bishops sat as a panel, listening to people testify about questions of social justice, world peace, and urban problems. I had invited Dorothy to offer testimony, but when she saw all these bishops sitting on a stage with television cameras, she got very nervous and spent a lot of time telling folksy stories about nice bishops she had known. To our great disappointment. Then, just before she finished, she said. "Well, there is one other thing I should say." Then she talked about the wealth of the church and the many properties it owned. And why couldn't the churches in the inner city be open for soup kitchens? And what about the land the religious orders owned? Couldn't it and the land of the monasteries be made available for gardens for inner-city poor people? So she did finally move to challenge the wealth of the church. Now, having been with the bishops as they prepared for this, I knew a lot of them [were] in awe of Dorothy Day. As she got older, she became a kind of icon and was widely admired even by people who had no intention of doing what she did.

Good Shepherd Sister Teresa Murray also attended that meeting and remembers that when Dorothy entered the room, the bishops gave her a standing ovation. This applause might have merely unnerved her, as she was still afraid of public speaking. But I also think that her aversion to any hint of a cult of personality ensured that she actually didn't recognize her own status at that time.

In an earlier era Beth Rogers remembers being at Tivoli one day when Dorothy got a letter from the archdiocese.

She said, "Oh, dear! Now what fault are they going to find with me?" And she opened the letter, and it was asking her to participate in a revision of canon law! And of course she said that she couldn't, because she knew nothing about canon law, and it wouldn't be appropriate. But she read the letter aloud, and Ammon Hennacy heard her, and said, "Dorothy, you've failed. You have been approved officially."

Many point out that Dorothy was ahead of her time as an American Catholic, largely due to the influence of Peter Maurin and his building a bridge between the contemporary situation, the papal encyclicals, and the work of European intellectuals such as Jacques Maritain, Eric Gill, and Emmanuel Mounier. Jim O'Gara was with the early Worker in Chicago and was later editor of *Commonweal* for many years. He comments:

Dorothy was not radical in the way that many people are in the church today. She was only at odds with Catholics who were not familiar with the encyclicals and other avenues of Catholic social thought. She read things that most people don't bother to read, so she was for an orthodox position. She was for a papal position. She may have differed from the majority of American Catholics, but she was completely orthodox.

Kassie Temple told me that she thought Dorothy "saw the church as the source of her liberation, not as the limiting of her liberation. She accepted church teachings, but it wasn't blind obedience." Chuck Quilty, who shepherded a house in Rock Island, Illinois, through the tumultuous sixties, remembers that Dorothy thought [obedience to the church] was very important and that we should "stay close to the people in the pews." Jim Forest explains:

What she wanted us to do was absolutely and clearly part of the tradition. It wasn't like she was planning to invent a new sacrament. If you look back at the old issues of the *Catholic Worker*, there's a lot on the encyclicals. Also the work of modern theologians, like Jacques Maritain. Dorothy took on what was there [in the culture], saying, "What does this mean for us? How do we deal with this?"

As Father McSorley saw it:

Dorothy was Vatican II before Vatican II. And I think she was more important to the church than most of its structures because she had a great influence on all the controversial issues of the day. For fifty years she led the way within the Catholic church on solidarity with the poor, racial justice, union rights, ecumenism, and peace. All those big issues. She took a lead and brought the name Catholic to all of them. These issues that private Catholics see as politics, she saw as faith, and knew it had to come from faith and be alive with faith.

Her relationship with the liturgy was tinged at times with ambivalence. One can see from reading *The Long Loneliness* how much she loved the mystery of the Latin Mass, and she would sometimes attend Eastern Rite and Russian Orthodox liturgies. But she joined with others in anticipating the liturgical reforms of Vatican II. As early as the 1940s she was following Virgil Michel and the Benedictines with *Orate Fratres*, worshiping at dialogue Masses, reciting portions of the Divine Office, and encouraging the use of the missal. Jim Forest says the liturgical and sacramental life of the church "thrilled her. So it was heartbreaking for her, later in her life, to see that a lot of the people coming to the Catholic Worker movement couldn't . . . wouldn't open those doors for anything."

Her friend Nina Polcyn Moore says:

I think some of the new liturgies were hard on her, even though she had been active in the pre-Vatican liturgical movement. [Saying Mass] around the kitchen table and not having the proper accouterments and so forth. She found those things painful, but she was gracious about it. Very nonjudgmental.

Brian Terrell may have the most balanced view of an older Dorothy's attitudes toward the liturgy. First, he tells an interesting story:

Charlotte Rose, Dorothy's great-granddaughter, was baptized at Tivoli. The presiding minister at this affair was Archbishop Francis from Woodstock, New York, an Old Catholic Archbishop.[3] He came with one of his priests and did a great liturgy. Dan Berrigan was there, too, and there was this marvelous celebration. Dorothy was very cordial [to the archbishop], who was an old friend of the family, and it was just a lovely day all around.

Now this man was a schismatic, supposedly. According to the rules, we were all in mortal sin just for being there. So for Dorothy, this wasn't just an openness to other faith traditions, it was openness to a schismatic priest. To take part in a schismatic liturgy is much more serious [than going] to an Episcopal church or a Lutheran church, so [her being there was] not just something ecumenical. But I think Dorothy was just happy to think that one of her great-grandchildren was being baptized at all. (Laughs.)

Then Brian tells competing stories about Dorothy's liturgical attitudes:

If you look at the book A Spectacle unto the World, with the photographs by Jon Erickson, there are beautiful pictures of Dorothy Day attending a Mass said by Dan Berrigan. He's wearing a turtleneck sweater and a cross made out of nails. No stole, no alb. And we see Dorothy sitting there, taking no obvious offense. I didn't come until a year or two after the picture was taken, but I myself never saw Dan

---

[3] Brian explains: "Archbishop Francis Brothers was an amazing, very charismatic man—a shrunken little old guy with lots of energy. He was the leader of the Old Catholics, a heretical sect. Some of the younger folks at Tivoli would cross the river to attend his Masses at Woodstock. That group included Dorothy's granddaughter, Susie, who had asked Archbishop Francis to baptize her daughter on the lawn at Tivoli."

pick up a missal. His Masses were all extemporaneous. During my first years in New York, we had a dining-room Mass every Monday night. Right there on that metal table. Some priests wore vestments and some would not, but Dorothy wouldn't be upset. She'd just be happy we had Mass.

Not too long ago, I was at the May Day Mass in New York. Father Dan Berrigan said the Mass, and this young priest, who had just read about Dorothy and never met her, was furious. "What an insult to Dorothy Day's memory! Dorothy never would have stood for this! Having Dan Berrigan say Mass in such a casual manner, without proper rubrics, without the proper vestments. She would never stand for it." On and on.

His complaining goes with the story Jim Forest tells of Dorothy being so upset about a common coffee cup being used as a chalice at Mass that she buried it in the backyard. Now if you've ever dug around in that back yard, you'd know it's not really a . . . a sign of respect for the sacred. *(Laughs.)* Burying an object in that hard ground is not returning it to nature. This is a New York City Lower East Side backyard; it's filth and garbage as far down as you can dig.

Another story, which I have been unable to document firsthand, was heard by Mary Durnin at a meeting at the cathedral in Milwaukee. Seems a friend of hers, who was a conscientious objector and spending time at the Worker, attended a Mass there. Here's Mary's version:

I don't remember everything exactly. But anyway, I think it was the time of the draft-card burnings, and there was a house Mass, and the priest was very young, and they all sat around the table. The priest used real bread and the crumbs fell on the table, and after the Mass, the priest just swept the crumbs away in a wastebasket. Dorothy took the wastebasket, picked out every crumb and ate it. Yes, yes. [My friend] was there, and he told us.

Both these stories of Dorothy's reverence for the Eucharist are more important for their metaphorical content—what they tell us about Dorothy's love for Christ and belief in the Real Presence—than for their adherence to actual facts. I frankly think Dorothy was too fastidious to go through a wastebasket at the Worker. So does Robert Steed, who, when I asked him about the story, commented: "Forget it! That never happened. Dorothy wasn't crazy." And I doubt very much if *anyone* would get a very big hole in the hard-packed dirt in the tiny back yard of St. Joseph's.

Richard Cleaver has a different chalice story, one about a priest who came to visit and didn't find a gold chalice, and so he wasn't going to say

Mass. It seems Dorothy held up a coffee cup to him and said, "Here, Father, use this. This is consecrated by the lips of the poor, by the lips of Christ. Do you want something better than this?"

Now both chalice stories story may be apocryphal but they're both also plausible as "Dorothy stories." She herself would be capable of telling and teaching with both stories because both say something true about the Eucharist. Brian Terrell continues:

T hose stories illustrate something else, too. Lots of people talk about her consistency, that the consistency between what she wrote and the way she acted was all of a piece. Well, sometimes she was consistent, and sometimes she wasn't. She was a very volatile person, and she published an awful lot. I think it's natural that you can find her saying how wonderful it is that people are saying Masses in living rooms with coffee cups, and you can also find her saying it's a terrible thing.

I'm past forty now, so basically I'm a grumpy old man, always harking to the old days, even though I realize that a lot of my feeling is simple nostalgia. I'm beginning to understand, though, how Dorothy, as a convert in the 1920s, would think [about liturgies] in the 1970s, "This isn't as good as when I was young." You've got to put it in context. She said things on both sides of the [liturgical] issue and both have some validity. People who are trying to pin her down to just one side are really taking their own position and making it Dorothy's.

And another thing that's often misinterpreted about Dorothy and the liturgy: People who come to the Catholic Worker in New York sometimes see that [the community is] always using liturgical books that have just been superseded. [The visitors] interpret this as a sign of liturgical conservatism, but it's not. It's simply the frugality of the Worker. You wear last year's fashions, eat date-expired yogurt, use the old stuff that other people are throwing away.

Yes, Dorothy had misgivings about the changes in the liturgy, and yes, she frequently criticized the church for its failure to live up to the gospel. But this strengthened rather than compromised her loyalty, as Jeannette Noel explains:

S he was very, very faithful to the church in a time when others were full of criticism. But instead of leaving the church, she gave to the church by her example. She made the church accept conscientious objection and [did this] without throwing stones. And it's amazing how many churches here in New York now have soup lines or places for the poor to sleep. Absolutely because of the influence of Dorothy and the Catholic Worker.

See, Dorothy always put God first. And she was very faithful to her prayer life—Mass every day, reading the office, praying the Rosary. She got all her strength from there. And her perfect trust. She trusted perfectly that somehow God would guide her in living out the gospel. And God did.

LILIES OF THE FIELD

She never considered that she owned anything.
—SISTER TERESA MURRAY

Dorothy's ready embrace of the poverty of the Bowery was a stark example of how completely she lived the gospel. One senses that the poverty itself excited the people I interviewed, especially those from the early years. For most of them, it was both new and unusual. And in reading her own work, especially *House of Hospitality*, one can sense this same exhilaration of the spirit in the face of adversity. But as Kathleen Rumpf once told a reporter, "Poverty was not pretty at the Catholic Worker." Nina Polcyn Moore gives a graphic description of the poverty in which Dorothy spent most of her Worker years:

She truly embraced a life of poverty. I remember once she lived in a small tenement with another lady from the house. Cold-water flat, no bath, maybe a toilet down the hall. The room was piled high with newspapers that this woman was collecting. No privacy, no amenities. But that was her choice. Everyday life was not easy for her any place.

Father Bernie Gilgun vividly describes the poverty he and co-Worker Jeannette Noel encountered in New York:

The first time we met Dorothy was at the Catholic Worker in New York in the late fifties. We went down to supper with her. Supper that night was a bowl of rice with a fish head. The eye and all were on the plate. Oh, I couldn't eat a thing! But I was ashamed to be seen not eating, so I fooled around a little with the rice and the bread.

Ah, but it was tough then. A "harsh and dreadful thing," as Jeanette Noel said when she first went down to try out the Worker in New York. She stayed for only a couple of weeks that first time. Bugs here, there, and everywhere. So she came home. Then she thought about it. "I had a vision of the judgment, and God asking me, 'Why didn't you go to the Catholic Worker when I called you?'" "Well," she said, "I'd be ashamed to say to God that I was afraid of the bugs." (Later, of course, she did go to the Worker, both with me in Hubbardstown and then for the rest of her years in New York.)

Terry McKiernan of South Bend remembers that someone asked Dorothy in 1949, "How do you manage to stay under these conditions?" She answered simply, "It's my work." Dorothy knew that it was more blessed to be poor than not poor, and she would often quote St. Vincent de Paul's prayer asking that the poor forgive us for the bread we give them. But she also wanted everyone to feel comfortable in accepting hospitality. Annette Cullen commented, "Wherever Dorothy lived looked like a place where the poor [would be] at home. There was never a feeling that you had to wipe your feet first."

We know from many sources that Dorothy's clothing came primarily from donations. Jean Forest commented that "Dorothy was not an aesthete, but the deprivations of her life were very difficult. She liked clothes and good food. Nice things, in general. The deprivations at the Worker included not only bad food and the absence of sometimes very basic material goods, but assaults on one's ears and nose, as well."

Even the few things Dorothy owned, she held lightly. Patricia Ann Bryon, an e-mail friend of mine who lived with Dorothy in the early seventies, wrote:

I can remember hearing Dorothy talking to a woman about our "belongings" being only ours on loan, waiting a time when someone else needs them more. And she was so generous with hers! Always leaving her books on my dresser, finding tiny surprises for my daughter Jennifer—lollipops, a tiny church, a child's rosary, children's books sent to her or discovered in donations. Thinking about her attitude toward material things made me realize that I had so much more than most of the women who lived in the house and that what I had was my way of showing others that I was better than they, because I had more.

Sometimes people thought Dorothy held things a little too lightly, especially if they had given Dorothy something special, which she promptly turned around and gave away. Ade Bethune talked about her mother, who loved Dorothy and used to hand knit her beautiful sweaters. Dorothy would give them away to the women she lived with. So one winter Ade's mother dug up an old sweater she had knit for herself back in the twenties. "Dorothy," she said, "I'm *lending* this to you. Try to keep it because it belongs to me."

Anne Perkins told similar stories, stories about gifts she had given Dorothy and gifts she had received from her:

Once, she gave me a nice little painting. On a block of wood, quite nicely done. I said to her, "Are you sure you want to do that?"

"Yes. Take it, take it!"

On the way out, I saw a young woman and she was looking at me through narrowed eyes. Looking very cross. I realized she probably had lovingly painted that little sketch and had given it to Dorothy and in Dorothy's casual way, she was giving away the painting, just as she'd given away the backrest I gave her. She seemed to have no feeling about possessions.

Dorothy would give little lessons about detachment, such as this small sermon to Dan Shay, who had a Catholic Worker house in Detroit as a young man:

I told her about loaning my car to a high school student for his senior prom. Now my car was kinda' special—a pretty little Ford with a new paint job and a beautiful grill. When he brought it back, the front end was all dented in and my nice little car wasn't nice anymore. I was telling Dorothy about it, and she said, "Can you still drive it? Then don't be so vain!"

In later years, the poverty at the Worker was not so stark. Jeanette Noel tells us:

Dorothy with Peter Maurin (reading May 1948 CW).

MARQUETTE UNIVERSITY ARCHIVES

I remember one time she was complaining about what she saw as luxury. She says, "I have a TV, I have an air conditioner! Now that's not living in poverty." She was just going on and on. And I said to her, "Dorothy, just say 'Thank you.' Thank God for gifts." She laughed and didn't answer.

Richard Cleaver has an unusual story about Dorothy and intellectual possessions:

This is maybe my favorite "Dorothy story," the one that was the most like a personal bit of instruction for me from her. She had gotten an honorary degree from the Jewish Theological Seminary up at Columbia, and she hadn't been there for it, so somebody brought it back to her, along with the program. The program was in English on one page and in Hebrew on the other, and we were sitting there at supper before the Friday night meeting or something. I said, "You know, I've always wanted to learn Hebrew, but I've never had a chance."

And she looked at me, and she said, "Well, you know, sometimes that's a form of poverty, too. You should embrace those kinds of poverty as well as the purely material poverty."

I've thought about that from time to time since. You know, I doubt that Dorothy would want anybody to carry that too far. She certainly wasn't a know-nothing. [She wasn't saying] that you should have no brain at all, but there's a certain kind of intellectual covetousness that's worth thinking about, too.

A perceptive observation about Dorothy's giving up the things of this world came from Marjorie Larney. Marjorie comes from a working-class family in Brooklyn and grew up hearing about Dorothy Day. She wrote me once:

My Dad saw her as having a kind of purity that most folks don't have. In other words, because she was middle-class, it didn't come naturally for her to be among working-class folks. Something else made her do it, and my dad thought that was a higher motive than just taking care of your own people, your own community. We can't separate our hearts from the people who loved us and taught us to love—it's natural to take care of the "village that raised us," to do it out of love for our own. But Dorothy grew to know, work for, and love a different community than the one she was raised in. And she gave up privilege to do so. Gave up status. Giving up material things is hard, but giving up status is even harder.

4.

Family and Friends

TAMAR AND FORSTER

Dorothy was the center not only of the Worker but of the Day family.

—TAMAR HENNESSY

I drove to Springfield, Vermont, on a beautiful green day in 1998 to meet Tamar Hennessy, Dorothy's only daughter. When Tamar greeted me at the door, I was momentarily speechless. The resemblance to her mother was uncanny. Tamar is a bit shorter but has the same moving-into-square figure clothed in a shapeless house dress, wears her hair in a similar white-braided coronet, has the same quick and intense eyes. We had a wonderful chat and were joined for part of the day by one of her daughters and by Rita Corbin, a Catholic Worker artist who lives in nearby Brattleboro.

Two years later I visited her again, learning more about the complicated and intense relationship between Dorothy and her daughter. Tamar is not well—crippled with arthritis and other ills of an aging body—yet her mind is agile and she laughs frequently with what people say is Dorothy's laugh, so our time together was delightful.

Dorothy was afraid she would never be able to bear a child, so the arrival of Tamar Teresa was greeted with great joy. Dorothy had Tamar baptized a Catholic, a decision soon followed by Dorothy's own baptism and decision to leave Tamar's father, Forster Batterham. Tamar means "little palm tree," and friends remember that Dorothy first heard the name from Tamar Katzman, a Staten Island friend. Dorothy rarely referred to her by name, though, instead calling her "my daughter," or "my child." Tamar called her mother "Dorothy" as far back as she can remember.

When Tamar was a year and a half, Dorothy herself was baptized and left Forster. For the next several years the mother and her daughter lived in many places—New York City, Los Angeles, Mexico—as Dorothy searched for a way to put her newfound faith into practice. One summer she cooked for a monastery on Staten Island and wrote garden articles for the *Staten Island Examiner*. Tamar remembers that she loved visiting the gardens and that she used to tell her mother stories, which Dorothy would record for Tamar to illustrate. It was while they were staying in New York with her brother John and his wife, Tessa, that Dorothy met Peter Maurin and found a way to combine her thirst for social justice with her Catholicism. As a working single mother, Dorothy was often forced to leave Tamar, and Tessa tried to fill in the gaps. Patricia Ann Bryon, who lived at Maryhouse with her young daughter in the seventies, said that Dorothy told her "to treasure the time I spent with Jennifer, that if she had to live her life over again, the only thing she would change would be the amount of time she devoted to her daughter."

After the Catholic Worker began, Dorothy and Tamar lived either at the Worker or in nearby apartments. It's hard for us today to imagine the grinding poverty of the Depression-era Worker. Poor food, cold-water flats, crowded rooms shared with others—and always, always, people who had less than Dorothy and her daughter, people who needed Dorothy's succor and guidance.

Tamar remembers her childhood as unconventional but rich in associations and in experiences. Rich sometimes even in material goods, in the form of presents from Dorothy's family or from Forster. And Dorothy herself compensated for the poverty as best she could. For instance, when they would visit friends, Dorothy would ask for a bathtub to bathe her daughter. When Dorothy was on the road, spreading the word and raising money for the work, kind people at the house cared for her daughter. Tamar speaks fondly of the people on Mott Street who helped when she was unable to travel with Dorothy:

It was wonderful to grow up there. So much enthusiasm! And everybody had found something they really wanted to do, so it was just so . . . so hopeful. I loved the spirit of that first ten years. But Dorothy would be away a lot, and I had a hard time with that. I even nicknamed her "Be-going." I wanted Dorothy so bad! When she came home, she lit up my room, she lit up my life.

When I went away to boarding school, I always wanted to be home, but at the same time it wasn't good for me there. There were just so many things that were precious to me about Dorothy. She'd love to make little treats for breakfast. Rumor goes around that she didn't cook. Ha! She was a very good cook!

But people get her all wrong sometimes. For instance, in the movie "Entertaining Angels," Dorothy was kind of grim. In real life, she'd walk into a place and throw her arms around the cook and say, "What are we having for dinner?" You know, cheer everybody up beautifully. And in so many of her pictures, she looks stern and convent-like. Well, she wasn't that way at all, but was wonderfully warm and loving and created a real home for the poorest of the poor.

Sometimes Dorothy was able to take Tamar with her when she traveled. In fact, several early issues of the *Catholic Worker* contained pictures that Tamar drew, including one of a prison chain gang she saw on the way to Florida to see Dorothy's mother, Grace Day. Eileen Egan told me:

In those times, it was rather bold of Dorothy to explain, "Yes, this is my daughter, but it's a daughter of a common-law marriage." You say this now without thinking. You didn't say it without thinking then. But she had a lot of presence, and people just accepted it.

Tamar remembers a trip to Alabama:

Sister Peter Claver took us all around. Alabama was still under the Depression and she took us to visit the Hoovervilles. The people had built their little shelters out of old car bodies, even laid out streets. Traveling with Dorothy was always amazing, always a rich experience!

When she was eight, Tamar went to the first of several boarding schools, including one in Canada that concentrated on the crafts of homemaking and one that taught methods of farming. Tamar:

I had confrontations with teachers who wanted me to be just

MARQUETTE UNIVERSITY ARCHIVES

Tamar, Dorothy, and Peter Maurin, circa 1935.

like Dorothy. From the time I was eight or nine, they began to ask me if I was going to take over the Worker when I grew up. I would cringe, because I'm temperamentally the opposite of Dorothy. My father is responsible for who I am. He kind of turned away from the world, and I'm not much of a people person, either.

My father just thought the world was a losing proposition. He didn't want a child. But when he had one, he loved me. I wish I'd known him a lot better. We were both shy people, so we didn't reach out to each other. We would meet together for holidays and not have anything to say to one another. *(Laughs wryly.)* But he sent me all kinds of books on biology and microscopes and things like that and . . . he was wonderful. He knew what my mother was going through. I guess we'd been very close when I was an infant, but of course I don't really remember that. I think I missed him terribly, you know, in an unconscious way.

As Tamar entered her teen years, Dorothy, like mothers everywhere, worried about her growing into adulthood. In fact, similar worries may have been partly responsible for her having Tamar baptized. She writes in *The Long Loneliness*, "I knew that I was not going to have her floundering through many years as I had done, doubting and hesitating, undisciplined and amoral." Perhaps in Dorothy's eyes, the "Great Retreat" given by Father Hugo was the linchpin in the mooring she felt Tamar needed. Tamar felt otherwise and holds Hugo's detachment as at least partly responsible for her hardscrabble adult life of rural poverty. Tamar told me:

Dorothy knew exactly what she believed and what must be done. She could be difficult, but that was all right, too. We were both strong people, but there was that period in my teens when Dorothy got very religious and severe, all because of that dreadful retreat.

When she was seventeen, Tamar fell in love with David Hennessy, a man who had come to the Catholic Worker farm because he was attracted to one segment of it—the ideas of the Distributists. Dorothy told her she could not marry until she was eighteen. Tamar remembers her mother going to Forster for help. He didn't see marriage as worth being concerned about and was no help to Dorothy. Worried that her daughter might make the same mistakes she did when she was young, Dorothy let the marriage plans go forward.

During the year she asked Tamar to wait, she sent her to Ade Bethune's in Newport, trusting Ade and her mother to provide a stable family for Tamar and wanting to be sure that she was prepared in the homemaker arts she herself did not possess. Tamar told me this was the happiest year of her life.

In April 1944 Tamar and David were married. They moved from one unworkable farm to another, had nine children, and apparently lived in a tension-filled marriage. Tamar summarizes her married years:

When I married I thought we were going to be back-to-the-landers. That whole foolish trip, you know. But we were neither of us adequate to that. He sort of collapsed under the burden. Couldn't handle the responsibility. It was too much. Very, very hard, long and hard, and no way to raise nine children. I think it takes its toll.

Dorothy would visit frequently, however, especially when new children were born. These visits and the contributions of the royalties earned from her writing may have bolstered Tamar's spirits but were never enough to counter the poverty. Dorothy loved her grandchildren and petted them and spoiled them as any grandmother does, and so did Forster, despite his pessimism about the world they were inheriting. But Tamar's life was difficult. When she finally left her husband, Dorothy said, "I don't know how you stood it for so long!"

Tamar concludes: "I live now in a small town and five of the children live nearby. Even some of the grandchildren and great-grandchildren. It's been very nice, as it worked out."

There is much complexity in this most compelling and passionate of all Dorothy's relationships—her love for her only daughter—and it was comforting to know how close they were in Dorothy's final years. Tamar is a private person, and we can give her and her mother no better tribute than to respect that privacy.

Besides seeing her family often, Dorothy remained connected with Forster Batterham, the father of her child. As she recounted in *The Long Loneliness*, Dorothy left him because they could not reconcile her new faith with his agnosticism and anarchism. While Dorothy was careful not to speak casually of Forster, it was clear to her friends that she remained her whole life in love with him. Robert Ellsberg speaks of seeing letters Dorothy wrote to Forster after her conversion but before starting the Worker. From these letters Robert sees that "in a sense, she wanted to have it all . . . Her hope was that he would soften and say, 'Come back,' and they would marry." Robert remembers her writing something like, "I really don't think I'm asking for all that much. Just that you permit me to bring up our daughter as a Catholic. I'm not planning to fill the house with all kinds of creepy statues or anything." Joe Zarrella comments that her human love for Forster "intensified her spiritual love of God."

A part of her craved marriage and motherhood and a relationship with the man she loved. While these dreams didn't happen, she was able to end her days in close and friendly contact with him and with their daughter. Until these final days, however, Dorothy kept her family life separate from her Worker life. In earlier years their relationship was not tranquil. Tom Cornell explains:

She wanted to avoid scandal. Very, very seldom saw Forster, although they were on the telephone often. (She really had to go after him to pay for Tamar's schooling.) Forster always had a woman. Once she saw him with one on the street. Dorothy said, "You should have seen her. Painted hussy! Red hair. Large breasts." Forster was embarrassing her by playing to this woman. [Her reaction] was also, it seemed to me, pretty girlish. It was part of her charm that she could lapse from grande dame to girl.

She knew that she had to lead a celibate life in order to continue, but she really missed the company of a mate. She often alluded to this. Remember the passage [in *The Long Loneliness*] about getting into bed with Forster's cold limbs? It's a wonderful image. You can almost . . . You can almost smell the salt. In her bed. (*Laughs heartily.*)

In 1959 Dorothy gave the use of one of the Staten Island beach cottages to Forster and Nanette, his companion, when Nanette was dying of cancer. She herself moved to the island to care for Nanette and asked Jean Walsh, a nurse, to help her. Johannah Hughes [Turner] was living nearby. Johannah remembers Dorothy bursting into the Hughes's bungalow one morning, "beaming and bubbling and giggling, carrying on like a young girl." She had been dreaming that she was in bed with Forster and she was crowing. "You can't be held responsible for sinning in your dreams." Johannah recounts:

She said that to my mother right in front of us. I thought that was a pretty risque thing for Dorothy to say and her high glee was infectious. That might have been one of the rare occasions when we jumped into the car with her and drove into town to buy some cinnamon buns to go with breakfast.

Another time during that same period Forster was doing or saying something to get on her nerves, and she was stomping around her bungalow raging about his ways, maybe accusing him of being selfish and demanding. I was sitting at her kitchen table, listening in awe, not having any idea what was really going on, and I started murmuring sounds of agreement as a gesture of support. Whereupon she turned upon me ferociously and defended him and gave me to understand I was not to criticize that wonderful man when I had no idea what a sterling character he really had and what kind of a strain he was under.

Jean Walsh remembers her time with Nanette and Forster and Dorothy:

Nanette was a sweet, sweet woman—beautiful and childlike. And stylish, too. A good fifteen years younger than Forster. There would be Dorothy and Forster and Nanette sitting there, and they'd talk and look out at the water. Nanette was so innocent and so uninhibited. Precious. I remember one day Nanette was all excited, telling me that when she got well, she was going to give all her clothes away and her jewelry and live like Dorothy did, like Jesus.

The night before I had to leave, Nanette died unexpectedly and very suddenly at 4:00 in the morning. I went next door and told Dorothy, and told Forster, and then I had to go back to my work. (A woman from Grailville had come to replace me.)

A few months later, I was visiting Dorothy and she told me that she went on a long speaking tour right after Nanette died. She said she was fleeing from Forster. She always used the word "flee." "When you get into a very hard situation, you flee."[1]

Sister Teresa Murray recalls Dorothy speaking of Forster while Sister Teresa was helping her move into Maryhouse:

I was helping her unpack. Forster had sent her these holy pictures, which he had cut out of an art book and framed, and I could tell she was just thrilled to get them. I said, "It must have cost you to leave him." And she said she had found that if you do what you think you should do—if it's a sacrifice—then the Lord fills the gap and gives you much more. It was one of those things that she said spontaneously, and you could tell she had a great affection for him.

Some of Dorothy's friends feel that Dorothy would have tired or outgrown Forster, saying that "he was good for her while they were together." However, the evidence pretty clearly points to her continuing love for him. At the end of her life they were in almost daily contact, and Forster walked with Tamar in the funeral procession. Tom Cornell remembers the later public Mass the cardinal said for Dorothy at St. Patrick's Cathedral:

---

[1] William Miller gives a different chronology in his biography, but this is how Dorothy remembered it and told it to Jean. Judith Gregory also remembers that she canceled a speaking engagement at the New School of Social Research and left abruptly on a bus trip.

I was sitting where I could see Forster, who was in the front row with some of the grandchildren and great-grandchildren. Tamar was not there. I remember thinking, What's going on in this guy's mind? He knew Dorothy in a way that none of us knew her. Loved her, evidently. She certainly was crazy about him. Never got over it. Who is Dorothy to this guy, and what does he think when he walks into this space, and hears the choir singing, and sees something like twenty-three identically vested priests up there with the Cardinal? All for this woman.

At the end, someone comes to Forster and says, "The cardinal wants to see you." Forster's frail. He's so old, he's so frail. And the cardinal comes and shakes his hand.

PETER AND AMMON

She loved Peter in her way; I would not speculate on "liking."

—FRANK WALSH

Dorothy worked closely with several strong-willed men throughout her Catholic Worker life, particularly co-founder Peter Maurin (1877-1949) and "one-man revolution" Ammon Hennacy (1893-1970). The accounts below explore what her friends thought about her relationships with these two important influences. Mary Alice Zarrella, herself very close to Peter when she was at the Worker, explains the symbiosis between the two co-founders of the movement:

Peter was Dorothy's teacher. He taught her about the church, taught her how she could put her ideals into action as a Catholic, guided her reading, gave her the grounding for what she became. People used to say, "Man proposes, woman disposes." That was certainly true of Peter and Dorothy. He had the ideas; she put them into action.

I wouldn't say Dorothy was intimate with Peter, as she was with some who came to the Worker to live the ideas. For instance, I never saw them whispering together, although they probably took walks together. Dorothy loved walking the streets of the city, and of course Peter never rode any place unless someone took him.

Eileen Egan elaborates:

She got her ideas from Peter Maurin, and it was a remarkably humbling thing for a woman to do because Peter . . . if you saw him, he looked like he slept outside in his clothes. But he had what she needed, which was a good knowledge of the church, and she chose him as her mentor and stayed with it. He was able to teach her about the encyclicals. Most people in the Catholic church know only that there *are* encyclicals, period. They don't know what they contain, don't know about the encyclicals [that] consider the rights of the worker and the evils of finance capitalism.

Joe Zarrella says he wouldn't have come to the Worker if it were just Peter:

She would talk about Peter, telling all of us "young Turks" that we didn't "respect" him enough. I was impressed with his mind and his grasp of history, but he would not have moved me. Dorothy was the— she'd hate this word—the *heart* of the movement. Now I'm not saying he didn't move some people. He made the one big convert, and that was Dorothy.

Some of the ways Dorothy would talk about Peter send double messages, however. For instance, Jane Sammon recorded in her diary a story Dorothy told her about Peter. Jane had asked Dorothy if she thought Peter was a saint, and Dorothy answered:

"Oh, yes. He was single-hearted. He had a vision. For instance, once in Tessa's apartment, we were listening to a concert on the radio, and I put my finger over my lips. I didn't tell him to keep quiet. I just put my finger over my lips. Well, he got up, went over, knelt down at Tessa's feet, and began whispering to her one of his [Easy Essays]."

Another example of her wry humor about Peter was recounted by John Williams of Seattle:

When we started our Catholic Worker here in '79, we wrote to Dorothy asking for permission to call it the Dorothy Day House. Dorothy wrote back, "Please, no. 'Fools' names, like fools' faces, always appear in public places.' Call it Peter Maurin House."

Dorothy wrote and talked constantly about Peter, and it occurs to me that she herself built the legend that he was the backbone of the movement. Michael Harrington noted:

MARQUETTE UNIVERSITY ARCHIVES

Dorothy, with her grandchildren and Ammon Hennacy.

Dorothy used to talk endlessly about him, but in very revealing terms. About how Peter just assumed that he'd write the entire newspaper and was sort of taken aback when it turned out that Dorothy was actually a journalist of some substance, that it was not going to be just *his* paper. As Dorothy told the story, it was sort of, "Isn't that charming of Peter?" Well, it occurred to me that if you're a writer, it might not have been such a charming . . . you know, [his was] a rather arrogant assumption. Dorothy would give whole lectures on Peter. It seemed to me she got very boring when she talked about Peter, and that also made me suspicious.

Another man important to the Worker who had an ambivalent relationship with Dorothy was Ammon Hennacy. In 1952 Ammon came to the Worker and eventually even for a time to the Catholic church. Dubbing himself "the one-man revolution," Ammon brought to the group an enthusiasm for protest that was a refreshing antidote to the Cold War, which permeated the country. A real charmer, he was most likely not only in love with Dorothy but with several of the Catholic Worker women, including Mary Lathrop.[2] In fact, many feel Ammon became a Catholic only to try to win Dorothy's love. As Michael Harrington put it, "It had very little to do with the Holy Spirit and very much to do with human love."

Robert Steed speaks forthrightly about Ammon's relationship to Dorothy:

He came here with the idea that he was going to marry her. And it was never going to happen, but it took him a while to catch on to that. He worked hard for five years, out selling papers every day, answering all the mail. Worked like a slave! She put up with his . . . he would just constantly say things that she considered anti-Catholic. He was a born *Protest*-ant. He became a Catholic 99 percent to please her, and I don't think he ever understood Catholicism. He would aggravate her, saying things about the clergy or about not believing in some dogma or other. She thought if you became a Catholic, you accepted it all. He worshiped Dorothy and anything she said was law. But she only admired him.

Karl Meyer, a lifelong Catholic Worker and resister and protege of both Ammon and Dorothy, feels that Dorothy at one time was herself in love with Ammon. He elaborates:

Dorothy often spoke of him very affectionately, but she knew about his blabbing tendencies and may have been exceptionally cautious not to give him anything concrete to blab about. Ammon was a gentle pussycat in certain ways, but he was also stubborn and single-minded, not the kind of gentleness that was mature enough to absorb Dorothy's moods and fluctuations.

Most people I spoke with believe that Ammon and Dorothy were close because of shared ideals and interests, but that their personalities clashed in ways that would preclude any lasting emotional attraction.

Father Bernie Gilgun also remembers that Ammon would tease Dorothy about the church. He said that he once went with a fellow priest to New York and when they walked into the Worker, Ammon called Dorothy over:

---

[2] Mary tells the story of going on a trip with Dorothy: "I was driving poor Dorothy crazy. 'Should I marry Ammon, or shouldn't I marry Ammon?' On and on and on and on. Poor Dorothy. She told me once, 'You will get tired of that old flesh and start chasing after younger men.' Finally, I opened the Bible at random and put my finger on this message: 'Woe, woe unto you that you should play the harlot and be his.' That was the end of it. Not the end of my friendship with Ammon but the end of that problem."

"Dorothy! Dorothy! Come here! You have to see this. Two skinny priests! You're not going to see anything like this again."

She came over and said, "Oh, Ammon! Hush up! Father Bernie, don't listen to what he says but do as he does."

Folksinger Utah Phillips, who was converted to radicalism by Ammon, gives us concluding insights on the relationship:

Ammon was a deeply passionate man. I know she had great affection for him and was moved by him. And I wish they could've gotten it together. No one could have lit any brighter candle than those two!

He also talked about the disagreements and differences between the two leaders:

One of Ammon's prison rules was, "Never go into the slam with anything that you can't give up." Because if you've got something like an alcohol addiction or a caffeine or a nicotine addiction, they can take it away from you. Now it was probably just petulance over their seemingly deteriorating relationship, but the flaw Ammon fastened onto in Dorothy was the little jar of instant coffee she always had in her purse. She couldn't get past the caffeine addiction. She'd given up smoking, but he thought that, in terms of doing time, coffee is what they'd eventually get her on.

Later, after they'd had a real falling out, he said a little bitterly, "Oh, she's talking to the bishop too much." And one time he showed me the original manuscript to *One Man Revolution in America*. And Dorothy Day wasn't in it.

I said, "Ammon! Dorothy's not in the book."

"Well, she's still alive. She's could chicken out at any time."

The book as it was published includes a chapter on Dorothy Day.

CONNECTIONS

Dorothy had the very great gift of really entering into your situations. Hundreds of people felt that they knew her personally because she gave them her total attention and really entered into their lives.
—BOLEN CARTER OF ST. LOUIS, MISSOURI

Dorothy Day was above all connected, with God and with all those in whom she saw God, including the people who came for food and shelter—

those that Peter Maurin called "the ambassadors of Christ." She was also connected to her many, many friends. Perhaps it's the nature of the interviews and the people who consented to them, but Dorothy as a friend stands out predominately for most of the narrators. She thrived on community and relationships and was able to let people know that they mattered to her. Even people who didn't live with her could be profoundly affected.

One of the longest and deepest connections was with Stanley Vishnewski, the Lithuanian boy who came to work with Dorothy when he was seventeen and never left.[3] She often told of his Sancho Panza style when he protected her from unruly horses in a demonstration. He was truly her "knight for a Day," defending her physically and healing her emotionally with his constant joking. One does not go to Stanley's book about the Worker—*Wings of the Dawn*—for the facts but instead for the human nuances, the humor and shared community in the day-to-day life. Stanley's presence provided both leavening and stability. As Tamar says, "Stanley would always say exactly the right thing to diffuse the tension." Sheila Dugan explains:

Dorothy absolutely adored Stanley. He came when he was just a Lithuanian kid and he stayed one. Real working class. The real thing. Stanley was . . . of all the people there, Stanley was the very closest to her. Never left her, all those years. Sure she'd get irritated with him and sometimes try to shove him out of the nest, so to speak, but she both depended on him and mothered him. Actually, the only person she was really, truly motherly toward was Stanley.

He'd stay up nights thinking of stories to tell her, and he'd tell the same stories, over and over and over again, but she'd actually laugh out loud at them. Oh, and his sayings—"The Christians know each other by the breaking of the heads," that sort of thing!

The connections of Dorothy Day's friendships were legendary. Mary Lathrop told me that she saw a book of Dorothy's inscribed to her as "the mother of thousands." Jim Douglass has this analysis of Dorothy's attraction to so many:

She had a kind of unique faith in people. She would frequently say that so and so "is a wonder." And she really meant "full of wonder," that there was that of God in them. You had a real sense of grace in the way she looked at people. She had a deeply moving sense of people's possibilities, a sense that often went deeper than their own sense of those possibilities.

---

[3] It is ironic that she outlived the much younger Stanley, who died in 1979.

Several of Dorothy's friends tell about her being able to know what was needed in a relationship. Kathleen Rumpf told me:

She knew my vulnerabilities and I sensed hers, so I'd try to protect her and not impose myself. We were taking care of each other, in very simple and unspoken ways. For instance, she was never critical of me. I think she knew my fragility. That's the thing I most respected about Dorothy. I never saw her strike out at somebody who was hurting. With me, she'd try to point out the beauty of the world, because she knew that was what I needed.

Ed Turner proposes that Dorothy's responses might have come from family values:

Dorothy was supremely loyal to her friends, both old and new. When Peggy Baird was dying of cancer, Dorothy brought her to Tivoli. However, Dorothy had the Day family characteristic of feeling that one should stand on one's own feet. If one really needed help, then one should ask. The Days would be generous in responding, but they did not reach out. Perhaps because to do so would be to intrude. This might be attributable to the Victorian values of the middle class. Dorothy was the soul of generosity, the most generous person I have ever known. But you had to ask her.

Dorothy was godmother for psychologist Clare Danielsson when she came into the church as an adult. Here's the story Clare tells:

In 1967, I finally admitted that I was interested in becoming Roman Catholic and decided to ask Dorothy how I should proceed with getting baptized. We talked, and she told me to read C. S. Lewis's book *Mere Christianity*. I told her I understood that I needed to take instructions, and she said, "Never mind about instruction. Just get baptized and keep right on doing what you're doing."

Of course, I bought the C. S. Lewis book and fell in love with it. I've always found it amusing that Dorothy referred me to a writer who identified himself as Episcopalian, but it was exactly the right book for me. Because I had the feeling I needed to be baptized in a "local church," I found Holy Name and Father Bradley. [After a couple of meetings] he agreed to baptize me and told me to come back the next Saturday with my godparent.

Godparent! Who was I going to ask? I thought and thought and finally called Tivoli and asked Kay Lynch if she would be my godmother. She declined and said she would ask Dorothy. Well . . . Dorothy was visiting Tamar in Vermont, but she drove all the way down to stand up for me. It's hard to estimate the power of that unexpected approval, what we psychologists call unconditional love—that unconditional love I received not once but many times from Dorothy Day.

Tom Cornell called her "a reader of souls":

She sensed people's condition and she spoke to their condition. I'd see a person saying, "How did she know?" Now I might know because I'd had a few drinks with the person the night before, so I knew what was on his mind. She didn't. How did she intuit it? How did she say exactly the right thing that person needed? Reading souls. Yes, she could do that.

Jean Forest, who was at the Worker in the early sixties, discovered this quality, as well:

Dorothy sensed that I was interested in issues around men and women—in issues about equality. And so we'd talk about these things. I did not find her to be a prudish person. She thought it was up to the young women to demand sexual responsibility from men. She was not a . . . I don't think she believed in sexual license per se, but I think she believed in sexuality.

Ned O'Gorman gives us another view of a friendship with Dorothy Day:

I wasn't an intimate. It would be crazy for me to say that I was, but I knew her very well, and to me, she was one of the most sophisticated women I've ever met. Certain women transcend class. Dorothy transcended class. I would write her soupy letters, like "I'm going to Europe yet again, I feel so guilty!" She would write back, "Stop being foolish. I have a place on Staten Island. [Everyone has] to get away."

Did you know she was also vain? I remember interviewing her for the *New York Times*. She told Charlie Harvard, who was the photographer, "Don't photograph me from that side; that's my bad side."

She was immensely polite. But more than polite. Dorothy had an awesome quality of charming men. For my money, it was a feminine quality, and I don't care if a feminist would shoot me for saying it. First of all, she's immensely beautiful. I have a picture of her at home. Little straw hat on her head. Gorgeous! I don't think anyone—any cardinal, bishop, or pope—could possibly have inveighed against Dorothy as they would a recalcitrant priest. Dorothy had this tremendously balanced and exquisite . . . I keep going back to her femininity. I imagine she was a bit like Teresa of Avila. Or one of the great Benedictine abbesses. She had a tremendous self-possession, just was a tremendously whole person. She was a mysterious and extraordinarily beautiful . . . umm, an extraordinarily beautiful *event* in anybody's life. Because she confounded expectations. It's kind of a cliche, I guess, but I have to say I found her authentic. There was in her a radiant, transcendent authenticity. It's an authentic, transcendent, vibrant thing. Did I love her? Yes, I did.

Sheila Dugan was very young when she met the Catholic Worker and Dorothy Day at Peter Maurin Farm on Staten Island. Her memories include an insight about the relationship Dorothy had with the woman who shared her room:

Dorothy always liked to talk about the pies I made, the cherry pies with the cherries I picked from the two cherry trees at the farm. Actually, I think I picked enough cherries during a summer for one pie; most of the time I was baking pies from Jell-O pudding mixes. I made about nineteen pies the first day I was there, and everybody was so crazy about them that I just kept doing it. I made pies the next day. And the next day. Who knows how much this pudding mix was costing the Worker! So everyone was talking about these pies and before she even met me, Dorothy wrote me a letter telling me how wonderful it was that I was doing all this baking. She even wrote an article about it later on that year.

I met Dorothy after I'd been at Peter Maurin Farm for about three weeks. She was charmed that she had met another Minnesota woman, like Georgia Kernan, the woman who had told me about the Worker. And I was charmed with Dorothy. Anything she'd ask me to do, I'd do. Anything. It was just delightful to be there. Such a completely different life than I'd had ever dreamed up for myself. *(Sighs.)*

Everybody at the farm worked at getting ready for her homecoming. Agnes Flynn . . . oh, my goodness, such a cute old lady! She lived with Dorothy, shared her bedroom. Dorothy never had a room of her own [while I was there]. Never! She'd start off with a room, and everybody would make it all nice for her, and then she'd take someone in. Then another. Two or three of the "shopping bag ladies." Agnes must have been about seventy years old.

Anyway, Agnes had this thing about saving blue dishes for Dorothy because Dorothy liked blue dishes. Dorothy must have said once how pretty a certain blue dish was or something, and Agnes remembered that. She would put them on a tray and give Dorothy breakfast in bed.

And then we'd all come in to see Dorothy in the morning, and she'd share her breakfast with us. So much for private mornings!

So, before I met Dorothy, I knew Agnes, and Agnes thought of herself as "Miss Day's" personal maid. She saw that as her duty. When any packages would come in, Agnes would be right there, going through the packages. And if there were any blue dishes, she'd take them up to Dorothy's room.

Dorothy's room was just charming with all of these madras throws on the chairs and beds and floral things, like pillow shams. Braided rag rugs. Her room was covered with these rugs. Covered! Overlapping each other. And lots of books. Dorothy slept in a double bed. Agnes's corner was in back of one of those folding screens.

I seem to recall that Dorothy came home just before lunch. We used to get leftover soup in a garbage pail from the Sisters of Loretto, who ran an orphanage near the farm. I was pouring soup out of the garbage pail when I met Dorothy.

She looked like a grandmother. I was really afraid of meeting her, kind of thinking she would be so awesome. But she wasn't. She never struck me as a fearsome person. She just seemed like a really gentle grandma. And she was. I think that's what Dorothy and I talked about, more than anything else—her grandkids. There were nine of them.

Sometimes Dorothy would talk just to me and sometimes it would be in a whole group. And whenever she wasn't reading, she was knitting. She'd knit all the time she was talking. She had wool in a big wooden bowl in the dining room, and she'd knit whenever she was there. Then there was another room, which Dorothy called the "loom room." It was just about the most wonderful room I had ever seen in my young, Minnesota-bound life. It was a little room with a fireplace and a big bay window off to the side. Under the window was a big box.

There were two kids at the farm at the time, and this box was being used as their toy box. Six feet long and three feet wide and full of kids' toys. This box had been made at Dorothy's request, to be used ultimately as her coffin, but, now that I think of it, I don't think it was wide enough for a human body. It looked just like a window seat, not gruesome at all.

Dorothy and I would sit around the fire and talk. People didn't group around Dorothy, at least that I was aware of. I would be in there because I babysat for these two little kids. Dorothy would come in and start knitting, and it would be a family scene. She would let the kids play with her, if they crawled into her lap. Actually, she was more like a grandfather than a grandmother. Grampa-ish, if you know what I mean. She would not turn them away—she really liked kids—but she didn't court them, or go after them, as a grandmother might. They'd go up and talk to her, and she'd talk to them as though they were adults.

Sheila met Kieran Dugan at the Worker and soon they were married. Here are her memories of Dorothy's role in the wedding:

Stanley gave me away and Dorothy . . . let's see, what was her role? Kind of like a maitre d'. She didn't fuss. I don't think Dorothy participated in things as a woman traditionally does. For instance, at my wedding, she was more like the father of the bride. Not real involved in the details. Which, in a way, was teaching me how to be a woman in the world. She didn't do any of the organizing for the wedding. (I did all of that. Ordered the cake and everything.) She just made sure the place was orderly. We got married at 11:00 Mass on August 30 at Old St. Pat's and then had the reception at the Worker at noon, when the men would usually be eating their lunch. And that day the lunch was already finished, so they were part of the reception. Everybody was involved, and that was very nice.

Dorothy was so ahead of time, without even realizing it. She would probably be the first to deny that she had any interest at all in women's liberation, but she didn't have to because she was a liberated woman before she was anything at all. She was the generation before us, and even in our time, unwed mothers were still giving their babies away to Good Shepherd convents without ever seeing them. She was always befriending single mothers. It wasn't just that she tolerated them and thought they should be married; she absolutely understood them and would seek them out and help them.

Dorothy absolutely changed my life. She was the very first woman I ever met who wasn't afraid to put career first. In a very odd sort of way, Dorothy was a career woman.

Even more important, though, was that she expected us to be adults and to act like adults. And so she was just the greatest teacher of all time. She *never* backed down on telling us, "Follow your conscience!" The priests would say, "Follow your conscience," but at the same time they'd give out all these rules. And Dorothy would simply say, "Follow your conscience." Her conscience was what led her to the Catholic church. Past the Catholic church. A lot of people think that you can't think you're following Dorothy without being Catholic. Well, I'm not a Catholic any more; I'm following my conscience, and I absolutely attribute that to Dorothy.

One of Dorothy's most fabled friendships was with Sister Peter Claver, whom I was privileged to interview when she was over one hundred years old. Sister recalls:

When I met Dorothy, my ministry as a Missionary Servant of the Most Blessed Trinity was with the African American people of the Archdiocese of Newark, New Jersey. I had no idea who Peter Maurin and Dorothy Day were but when I heard about them from Father Harold Purcell, I went to New York to meet them. They had not yet published the first issue of the paper. Dorothy always claimed that the first dollar she ever received as a donation came from me.

Dorothy and I came to be real friends. I think it was the ministry among the blacks that attracted her. The blacks were powerless people. This was the desire of her own heart. She had a love for the poor, the disadvantaged, and the street people. She used to tell me her work was one step below mine. Whenever we had any kind of affair like a communion breakfast or something special, she would always come out for it. This was the beginning of a lifelong friendship.

One can see from these differing relationships that Dorothy was more than "friend" to many people. One sees instead something more complex and personal. Many, of course, saw her as mother, because even at the beginning of the movement, she was older than the young who came to work and pray with her. Mary Lathrop says directly, "She really was my mother. I suppose a psychologist would call it some sort of a bonding." And it was as a dutiful daughter that she would carry food to Day during the last years of her life. Mary remembers, "One time she said to me, 'You're taking care of your old mother.'"

With some of the men, the relationship assumed conventionally gendered roles. Michael Harrington remembers that Dorothy liked his manly courtesies toward her, such as standing up when she entered the room. Former editor of the *Catholic Worker* Tom Cornell describes their experiences together as sometimes fraught with tension but says,

It was a very mother-and-son relationship, really. She was very modest. She didn't like . . . she would be in her bedclothes, and some seminarian or young priest would show up. Some fool would bring them right into her apartment while she was sitting there in her nightclothes. That embarrassed her terribly. But she would entertain me in her nightclothes.

While many of the men would talk about arguing with Dorothy— about the paper, primarily—Nina Polcyn Moore said the two of them "never had any reason to squabble. Maybe there was competition with the men not wanting the woman to dominate." Ruth Ann Boylston, who married Larry Heaney of Holy Family House in Milwaukee, saw that single women got along with Dorothy better than some of the married ones:

I think I saw her as interfering with my marriage a little bit, and I resented that. Telling Larry to do this or do that when we were living at the farm in Easton, and he wouldn't have a chance to consult with me. He didn't entirely like it either, you know.

As she became older and more secure in her leadership, Dorothy's relationships with couples became closer, as well. I spoke with Pat and Kathleen Jordan one memorable summer day in 1988 when they were living in one of the beach houses at Spanish Camp. Kathleen remembers:

We were blessed to have the time with her out here on Staten Island. With one baby and another on the way and spending day after day with this elderly woman on the beach. We miss her very much. I remember when we were getting married and ready to leave the Worker. We were very close to her by then, and it was hard for us that we were leaving. At one time she actually asked, in an indirect way, if we would stay. Then she immediately stepped back and just sort of fell against me. I was patting her on the back but she quickly straightened up and said, "Don't pity me." I felt she was saying something to herself, but she certainly was saying something to me, also. So it was very hard to part.

Pat joins his wife:

I got my life through Dorothy Day and the Catholic Worker. Got my life. We so very often think about her. Our son Justin just loves to go down and fish and catch eels. I think of Dorothy telling us about being right out in back of our cottage with her brother John in a boat full of eels and it tipping over. And she writes in *The Long Loneliness* about the fellow who did the beach combing right below where we live. You know, I came from California, where there were lovely beaches. When we came out here, I was quite disappointed because it's very rocky and . . . not Malibu at all. What I saw at first were the old tires, the refrigerator somebody had left down there, whatever it was. She taught me how to see the beauty in this beach, and in everything else.

All these gifts . . . Well, obviously the gift of our own family. We came from different parts of the country and happened to meet at the

Catholic Worker. And now we happen to know these children. It's thanks to Dorothy and the Catholic Worker that any of these good things happened in our lives.

Johannah Hughes Turner knew Dorothy from the time she was a child and thus gives an unusual perspective:

I remember her as physically warm and accessible when I was a child, with me and with other kids. Plenty of hugs and kisses and affection in her voice. Dorothy was a very powerful person, and she was the founder and director of the Catholic Worker. But she was also very vulnerable, really vulnerable, and I learned this at a very young age. You could easily hurt Dorothy's feelings. I've seen her in tears, and that was a revelation to a young person to see that vulnerability—that everyday vulnerability—in a powerful person, a powerful, influential, strong-willed person.

I remember once we were living on Staten Island, in one of the bungalows. And she came in all bubbling. She'd been reading about some saint and some miracles, and she was impressed by it, inspired by it. Well, my brother and I exchanged looks and snickers and rolled our eyes and when she saw what we were doing, she walked out in tears. We were immediately sorry. We were used to doing that kind of thing with each other and had no idea we could hurt an adult that way.

I have to tell you, though. I was very disappointed in her once. I was in anguish over the breakup of a relationship, and Dorothy was trying to comfort me, trying to say that it wasn't a right relationship to begin with, and that it could be gotten over and wasn't the end of the line for me. She expressed it in her own terms, using a parallel that made sense to her regarding inappropriate feelings and doomed relationships.

She told me that at one time she'd had to "pray down the lust," as she called it, for a man who was unavailable to her. She said that the process of "praying down" had been long and hard and painful, but it had been ultimately successful. She didn't go into any detail about the relationship but told me about it, I think, to show me that I could do it, too. I don't remember saying a whole lot in response. Or wanting to. I suppose I thanked her for trying, but the words she gave me couldn't help me at the time, partly because I'm not a believer.

Anyway, there are a couple of points here. One is that for Dorothy, this [confession] was another frustration of affection, another personal and particular relationship sacrificed to the life she'd chosen, and another painful secret and complicating factor in her relationship with other people.

She was also more important than she should have been in some . . . in a lot of our lives. She was the protector. If you come to the Catholic Worker because you're broke, or because you've been injured, or because you need a place to rest, or you've been in a mental institution, or whatever it is, you come there to heal. You come there without power and Dorothy becomes—there's transference with all this, I think—Dorothy becomes the mother and the . . . the everything to a lot of people. When she's imperfect in any way, it hurts. It's devastating.

So she carried that burden of being everything to everybody and not meeting everyone's needs as they saw them. She offered a world of compassion to a zillion individual people and yet couldn't provide enough to satisfy them all. And of course, because of that, she caught—from me and from other people—a lot of hostility and resentment, a lot of accusations that were inappropriate.

Johannah's mother was the late Marge Hughes, whom many people mention as one of Dorothy's dearest friends. Marge came to the Worker in 1939 when she was only nineteen. I was able to speak with Marge the year before she died, and she told me:

I'm glad you're doing this book because I'm sure it will speak to a lot of people, but there are a lot of things I'm not going to tell you or anyone else. The public doesn't need these confidences between Dorothy and me. But I will tell you some things. For instance, she worried about the young girls at the Worker and wasn't at all hesitant to speak to them about it, including me, but I didn't pay any attention. Once she said to me, "We don't go out with such and such. Or with so and so."

And I said, "Maybe you don't, but I do." (Laughs.) I said it a little more politely than that, but nevertheless, I very firmly said it. I guess this was a refusal to be the daughter. I was still too insecure in my independence. But I was [a daughter] in every other way. I was just crazy about her.

You know, she adored Tamar, but maybe she thought of me somewhat as a second, older daughter. She made me a friend right away. Took me to meet all her own personal friends. Pointed out places where she had worked or where this or that had happened. She took me through the last of the dark old tenement streets that hadn't quite fallen down. Those dark, dark, little tiny tenements, and all those people had their own ethnic festivals every year. I got in on the tail end of that, and I'm so glad that I didn't miss it.

In the summer we went to the public showers and to the public baths. Then we'd go around the corner to a little Jewish restaurant,

where for fifteen cents we could have a nice big bowl of kasha and a
cup of Russian tea. And she talked to me very frankly, about herself,
and . . . and everything else. She took me to rallies. She took me to
libraries. Sometimes we got standing room at the Metropolitan Opera.
She made me a friend, and I've always been so grateful for how much
time she spent with me.

I was able to speak with several people who had been greatly influenced by Dorothy—"on the hook," as Jim Douglass calls it—even if they
didn't live with her. Pat Murray has also been "on the hook" through his
whole life; he, like many others, met Dorothy through the written word:

I first saw the paper when I was fifteen years old. In the public library
of Erie, Pennsylvania. And even then, it costs a quarter for a lifetime.
You send them a quarter and the paper comes forever. So I sent away
for my own subscription, and it came to the house. [My] father was
Irish Catholic, and when he saw that logo with the black man and the
white man with their arms around one another, right away he said,
"This is a communist paper!" He just raised hell with me, and of
course that confirmed to me that I was onto something good.

In contrast, Dale Wiehoff of Minnesota was hooked by Dorothy when
he saw her in action. He describes the trouble she took to reach young
people:

It was a long time ago. I was in high school and on my way to get my
hair cut. My parents were upset because I had a Beatle hairdo, and I
was being sent to get it cut off, and I was really in a foul mood. It was
in the fall, maybe in November. I could see this small bundle of women
coming down the middle of the street. Now this is St. Cloud, a small
town. In 1966. From blocks away I could see them walking in the
street. I had never seen a demonstration in my life. And as they got
closer, a man stepped out from the group, Wilford Mische, and he invited me to join the march. It was an antiwar march, and Dorothy Day
was in the lead. Protesting the war in Vietnam. I had no idea what
Vietnam was, or even where it was.

But I got a quick history lesson as we marched down the street. We
ended up in front of a federal building and got our picture taken by
the newspaper, and then I went off to get my hair cut, and the next
morning my picture was in the paper. But in that short time, I had been
introduced to Dorothy Day, and she asked if I would come over to the
[home of Donald and Mary] Humphrey.

I didn't know them very well, but I went. It was kind of a formal meeting, with Dorothy introducing herself and talking about the Catholic Worker and giving me a copy of the newspaper and asking about my interests. I didn't know anything about this stuff, but I knew I was in big trouble for getting my picture in the newspaper.

In the spring of '67 I was invited back to the Humphreys because Dorothy Day was back in town. She spent the whole afternoon with me and all the Humphrey children. Dorothy Day was trying to . . . she talked to us about King's speaking out against the war at Riverside Church in New York. It was a historic speech, and I felt . . . you know, I was just this kid in a small town, and no adults had ever talked to me about the big issues. The war. Or the civil rights movement. So this was an unusual experience. She wanted us young people to understand the connection Martin Luther King was making between the war and the treatment of blacks in the United States, and how important it was not to separate these things.

Then she moved on to religious beliefs—our morals—how we viewed the world and so forth. Well . . . we started joking about the rosary and she got very upset with us. One of the girls had put on a record of Tom Lehrer singing "Vatican Rag." We just thought it was a riot. We were rolling on the floor, but she was getting more and more upset by the second. As soon as the song was over, she provoked a long discussion about symbols and stuff like that. But it was a great night for me, and I think for all of us. She treated us as adults, but more than that, as people whose thoughts mattered.

Michael Cullen, who came to the United States from Ireland and founded Casa Maria in Milwaukee, is another Midwesterner who heard the call of the Worker:

After we started Casa Maria we, of course, went to see Dorothy in New York. But I'd heard all the stories from Bob Gilliam, from the days of seminary. I thought I'd see an eccentric woman but at least a very structured . . . an administrative building, you know. *The* Catholic Worker. I'm going down Chrystie Street and I find this building. I mean, you could barely see through the windows. But I see the statue of Mary through the dirt, and St. Joseph and the cross and the big room where they're making soup. Dorothy was upstairs, on the third floor, waiting to meet me. Going up these narrow rickety old stairs. Still those impressions are with me.

And oh . . . experiencing this stench and wondering where this stench was coming from. And then very graciously, lady that she was,

Dorothy meets me at her door. This tall lady with her hair braided on her head. She had immediate presence. Yes, presence. You always knew she was a holy woman. Always. Knew from the very moment that you were in the presence of a saint, although I wouldn't have used that language at that time.

Then immediately she wanted me to meet her roommate. She had brought her from the street. It was later that I found out that the stink was [from] the lady's ulcerated legs. She had gangrene legs, and Dorothy had given her a cot in her room. After that, you didn't need to know any more.

Anyone who has ever lived in the New York house can remember when he or she met Dorothy, but many of them worked and lived there for a time before seeing the founder. Terry Rogers's story is different:

How I came to the Worker is the most wonderful story. I mean to me. We were coming through New York on our way to a camping trip in Canada. I said [to my friend], "Let's just walk past the Catholic Worker and look at the outside." So we did, and my friend said, "Let's ring the bell."

"Oh, no, no, no!"

"Come on, come on, come on."

So we rang the bell. Dorothy opened the door. My friend says, "We're here because my friend has always been interested in the Catholic Worker, always wanted to come live here." This is like in the first minute of the conversation.

And Dorothy said, "Well, we have a bed upstairs." Just . . . like . . . that. That complete acceptance. And so I moved in. I'd come East thinking I was going back to Texas. But I never did.

Pat Rusk also remembers that ready no-questions-asked acceptance:

The first time I saw her, she was leaning against the back of her desk chair in the half light from the hallway after a Friday night meeting. I came back into the office and there she was in a navy jumper and white blouse to go with her braided white hair. She had large, deep blue eyes. You felt she could see into your depths, and maybe she could. Dorothy was a magnet. She pulled me right out of myself. Dorothy was deeply welcoming to me, a shy, devout girl who had come to pop the big question, but my hand shook so much I could hardly drink the tea she offered me.

"May I come to the Worker and live with you and work with you?"

Dorothy's answer was simply "We'd love to have you."

Chuck Matthei felt this welcome, as well. He first met Dorothy at Tivoli, during a Peacemaker orientation to nonviolence. He had just burned his draft card and "that, of course, was enough to awaken her maternal instincts. So her immediate response was, 'Well, you're one of us. Part of our family!'"

The late Ade Bethune was one of the first members of the Catholic Worker family and contributed the masthead for which the newspaper and the movement are known throughout the world.

The first time I visited the Catholic Worker, in the fall of 1933, Dorothy Weston gave me a tour of the little storefront on East 15th Street and sent me home with copies of the *Catholic Worker*. All the way home, on the Third Avenue El, I read Dorothy Day's stories, and, ah . . . fires were being kindled in my nineteen-year-old heart.

I also noticed that the paper was not very attractive looking. I was acquainted with beautiful black-and-white illustrations in the *Masses*, and I thought, "If only we could have something on that order for our Catholic paper!" So I made four black-and-white pictures and sent them down to the editor. After some time, a postcard came back, "We love your pictures and will print them. Thank you, The Editors." Oh, I was thrilled!

Then I found a notice that they could use old clothes. Before you know it, I had gathered old stuff and was on my way downtown again with two bags of clothes. I was horribly shy and must have appeared petrified when a tall woman who looked as though she had been carved with an ax strolled across the room.

Hey! I was scared. But she was kind.

"Are these your things?" she asked. "I'm awfully sorry we don't have any room, but we'll try to put you somewhere." She thought I needed a place to stay. Hospitality was being practiced on me!

"But, but, but . . . " I spluttered, "I'm the girl who made the pictures."

"Oh, you are? Well, sit right down." She sat me on a pile of newspapers, and sat herself on another, and started telling me what saints' illustrations would be needed for future months. So I was happily launched into being illustrator for the paper, with many projects ahead. At first, Dorothy seemed bossy. But she saw God in people, and she taught me how she loved them. In the saints she saw real people doing real works of mercy to those in whom they saw God. Not abstract personifications, but real people—St. Vincent de Paul and little babies for whom he made homes, St. Martin de Porres, feeding a sick man.

When Dorothy owned the two cottages on Poillon Avenue in Staten Island, she made the acquaintance of Walter Stojanowski, who owned a

Dorothy and her granddaughter Rebecca Hennessy, circa 1946.

hotel across the street—the Beachcomber. Walter has fond memories of
their times together:

See, Dorothy Day was a regular, special person. I can't really explain
that, but she was—both regular and special. She'd often come into the
Beachcomber to talk and mingle with the customers. Have a glass of
wine and a chat about the day's events. She always had so many responsibilities to think about, but she always had a calm demeanor and
never had anything bad to say about anyone. In fact, that's the main
thing I learned from her—not to let the details of life upset me. She
would get things done without getting upset, and that's hard to do.
Also, to try and see the big picture, if you understand what I mean.
Because of her, I'm really much more involved in the community—
delivering food to AIDS patients, things like that.

I didn't see her laugh very often, but I think she genuinely loved life
and loved being with people. At Staten Island she got away from the
responsibilities and the hustle and bustle of the city, so she could write
and contemplate her calling. Take long walks on the beach and enjoy
the sea air. Oh, she loved Staten Island. Loved it! When she sold the
houses across from the hotel, she asked me to look for another one.
The only place was in Spanish Camp, where you own the house, but
not the land. But she bought the two little end houses and later the
third one across the street.

I remember once we had a birthday party for her at the Beach-comber. (This was after she was already living in Spanish Camp.) We had a cake and she was swinging along to the music and just real happy about it. Dorothy also went to my niece's wedding reception at the hotel. The wedding had an ethnic flair—many Polish touches—and Dorothy loved all the symbolism and the polkas.

Father Dan Berrigan explains Dorothy as one of the sources of his life-long activism:

Dorothy opened up all sorts of connections that I had never gotten in the seminary. And at the heart of it, the connection between the ur-ban misery that she was experiencing on the Lower East Side of Man-hattan and the world of war and the waste of the earth. It sounds simple on its face, but it was an absolutely stunning insight for me, as was the fact that she rejected absolutely the idea that God was willing this kind of suffering for people, when it was the result of social, eco-nomic, and political nonsense. Not without reason did she speak of what she called a "filthy, rotten system," a system she saw producing misery in every direction. So that got me started. I got it both from reading her column and from knowing her and calling her a great friend. I was very privileged in that regard, and so was my family.

Even one-time connections would hold deep meaning to the people she met. Joan Montesano remembers when Dorothy met Joan Baez in San Francisco:

Joan Baez and Dorothy were united on Farm Worker stuff, and I re-member when they were together on the podium at St. Mary's Cathe-dral. Dorothy just loved Joan and loved her voice. Afterward, the two of them walked off to have a private conversation. You could really see the tenderness in Dorothy. Like a mother, taking her arm so fondly. I remember Joan saying how ashamed she was of her shoe fetish—she had seventy-five pairs of boots in her closet and here's Dorothy living out of the rag bag.

Almost everyone I interviewed listed Dorothy as *the* significant person in his or her life. Part of this, of course, was due to the interviews them-selves—I was asking only about Dorothy and the narrator's relationship to her. Still, her influence on individual people was remarkable in its va-riety. Kathleen Rumpf was the one who first pointed out to me that Dor-othy gave the part of herself that people needed at the time. Perhaps that's why so many remain truly connected with her—in memory, in faith, and in lived convictions.

5.

What Was She Like?

A SEARCHING INTELLECT

She herself was a student, and that's why she was such a great teacher.

—NINA POLCYN MOORE

Dorothy was sharply intelligent and eternally curious, but her intellect wasn't what most would call theoretical. Robert Ellsberg says she had a "practical mind" and that she thought such practicality was characteristic of women. "'Men,' she would say, were 'purer,' more capable of operating in the realm of ideas. But she didn't see that as a compliment." Her intellect fed her spirituality and vice versa, and both were concrete and specific to the person and to the occasion, whether the natural or the supernatural world.

Dorothy was curious about the world and the people in it, and this intensity remained with her even in old age. Pat Jordan recalls:

W e'd be driving along and she'd see a stand of wild clover and she'd say, "Stop the car. That is wild clover! When I was a girl, my mother used to pick the wild clover and put it in pillow cases to make the house smell good." And she'd pick it and bring it back to the beach house. Even in her seventies!

Some call this a writer's curiosity, but it seems to me also the curiosity of someone in love with the world and the God who created it. She liked listening to people as much as she loved telling stories. I remember seeing evidence of that interest in other people's ideas in my own very brief glimpse of Dorothy in 1969 when she visited the Thomas Merton Catholic Worker in Saginaw. That evening, she paid little attention to the "peace people" gathered to do her homage but instead spent most of her time in deep conversation with a young black woman who was describing

Eileen Egan, César Chávez, Frank Donovan, Marion Moses, and Dorothy at Maryhouse, circa 1978.

her work with the Welfare Rights Organization. In a similar story, Nina Polcyn Moore remembers Dorothy talking to her parents:

My parents liked Dorothy, and Dorothy was, of course, very interested in regular people—people like my father, Max Polcyn—and they had very long conversations. She wanted to know about the work my father did as a railroad switchman. She wanted to know about ordinary people and about their hopes and dreams and fears.

I also think she had what I would call a narrative mind, illustrating by way of stories or examples rather than proving by logical argument. Here's how Eileen Egan explains Dorothy's thought process:

You can take course after course after course in so-called theology and never hear the message at the heart of Christianity—the message of Jesus, which is indiscriminate love. This includes loving the enemy. This is the simplest of theology. Somebody has said that much of theology consists in getting around the Sermon on the Mount. Well, Dorothy and Peter didn't get around the Sermon on the Mount. They accepted it straight on.

I think the closer we get to simple thinking, the better Christians we become. Men are so easily fooled. A man will say, "It's a sign of great patriotism and power to lay down your life for your country." And a woman simply says, "But you're going out to kill, to kill somebody else's son or father." It's an entirely different approach. One is the abstract—lay down your life for your country. The other is the concrete—you'll be killing a real human being. Dorothy was always simple and always concrete.

Perhaps because of this attachment to the concrete, much of her learning came from novels—the great Russian novelists, Sigrid Undset's *Kristin Lavransdatter,* Dickens, the American realists. Gary Donatelli, who was with the Worker in the seventies, says, "We were always sharing books with each other. It could be Dostoevski. Or *The Cloud of Unknowing.* Butler's *Lives of the Saints.* The Catholic Worker reading list is very eclectic."

Through Dorothy and Peter Maurin, the Catholic Worker united different intellectual currents. Workers who were with Dorothy and Peter in the formative years of the movement speak of their excitement in finding a place where lay Catholics could address intellectual problems from a Catholic perspective. Ed Marciniak explains:

It was an exciting time. Lay people and religious priests didn't wait for the bishops of the world to give them the go-ahead. Virgil Michel was working with the liturgy, and Eric Gill was working in England and Emmanuel Mounier in France. Dorothy Day and Peter Maurin intersected when these ideas were floating around. They crystallized them in the Catholic Worker, in a place where Catholics could come together and understand what was really happening.

Nina Polcyn Moore remembers:

She brought such richness to the work. Larded her conversations with so many references that she was a delight just to listen to. Such a school it was! You had scripture. You had music. You had archeology. You had all phases of culture, just in an afternoon.

She had that global concern, and shared that with the person in front of her, and so we became less parochial and less insular. She read the *New York Times* every morning and to her it was not just news, it was people. It was people in Bosnia. It was people in Africa. All these people, and connected with the gospel! The wealth of her mind was . . . was staggering.

I'm always startled by the fact that she came as a convert and came with this vast bedrock of the importance and dignity of the human person and this great sense of revolution for the world, that it is not as it must be. She was able to translate these surging feelings and this thirst for justice into a Catholic tradition.

She learned so much from Peter, and she really paid him his due on social questions. Yet she continued learning all her life, and I think you don't usually see this in adults. For most people, their notion of the church is whatever they finished grade school or high school with. They're illiterate on so many topics, but she had this tremendous mind, this tremendous spark. She was able to relate everything to the infinite because she herself was always reading and making connections. She herself was a student, and that's why she was such a great teacher.

While she admired people who did the actual work—making the soup, sweeping the floor, proof-reading the paper—she loved to talk with those who came to the Worker for answers to their intellectual questions as well as for a place to practice the works of mercy. In other words, she wanted people to emulate Peter Maurin's ideal of being both scholars and workers.

Judith Gregory muses on the way Dorothy's mind worked:

I never heard Dorothy talk about people's psychological complexities, except in literary terms, maybe. You have Dostoevski but you don't have therapy. Do you see the difference? Dorothy was willing to accept people who were abnormal in all kinds of ways. But she didn't want to look into it, didn't want to speculate as to why. It just was.

Instead of rules, she had these deep references. She read a lot and prayed a lot, so that kept her focus and whatever she did couldn't help but be related to these benchmarks. When you make choices all the time with that constant inner reference to something like the gospel or the way Dostoevski sees the world, you're going to land in the same place over and over again. So it's not rules exactly, but something deeper.

That "something deeper" produced a compassionate and searching intellect, one that showed through her writing and her conversation.

MAKING DEMANDS

Psychiatrist Robert Coles was able to spend hours recording his conversations with Dorothy Day, and his book Dorothy Day: A Radical Devotion *was one of the results. I have learned much from this text and others of his that I've read over the years, so I was delighted when we were finally able to arrange a phone interview. His infectious chuckle and easy style put me at ease, and I continued to learn as we talked. Here's what he told me:*

My mother was no stranger to the Catholic Worker movement, although she was Episcopalian in background. She had been urging Dorothy on me all my life. My father was Jewish and Catholic both, but he was much less interested in Dorothy Day.

I was in medical school in Columbia and not enjoying it much. Kept complaining about it to my mother, and she said that what I needed was to go down and work at a soup kitchen for Dorothy Day instead of complaining. I understood what my mother was getting at. She used to say that there are things more important than the troubles you're having, and there are people who might help you to understand that and especially help you to get some distance from your complaining and from the rather privileged position of being a medical student. The long and short of it is, I eventually went down there and met Dorothy Day.

Incidentally, Chuck Matthei tells how Coles's writing of this incident impressed him:

The moment in Robert Coles's book that really touched me most came not from all the interviews that he'd done with Dorothy, but from the story he told about his first encounter with her while he was a medical student.

The soup line is over, and there sitting at a table in the kitchen is Dorothy, engaged in a conversation with a rather drunken woman. Coles recognizes her from photographs and feels if anyone can help him in his spiritual agony, it will be Dorothy Day. So he's standing at a respectful distance, waiting for her to finish this conversation. The woman, who is inebriated, goes on and on and on. Every time it seems that she's finally run out of steam, Dorothy makes some little comment or touches her arm or does something and it starts all over again. Coles is waiting, trying to be patient. Finally, Dorothy looks up. She reaches over and touches her companion and says, "Wait a moment, dear." And she turns to Coles. "I'm sorry. Were you waiting to talk with one of us?"

To return to Coles:

I remember after that first visit, my mother asked me what I thought of Dorothy. I said, "Well, she's very demanding. She asks a lot of people." That was the first word I used to describe her—*demanding*. I said it with a certain innocence, the innocence of youth, but maybe there was some intuition there that wasn't totally off the mark. And my mother said—I'll never forget it—she asked, "Demanding of what?"

I said, "Of your time, commitment, your energy."

Years later, when I was writing books based on long interviews with interesting people, my wife, Jane, kept saying to me, "If there's anyone you should tape, it's Dorothy Day."

I said, "How could I ask her?"

She said, "How do you ask anyone?"

When I did ask if I could tape her, she smiled and said, "If you want to hear me, I'll speak." That's word for word.

Years later my wife was diagnosed with a brain tumor, and they told me she was going to die within a matter of months. I told Dorothy this, and I then got a letter from her telling me that she was praying for her, and that the whole community there was praying for her.

I bring this up because most recently there was some distorted version of this incident that got into the newspapers. The article had my wife praying to Dorothy Day, and that's not true. Dorothy was praying for my wife's recovery. Anyway, at first the doctors told me that my wife had four or five, six months at the most. Then it was extended to a year, then two or three years. One of the doctors said to me, "It's a miracle."

Yes, it was a miracle, but I don't think the doctor meant it the way my wife and I saw it. We thought Dorothy somehow did this, but we had no proof. We do have a medical story that went one way and then reversed itself.

There is no question that Dorothy wrote that letter, and that she and others at the Worker were praying for us. And no question that the doctors changed their view of what would happen from their initial prognostication. And indeed my wife lived for over twenty-five years after that. Certainly something happened that the doctor said wasn't going to happen, and Dorothy and her friends at the Catholic Worker were the only ones I know who were praying for my wife. I wasn't praying for her; I was worrying and doing the medical thing, and my mother, who was the more religious person, wasn't religious [in] that way.

Let me tell you another story about Dorothy. You know I used to bring my students from Harvard down there. I'd drive them down for the Friday night "clarification of thought" meetings. She would meet with them. Now this was in the late seventies, and she was then into her congestive heart failure, and she was not well. But she came downstairs and they met. She told me later how much she'd enjoyed talking with those young people. Their moral earnestness, I could sense, had reminded her of her own young idealism.

I did it three years in a row, and to this day that is what some of the students remember about their Harvard education. They don't remember all the teachers, they don't remember all the books, but they remember that trip down to the Worker. And they remember Dorothy coming down and talking to them. She wrote me afterward. "It meant so much to us here, the visit of your students." I said, "Listen, it meant so much to us here, too."

I saw her change over the years. She became . . . oh, she was always demanding, if I may go back to that first word I thought of. But as she grew older, I saw a wry, ironic side to her that comes sometimes with age. In fact, she said to me—actually, this was the last time I saw her. She said, "You know. I'm no longer as impatient as I used to be." *(Laughing.)*

STORYTELLER

She was just a wonderful conversationalist, so in that sense, she was a master teacher.
                                                        —PAT JORDAN

Dorothy taught through stories, often giving her faults as a reference. She welcomed people and initiated them into the tradition by telling stories about others and about herself. Robert Coles says, however, that she "had a way of making her point by indirection—bringing someone else into it, a member of the community, say. She'd say, 'Well, if you ask Frank about this, he might say . . . ' She'd try to get the emphasis away from her."

Sometimes this teaching was casual, and sometimes it happened in the many, many public presentations she gave over the years. In contrast to their memories of other aspects of her life, all those I spoke with agreed that Dorothy's public-speaking style was personal, rambling, repetitious, and utterly engaging in its lack of artifice. Actually, it wasn't much different from her style when she was "just sitting around talking," except that she'd be very nervous before a public lecture. Professor David O'Brien of Holy Cross University in Worcester, Massachusetts, told me that Dorothy asked him to pray for her as she entered the stage for a public appearance. Pat Rusk noticed that she'd be so nervous her hands would twitch in her lap. Chuck Matthei pointed out that, like Gandhi, Dorothy lacked any polish in her oratorical skills. But she was convinced of the need, both to spread the message and to raise money for the work, and from the time the Catholic Worker was founded until ill health confined her to her room, Dorothy spoke often in public. In the early years she answered every request—even if she received no stipend, even if she was exhausted from a long bus ride—because it was one way to ensure both the survival and growth of the Worker.

Joe Zarrella remembers:

When she gave a public talk, she was very conversational, not dramatic at all. Very seldom did you hear a raised voice or a critical tone.

And she never prepared her speeches. She just spoke. She'd quote authors she'd read, and then just go on, talking in a normal way. Aiii! Her memory must have been unbelievable. She didn't enjoy the speaking, though, but spoke from a sense of compulsion. And then, of course, the talks would bring the money in.

Ade Bethune also speaks of the early years:

If Peter Maurin could have his way, he would have made everybody into a public speaker. But he couldn't "mek" Dorothy different than she was. Never mind, she made a terrific impression on people. She'd ramble around from one idea to another. And you'd think, "My Goodness! This is a talk without beginning, middle, or end." But it was deeply impressive because of her example, because of her being herself. She did not preach in any way.

She'd illustrate the points she was making with contemporary stories, usually taken from what she had just been doing. Jim Douglass:

Each time I've heard her speak, she gave a kind of "Dorothy on Pilgrimage" vision of the Catholic Worker. She'd just say what she was doing and the context was then an engagement with all the serious questions—homelessness, or nuclear war, or the farm workers' struggles, or whatever was going on in relation to the Catholic Worker.

Father Bernie Gilgun of Worcester, Massachusetts, remembers his mother hearing Dorothy in a Bill Moyers interview. When he asked her what Dorothy said, his mother replied, "Oh, just the same old stuff!"

That "same old stuff" was always told with humor and attentiveness to her audience. Jim Eder of Chicago recalls hearing Dorothy speak at DePaul University:

A couple of theologians were on the stage with her, and it was kind of boring. But then she started talking, in a real simple way. She looked genuinely dumpy, you know, like somebody's grandma, but I thought, "That lady knows what she's talking about." The clarity, that incredible clarity!

A couple of people from the audience asked really silly questions, and I was impressed because Dorothy thought these people were worthy of being listened to. Really treated the audience with dignity. There was one person with a speech impediment who wanted to know why the Catholic Worker didn't side with the IRA or something, and she was very patient. I would have thrown most of those people out on their ear if I'd been in charge, but she had respect for everybody.

Catherine Morris of the L.A. Worker remembers the day she became one of Dorothy's illustrations of anarchism:

It was so embarrassing, really. See, we were at Tivoli at the time of the Peacemaker Conference [the Peacemaker's Orientation Program in Nonviolence], and the place was a mess. It was a mess! The plumbing was all screwed up, and right in the middle of the driveway there was this huge pond of sewer water from the toilets, which were all backed up. I'm not into that kind of stuff, so Jeff and I decided to clean this bathroom. We hunted around and found a bucket. (Our toilets in L.A. are always doing strange things, and so I know all about gravity flushing. You fill a bucket and pour it down and get rid of all the stuff.) When we got back to the bathroom with our bucket and mop and sponge, who's there but Dorothy. I left the bucket, put my sign up, you know, this little directive on how to gravity flush. When we came back, someone had put a swastika on it. The next time someone had ripped it down. And the toilet was in the same condition as when we'd started.

Well, then at the section of the conference when Dorothy was speaking, she started going on and on about the visitors from the L.A. Worker. How they'd come, and they were exhausted. (Now, we never said we were exhausted. She just made such a story of it!) She said we'd come to rest and to visit. And what did we do but clean the toilets! "Now that is anarchism! When you see something that needs doing, and you do it, that's anarchism."

Chuck Matthei was also present at the conference, and heard this illustration. He concludes:

That's Dorothy. She always brought it right down to the simple, the ordinary, the accessible, the challenging. And also the humorous. I think that's an important part of it. You couldn't survive life at the Catholic Worker over any prolonged period of time without a sense of humor, and she had a very good sense of humor. She could be tough. She could be demanding. But she always had that profoundly personal and humorous perspective.

Rosemary Morse told a story Dorothy used to tell, one that illustrates her sense of humor. Seems Dorothy was giving a talk someplace, and when she went to sit down, the chair broke. She came back to the microphone and said wryly, "I guess it's time to give this chair to the poor."

Yes, Dorothy could be sarcastic. Harry Isbell tells this story of meeting Dorothy in the early sixties:

I was in graduate school at Notre Dame, and Dorothy was touring
about (by Greyhound bus, of course). She had developed a friendship
with Father Hesburgh, who was then president of Notre Dame. Well,
it was a miserable winter day with a storm blowing off Lake Michi-
gan. Dorothy was supposed to arrive at about 4:00, enough time to get
herself ready for the 8:00 lecture. But the bus was way late, so she
went directly to the auditorium, which was full.

Clearly she was tired, hungry, and sore. But the show will go on. She
spoke for about forty-five minutes and then allowed as how she was
done. The student who had introduced her cheerfully announced that
"Miss Day would be happy to take questions." Well, happiness was
hardly her reaction—more like astonishment, I would say. The first
question was from way back in the hall.

"Miss Day, this soup that is always on the stove. Just how is that
soup made?"

"You chop vegetables until your fingers bleed. That's all for tonight."

Perhaps the most famous "Dorothy story" is the one about the diamond ring. I have not yet found anyone who actually remembers being
in the room when the event occurred, but Dorothy told it often and others do as well. It seems one morning a well-dressed woman came into the
house. Walked up to Dorothy and said, "Miss Day, I have a little something I'd like to give you." It was a diamond ring. Jim Forest:

Dorothy received it with exactly the same appreciation she would
have given to a crate of frozen frankfurters and put it into her pocket.
An hour later, in comes the Weasel. (Everybody at the Worker had a
nickname. You rarely, rarely knew their real names.)

The Weasel lived in a tenement with her huge, mentally handicapped
son, whom she led around like an enormous watch dog. He was very
. . . he was a person with very little mental capacity. And she took care
of him. Heroically. On the other hand, she was one of the most unpleasant people we ever served at the Catholic Worker. We paid her
rent and we provided for her from time to time. Of course, she received
some aid from the state, but not enough.

Now, the Weasel was in a permanent state of rage. Had a voice that
could strip paint off the wall. She was the kind of person who makes
you wonder if you're cut out for life in a house of hospitality.

Dorothy took the diamond ring out of her pocket and gave it to this
women. Later, someone asked if it wouldn't have been better to sell the

ring and pay the Weasel's rent for some time in advance. Dorothy said,
"She has her dignity. If she wants to sell the ring, she is free to do so
and pay her rent. But if she wants to take a cruise to Bermuda, she can
do that, too. And then she said, "Or she can wear the ring, just like
the woman who gave it to us. Do you suppose God made diamonds
just for the rich?"

Dorothy's public speaking was the way most people first met her. It's
very lack of oratory is what supported the work, drew people to join her,
and helped everyone who heard her relate Christian truths to the contemporary world. But she also taught when she was at home at the Worker,
told the same stories and gave the same lessons but in casual conversation. Patrick Jordan recalls his time with Dorothy and the lessons she
taught:

> Dorothy often said to us that very few people understood the whole
> picture. We'd be saying, "What does this mean?" "How does this fit
> in?" And she'd say, "Well, you know, I didn't understand Peter's whole
> thing for many years." But when she did, she went the whole way.
>
> She was a very good teacher. Of course, it wasn't like you had
> classes. But you'd sit for hours, you know, opening the mail and talk-
> ing. She was just a wonderful conversationalist, so in that sense, she
> was a master teacher.
>
> Dorothy always called it a school. And she always stressed every-
> body's individual vocation. She would say to us, "You will know your
> vocation by the joy that it brings you. You will know. You will know
> when it's right." And she often would say that the gold moves on and
> the dross remains.

I told him that I had heard that as Stanley's Vishnewski's line, and Pat
replied: "No, she would say that about herself. That she was the dross."

As Pat mentioned, much of the teaching would come as Dorothy
opened the mail with other Workers. Jim Forest explains:

> She often read the letters aloud, telling a story or two about the people
> who had written them. This was the Dorothy Day University in full
> swing, though I didn't know it at the time. A good part of Dorothy's
> life was spent reading and writing letters—even her monthly columns
> were usually nothing more than long letters.

Often the lessons would come in a seemingly casual way, springing
from the deep roots of her Christian faith. Terry Rogers recounts one such
story:

I remember very soon after I had gotten there, a guy pulled a knife on somebody at dinner one night, so he was banned from the house. Dorothy hadn't been there when it happened, but later she asked me and I was telling her. I can't remember her exact words, but she said something like "Well, of course we have to see Christ in him." She just said it so matter of factly. She wasn't consciously trying to indoctrinate me. It's just what came out of her.

Johannah Hughes Turner:

Once in a great while she'd tell stories about her childhood. Or interesting things about other people. She rarely told a vicious story, I mean, engaged in really disparaging gossip, as the rest of us do. She could be uptight, but most of the time she was loving and accepting. She could soothe the most violent, angry people with her touch and a word, and when she made a statement she delivered it seriously and emphatically—in a lovely musical voice.

Dorothy was never "cute." She didn't toss off one-liners. She didn't use slogans. She didn't assume postures, didn't speak in falsetto, didn't exaggerate or use "newspeak." There was no grandiosity and by the same token no false modesty, no wiggling for approval in spite of the unpopularity of what she was saying. She could be informal, relaxed, intimate, humorous, even a little whimsical sometimes, but mostly she stated what was on her mind in a clear and straightforward way.

Dorothy spent a lot of time with Catholic Workers but also kept in touch with her old friends. Rachel de Aragon was the daughter of Paula de Aragon, one of the women in the Staten Island group Dorothy knew from her pre-conversion days. Rachel's memories:

I remember Dorothy as joyful. Not giddy, but joyful in a deeper way. And she'd just fill the room with her energy and her presence. She brought a lot of fun and charisma into every situation, with her sense of humor. Not Catholic Amish, as some of them are now, but "one of the girls." She'd kick off her shoes and hang out with [my aunt] Tina, who was close to Dorothy.

Dorothy would often tell stories on herself, such as the following. She didn't have the skill with knitting that her daughter, Tamar, had, and she knew it. Once, someone saw some socks she was knitting and asked her if she could have them to give as a gag gift. Chuck Matthei reports that Dorothy would often repeat a story Frank Sheed told her. Seems Bill

Buckley was talking to Sheed once and labeling all these prominent people "asses." When he got to Dorothy's name, he said "half-ass."

Once Dorothy was invited to visit a large family in upstate New York:

At that time, she was probably in her sixties or seventies. It seems the parents were preparing the house for an impending visit, cleaning, getting a room ready, telling the kids that all was being done because "Dorothy Day is coming." That night at the supper table, after Dorothy had finally arrived, one of the little fellows blurted out: "All day long I heard 'Dorothy Day is coming! Dorothy Day is coming!' Now she's here, and she's just an old lady!" At the end of this tale, Dorothy would chortle, her shoulders shaking.[1]

Chuck Matthei, a storyteller himself, told a "Dorothy story" that talks directly about her own storytelling:

At the end of the living room at Tivoli there was a good-size table for clothing donations. There was always a pile of old clothes, and people would take whatever they needed. One day I was standing idly at the doorway between the living room and the dining room. Suddenly Dorothy's voice comes from behind me. "Oh, my goodness! Stop him, stop him!"

"What's happening? What's the matter, Dorothy?"

She said, "It's Charlie! He's into the clothes. Get him out of those clothes!"

Now this guy was one of the long-time residents, and most of the time he was pretty quiet. He was simply sorting through this large pile of clothes and occasionally pulling out an item and trying it on. He was very heavy set, so very little of the clothing would have fit him, anyway.

I said, "Dorothy there's no real problem. He can't even fit into most of those clothes. He won't take very much."

"That's not the point. I don't care if he takes all of them."

And I said, "Well, then, what is the problem?"

She said, "He has lice. He always has lice. He'll get lice in those clothes. They'll spread. We'll all have lice. And I can't stand it! I just got rid of them last week, and I don't want them again. Not so soon." *(Laughs.)*

So I thought, "All right. I'll do something." But before I could move, Dorothy said, "Oh, this reminds me of that time in 1936." And this

---

[1] Retold by Ric Rhetor, *The Catholic Worker* (June-July 2000).

is so typical of Dorothy, that she would launch into a story and so actually undercut my ability to follow her orders and deal with the problem because I had to listen to her.

She said, "I was invited to address this august gathering of theologians. All the Catholic luminaries of the day were there—editors of this and that journal. Well, at the end of my humble little presentation, Jacques Maritain looked at me and said, 'Ah, Dorothy, you're always so serene.'"

Then she said, "Just at that moment, I felt this louse crawling across my bosom, and I thought to myself . . . if you only knew the truth!" *(Laughs.)* It was, you know, so typical of Dorothy. It was so absolutely realistic and practical with the full range of emotions, but with a sense of humor at the same time.

One of the stories Marge Hughes would tell concerns her youngest son, who was the only one of the Hughes children to call Dorothy "Granny":

After Dorothy bought the first Staten Island bungalows, across from the Beachcomber Hotel, my family lived in one of them and Dorothy stayed next door. My youngest son was four at the time and still small for his age. He came outside one day in his bathing suit. Dorothy was sitting on a bench between the houses. He climbed up on the bench and walked over to her and said, "Granny, are you a person?" She said, "Yes. And not only that, I'm a personage."

Robert Steed summarizes her wit:

She was fun. More interesting than most people you'd ever meet. She knew that she was . . . was somebody, and she might have played to that occasionally. But basically, she was a very . . . what we would now call an authentic person. She wasn't a phony in any sense. She wasn't dishonest or hypocritical.

She could take kidding up to a point, and we used to kid her occasionally, but she had a temper, too. I'm sure her religion helped her get that under control. But you could tell she was angry by looking at her eyes, which would get steely and cold. And when that happened you knew you'd best retreat, back off.

As Jim Forest reminds us, she said about herself, "I hold more temper in one minute than most of you will hold in your entire life."

Funny stories about Dorothy include one by Peter Lumsden of London. When Dorothy came to England in 1963 to speak at a Spode Conference sponsored by Pax, she wanted to see the grave of Karl Marx at Highgate, and Peter took her. He recalls:

Do you know what she wanted to do? She wanted me—me, not her—to steal some flowers from someone else's grave so she could put some on Marx's grave. I told her if she wanted to put flowers on his grave, she should steal them herself. But I ended up doing it!

Sister Teresa Murray saw a gentle Dorothy:

Never, never did she say an uncharitable word, or voice a negative opinion or . . . except for the Hells Angels, whose headquarters were just down the street from Maryhouse. She was afraid of them, I guess, afraid of violence, so she told us to avoid them.

Once I was in her room and Ernesto Cardenal of Nicaragua called her on the phone. I said to her, "How do you feel about the violence he's talking about?" She said—and this is paraphrasing of course—"You never know what you'll do when you're put in a situation." As much as she was a pacifist, she never, ever condemned anybody else for their attitudes, you know. Not to my knowledge, anyway.

Father Richard McSorley tells a similar story:

One example that impressed me very much, especially because I'm a Jesuit priest, is when a reporter asked her, "What do you think about . . . about your Jesuit friends? They have very nice rooms and very nice food, and you're living with the poor and the outcast. Don't you think it would be better for them to live here with you or to live at least this style?"

And she said, "Well, I know that the spirit calls people in different ways . . . I don't know what the spirit of God tells other people, but I do know what the spirit of God calls me to, and I know that there are other people called to other things."

Well, the reporter was very insistent and asked the same question again, and she gave the same answer. Now I think that's a real sample of the Catholic Worker spirit. If she had said that the Jesuits would be better off imitating her, she would be implicitly saying that "I'm better than . . . " Well, no doubt she was "better than." But she wasn't saying that, and she didn't think that. And that's the mark of all the saints, that they consider themselves the least of all. They not only genuinely feel that, they live it.

THANK GOD, SHE WAS HUMAN!

Once you get to know her, she's just another crabby old lady!
— STANLEY VISHNEWSKI

Most people would agree with Robert Steed, who said "her faults were minimal compared to most people." Yes, Dorothy had faults: she was often inconsistent, frequently short with people, and sometimes sarcastic, especially when she was tired or beset with difficulties. But Walter Chura said with a sigh of relief, "Thank God, she was human!"

Her inconsistency could be annoying to those who lived and worked with her; however, this inconsistency was never in principles but only in her style of leadership. In principles, her deep spirituality gave her more consistency than others could ever hope to have. Judith Gregory muses:

She used to say she wanted to stay at the beach house and spin. Sure. For a week or two. But then . . . she was like most of us, with many things going on inside. She did want that, but only partly. She also wanted to travel and do the other things. I think she was very torn, and pulled in a lot of directions, but not necessarily in a painful way. Also, she was like anyone who's sought out a lot. You can't help drawing back and wanting some time of your own. But I think she always felt guilty about that, always felt privacy was a luxury. I think she was always pulled in all directions by her conscience.

It's decidedly harder to operate according to conscience rather than rules, and her followers often demanded that she make decisions for them, begged and pleaded for rules, especially rules that those who disagreed with them must follow. Some of the Catholic Workers resented Dorothy's frequent absences and demanded that she arbitrate both serious and petty problems. Terry Rogers explains:

I think it was difficult when people would come and ask her to adjudicate things. "I'm mad at so-and-so because they did such-and-such." She hadn't been involved in it but would feel she had to respond and feel responsible; that would give her a great deal of grief.

The "butter crisis," one of Jim Forest's oft-told stories, can be seen as paradigmatic of such attempts to make Dorothy's word the final arbiter:

Different groups or factions would take to this or that aspect of Dorothy. Like the great butter crisis. Dorothy was away a lot, and all kinds of things could happen. She'd come back and sort it out, and then go off for another trip, or go on retreat or something. The butter . . . Sometimes someone would give us butter, or some other scarce goody, but not enough for everybody. The practice had been that [such treats] would go to "the family," meaning the people who actually were part of the Catholic Worker community. (I guess you'd call most of them permanent guests. They'd actually been there much longer than any of the so-called volunteers.)

Well, anyway, some of the young Workers decided that the butter should be given "to the line," as it is referred to in the Catholic Worker community. That is, to the anonymous people, largely, who came in just to eat and didn't have a regular place in the community. So you had these very new, very idealistic kids deciding what's going to happen with the little edible treasures that came into the community. And it was, of course, outrageous to the people in "the family" who were suddenly not going to be receiving the eggs or butter or whatever.

And I remember different people put quotations from Dorothy on the bulletin board to support their position. One of them had Dorothy saying that we should roll up in newspapers on the floor to make room for people. Well, nobody in the New York house when I was there ever rolled up in any newspapers. At this time, it was very unusual for somebody to even give up their bed, for God's sake! And somebody else had another quotation from Dorothy about how we have to accept our limitations, that not everybody can do everything.

Now these were the polarities that Dorothy lived within. You can't live on just one or the other of these extremes at a Worker house, you have to live within that tension, which we don't like to do. We want to have either the Dorothy Day who rolls up in the newspapers or the one who says it's okay not to roll up in the newspapers. But we don't want the Dorothy Day that has both of these messages because, rationally speaking, they cannot be combined.

In the actual experience of living, though, they have to be combined. You have to live in the tensions. It's not gray, it's . . . it's just flickering black and white. About the butter . . . Dorothy came back and made the decision that it was right to continue as things were. The regular household would get the goodies. Dorothy never was trying to mass produce a certain kind of Christian, or to give the correct list of possessions to people: "This you can have and this you shouldn't have." Rather, she was asking you to keep living with certain questions.

Jim Wilson, who was there at the same time as Jim Forest, explains it this way:

Dorothy wasn't the problem. We were the problem—all the struggles people have living in community. And somehow one leader was supposed to fix it all. She didn't want to be in that role, and if people wanted her to fix it . . . I saw two [responses] from Dorothy. I saw her just walk away and say somebody else was going to fix it, and then I saw—and this is the angry part that some people talk about—she would finally get fed up right up to her eyebrows and say, "You want a decision? Here's the decision! Bang!" Part of Dorothy not wanting to make a decision was that she knew she was going to get everybody all riled up. Part of it was sort of payback time.

But, like others, she sometimes doubted her decisions and changed them. Beth Rogers remembers Charlie McCormack saying he always waited for Dorothy to tell him three times before he'd go out on an errand, because he knew it would change. She truly "lived in the moment." Chuck Matthei reminisced:

She'd come into the house in the city one night and say, "Why is the basement empty? It's freezing cold outside. We're not here to barricade the doors and live a life of privilege in this warm, cozy house while others suffer in the streets. Open the doors and let them in." That would be one night.

Well, the next night there might be one poor old guy sittin' down in the basement. She'd come in tired and in a different mood and say, "Why do we have people in the basement at this hour of the night? We can't take everyone. You know we can't meet every need that comes our way." So, you see, she had the same range of emotions, capacities and limitations as anyone else, but she also had a certain strength and consistency and a good sense of humor about it all.

Several narrators spoke of Dorothy being what we would call today "appropriately angry." Jim Wilson told me:

I learned from Dorothy that anger isn't necessarily bad. Dorothy could be a very angry person, but she was angry about the right things. She was angry with the church and government and not afraid to stand up and speak out, particularly in her frustration with the church's response to the Vietnam War and to the poor and hungry. She never apologized for [that kind of anger], and I saw it as very appropriate.

Bolen Carter of St. Louis told a story that illustrates Dorothy expressing anger to teach a lesson. The incident happened while he was driving
Dorothy up to Granite City, Missouri, to address the steel workers:

W e were in a restaurant and a young man I knew came over to say
hello. He was a student at St. Louis University, which is Jesuit. I don't
know how it came about, but he said, "You know, a nigger can't stay
in this town overnight."
    Dorothy said, "Where do you go to school?"
    He told her and she said, "You ought to be ashamed of yourself!
Don't ever talk like that in front of me."

Perhaps the most famous story of Dorothy's anger was the "Big
Stomp," a clearing out of Worker hangers-on that occurred in the sixties.
The poet Ed Sanders allegedly printed a paper on the Catholic Worker
mimeograph called "Fuck You: A Magazine of the Arts." Jim Forest remembers the occasion as follows:

I was down at the Abbey of Gethsemani, staying with Thomas
Merton. Called up the Catholic Worker. Dorothy picked up the telephone, which didn't often happen. And she was mad. You could hear
that she was mad! She said, "Did you have anything to do with this?"
I didn't laugh.
    "With what?"
    "This, this, this, thing!"
    When she told me—it wasn't easy for her to say the name of the
publication, but she did—I could recall hearing people like Ed Sanders and Nelson Barr and Bob Kaye talk about it. It was a kind of running gag, you know, something people laughed about. I never actually
believed them. There was at that time at the Worker a kind of decadent quality that mirrored what was going on in the subculture in
New York at the time. But the magazine idea was so high school.
Sometimes high school students actually do some of the things they
joke about. And they did this. Dorothy felt furious because they were
using the poor. They were risking what the Catholic Worker was
doing. They were compromising her tolerance and her hospitality of
them.
    You know, I'm not sure that magazine was even printed at the
Catholic Worker, even though they claimed it was. Our mimeograph
machine was so dreadful that more likely it was printed on the War
Resisters League mimeograph machine. So I suspect that it was just a
. . . that it was just part of the bluff of the magazine to say that it was

printed at the Catholic Worker. But the cardinal wouldn't be interested in hearing arguments about whose mimeograph machine it was.[2]

On the other hand, she didn't want to bother the volunteers with a lot of this struggle. Volunteers would come and go. [The responsibility] was on her shoulders. See, she was very good with the young people. She really wanted to . . . she didn't want to blow her stack at us too much. She tried to work in a very gentle, storytelling, invitational way with us, by and large. But I think she felt used. And I think she was used, actually.

Her beloved Stanley Vishnewski was the one who would say, "Once you get to know Dorothy Day, she's just another crabby old lady." Dorothy would often apologize for losing her temper, as illustrated by the story Terry Rogers tells:

This really . . . this is my most favorite story about Dorothy. It was in the spring. A young runaway had been living in the house and that had caused some difficulty. Dorothy had been away, and when she came back, she got a lot of complaints.

She raced upstairs and . . . we had a fight, basically. She was really scolding me. I knew she was tired and aggravated and had gotten all this dumped on her, and that she needed to dump on someone, so as I remember, I didn't say anything like "Now Dorothy. Sit down and hear my side of the story." I just said, "Well, okay. I'll try to take care of those things."

I left. I got home late that night. At that point I had graduated from a bunk out in the big room to a cot behind the curtain, in a little cubby hole. It was dark and as I pulled back the curtain and walked into the alcove, I was just overcome with this gorgeous fragrance of lilacs. Just overcome!

I turned on the light and there was this huge vase of lilacs on my bed and a note from Dorothy: "Please forgive a crabby old woman. I know you work so hard and you're so wonderful." I mean she was just so extravagant in her praise. Just as unrealistic as she had been in her scolding. "Somebody brought me these lilacs today, and I want you to have them. You remind me of the daughter of an old friend."

---

[2] I was able to speak briefly to Ed Sanders in person when he visited Saginaw in 1999 for a poetry reading. He confided to me that the paper had *not* been printed on Catholic Worker premises. He also told me that he did not, in fact, print an issue on equipment in the offices of the American Friends Service Commission called *Fucketh Thee*, but said he would often joke about doing so.

Often the young Workers would "have a hard time understanding the grumbling of their elder leader as an expression of love," as Brian Terrell says. "For all its craziness, the Worker is a family, and in families it often happens that the elders complain about the [actions and looks] of the younger generation." Brian tells a generational story about Dorothy coming upon some young people at work in Maryhouse and listening to the Carly Simon song "I Haven't Got Time for the Pain." Dorothy shook her cane at them and said, "You've always got to have time for the pain." Other stories abound about her dislike for contemporary music. Jane O'Malley wrote me that she heard Dorothy yell from her upstairs room one particularly noisy day: "Holy silence!" And there's a story that she asked folksinger Charlie King if he couldn't "play something else."

Analyzing Dorothy was a favorite pastime for people who worked with her, especially during her absences from New York. She herself was more than aware of her failings. As Jean Walsh observes:

Her faults were so very obvious, but I always felt the presence of God so clearly. To me the miracle is that she stayed—spent fifty years living with the people at the Catholic Worker. She had no privacy at all, and the demand on her time was extraordinary! So much of her is lovable, but at that same time you could get pretty angry at her. She could criticize you—you could think unfairly. She would say that with God, you never get a hit amiss. So when you were criticized unfairly, you should take it. But hurt feelings were not uncommon around the Worker.

There was so much going on all the time and she'd sometimes be quite high-strung. I remember one day she was walking down the steps to the cellar and she was very nervous and annoyed about something and very vocal. Later she told me that Eddie Forand patted her on the shoulder and said, "Don't worry, we'll take care of it." She told me in a kind of wonder. And it seems so insignificant, but I realized that for once, someone else was stepping up and taking on responsibility, not just Dorothy. That didn't happen very often. We all depended on her, and just this tiny thing that Ed said impressed her enough to tell it to me.

ENGAGED AND ENGAGING

Dorothy would light up a room, cheer everybody up wonderfully!

—TAMAR HENNESSY

What would be a typical day for Dorothy? It depended, of course, on where she was. If she were in the city, she'd have less time to herself and be more "on call," both for those at the house and for expected and un-expected visitors. Opening and reading the mail was something she often did while sitting with young Workers, and her asking someone to help answer mail was one of the privileges of friendship. But whether in the city or on the road, she would find time alone to write and pray. Most of her friends recognized that she was most relaxed and conversational when she was at the farm, which would have been either in Easton, Pennsylvania, or Newburgh, New York, or Staten Island, or finally, Tivoli on the Hudson.

No matter where she was, she didn't start the day with a bang but "liked to sit around and read and maybe write and talk and drink coffee," as Judith Gregory tells us. Understandably, she loved the change [in the fasting rules before Mass], so she could have breakfast and go to a later Mass. Pat Rusk, who worked as an airline stewardess before becoming a part of the Catholic Worker family, conveys this atmosphere in an interesting way:

The Catholic Worker seems un-American to me, not so much in its thinking as in its plain living. It has a certain peasant quality, not the aggressive quality that marks the American way of life. Even Dorothy herself had that laid-back quality, as though time were endless. And it seemed to be at the Worker.

What do people remember about Dorothy's physical appearance and actions? Johannah Hughes Turner says she still misses Dorothy's beautiful voice, and describes her laughter as either musical or a "kind of titter." Some remember her laughter as a wry chuckle, what Brian Terrell calls a "doctor laugh," one matching her dry humor. Others have called it an "overflow giggle." Terry McKiernan of South Bend, who knew her in the late forties, called it a "nervous laughter" and said he noticed a shyness and that she'd "often put her hand up to her face." Joe Zarrella, one of the earliest members of the movement, remembers her young laughter as "hearty and infectious." It seems fair to say that Dorothy's laugh changed not only as she aged but also according to whom she was with and how at ease and free from worry she felt.

Terry Rogers recalled with affection:

She could be so *silly*. Sometimes, of course, she'd be enormously grim and sad and grieved and serious about stuff, but other times, she'd be just plain silly. Happy and very girlish and silly. I remember we were all hot and crabby one day, and she came in and said: "It's a beautiful day. Let's go up to the Cloisters. The guardian angels will look after the house."

Beth Rogers saw a romantic streak:

I've always thought that she had a streak of romanticism—a romanticism coupled with great practicality. These two impulses in her are an interesting combination, don't you think? She always said she wanted to have the Worker on a houseboat. And she hated central heating. Liked coal-burning fires, such as the house on Mott Street had. And of course they never really heated the place properly. I guess the first couple of farms had outhouses. So when she bought the farm at Newburgh, somebody said, "You watch. Dorothy will tear out the indoor plumbing and establish an outhouse." *(Laughter.)*

Dorothy loved opera, and Ned O'Gorman and others would sometimes take her to the Metropolitan, occasions she clearly relished. She told several of her friends, including Robert Steed, that if there were such a thing as reincarnation, she'd like to come back as a Wagnerian soprano. Robert remembers:

Then in the same breath, she told me that she had met the composer Prokokiev in Chicago at some party, back in the early twenties. They were talking about a particular piece of music, and nobody could remember how it went or something. And she hummed it for them. And Prokokiev said, "You have a very good ear but a terrible voice." So she could never be the Wagnerian soprano, in this life at least. *(Laughter.)*

Sister Teresa Murray remembers overhearing Dorothy discuss opera one day with some of the women who lived in Maryhouse. "Some of them loved opera, too, and she breathed life into them by reminding them of it." Tom Cornell remembers that she once said she didn't like Mozart and never talked about Bach, but the Romantics were another matter! One day he came into her room while she was listening to *La Bohème*. She exclaimed, "Oh, it may be silly, it may be romantic, but isn't it wonderful?"

Balancing her romanticism was a practical streak. Beth Rogers:

She had a sense of publicity that was very interesting, too, and that illustrates her streak of practicality. When the fire happened at Chrystie Street, she was the one who thought of notifying the *New York Times* about the fire. They ran it, and the story went all over the world.

The poet W. H. Auden was teaching at New York University at the time, and he read about it and came over to the Worker, all rumpled and messy looking. Dorothy [had gone] out early to go to Mass, and she said this rather scruffy-looking man stepped up to her and handed her an envelope. "Miss Day, here's something for you, for the fire." When she opened it up, she saw it was a check for $250 from W. H. Auden. And *that* story got onto the wires, too!

Common sense was Ned O'Gorman's first impression, as well:

Sometime around 1955 or 1956, I got the notion that I had to go down to Chrystie Street. I walked in with my Harris tweed jacket and decided I would work with the Bowery folks. So I took off my jacket, with my wallet in it, of course, and threw it down on the chair. Suddenly I heard a voice say: "Who threw this jacket down on the chair with a wallet in it? Don't you know that poor people steal things?" And that was my first memory of Dorothy. Giving me a lesson in reality.

Everyone I talked to agreed that Dorothy was a striking woman with a great deal of presence, even when she aged. Terry McKiernan says, "When she entered the room, you knew it." She was tall with what my mother would call "good bones," and people used words like *stunning* and *movie star* to describe her in her youth. Judith Gregory described her as having narrow shoulders, similar to the woman Marcel Duchamps portrayed in "Nude Descending a Staircase."[3] Pat Rusk commented that she was scrawny from her waist to her shoulders and thought that "perhaps that was why she wasn't a hugger, but would kiss people right on the lips."

Sometime during the early years, she decided to give up getting her hair cut and let it grow long. The braided coronet wound around her head became her unvarying look for the rest of her life. Like most of us, she took pains in choosing photo portraits for publication, but Martha Pickman Baltzell remembers her as being unconcerned with her appearance:

She was without pretense. She had a fine tweed suit, which came out of the packages for the poor. She was very proud of it, even though it didn't fit her very well. In her old age she had a beauty beyond the physical, a beauty that came through her.

Betty Doyle of St. Joseph, Minnesota, told me:

---

[3] Workers would often speculate on Dorothy's early life, and one such story, clearly apocryphal, is that she modeled for the Duchamps painting in her pre-conversion years. As Robert Steed pointed out to me, she would have been about twelve when it was painted.

Dorothy, of course, always just took whatever came in on the line, you know, so she didn't look very elegant most of the time. My aunt Molly Hastings was about Dorothy's age and pretty much the same size. Often would give her clothes to Dorothy, especially if Dorothy admired them, you know. And then my aunt was a wonderful seamstress, so she'd sew for her, too. She liked to dress her up.

Dorothy got saggy as she got older, like most of us do. My aunt was saggy, too, so Auntie used to give her girdles and corsets, real corsets. Dorothy was always so pleased. She'd look at herself in the mirror and say, "I really don't look too bad, do I?" She was a very feminine woman. Now she didn't look particularly feminine, but she had a lot of sweet, feminine ways about her.

She was always having trouble with shoes. She could get lots of other things from [the clothing that came into the Worker], but getting shoes was pretty difficult. She was a tall woman, a really big woman, you know, and had fairly large feet, so she was always glad when she got some nice-looking shoes. No, there was nothing masculine about Dorothy.

But Rose Morse remembers that Dorothy used to "shuffle along in those kind of cloddy shoes of hers, especially as she got older. And she worried about tripping on the carpet the day she received communion from the pope."

Dorothy had high cheekbones, and several well-known photographers worked with her over the years, including Richard Avedon, Robert Fitch, and Vivian Cherry. I was able to speak with Vivian, who photographed her extensively in 1955 and again in 1959. She remembers Dorothy as a gracious and natural subject, very cooperative and helpful:

She had an essential spirit. When she came into a room, no matter how she looked or how she was dressed, she was a special person, especially in her treatment of people. I liked her, liked her very much, because she thought of you as a person and didn't ask what your beliefs were.

Bill McDonough, who met her near the end of her active days, was impressed with the "etchedness" of her features:

Her face, at that time, was beginning to droop, so just her cheek bones stuck out and the strong chin. But when she smiled . . . Then there were no harsh edges, just warmth in the interpersonal connection. Perhaps an austere look but great personal warmth.

Janet Kalven of Grailville described her face as "very sensitive and centered and with a kind of contemplative quality to it, a serenity, even in the midst of chaos."

Brian Terrell, who came to the Worker before he was twenty and knew Dorothy at the end of her life, said:

I guess I'd sometimes feel intimidated by Dorothy. Her face was so strong and her height and her bearing was . . . uh, I think she would have been a dominant force in whatever she chose to do, whether politics or selling shoes.

Dorothy's daughter, Tamar, gives perhaps the most perceptive physical description of Dorothy:

Dorothy had beautiful bone structure. Strong jaw. And the eyes—her eyes were beautiful. She had a wonderful way with them, but they could be devastating, too, so when she disapproved of something, you knew it. *(Laughs.)*

Often, when Dorothy sort of settles back, she looks very sad, though, and they seem to choose those pictures whenever someone publishes something about her. There's a lot of truth [in those sad looks], but I don't like seeing only that when there's so much more.

Others also spoke of this sad look, as these memories illustrate. Johannah Turner muses:

I have also perceived Dorothy as lonely and as needing the approval and affection of others, as being very easily hurt by ridicule and by rejection. I saw her often as vulnerable. Not just [being hurt by] little slights but doubting herself. However, at the beach she was usually very sociable and jovial, or at least indulgent, in the company of others. But there were other times when you could see her just looking silently at the water. Maybe she was thinking of the endless cycles, the changing world, her youth and her losses. I'm sure if she felt bad enough, she'd "pray it down." But I wonder sometimes at the sadness she felt.

MARQUETTE UNIVERSITY ARCHIVES

Ed Forand gives one probable reason:

You know around the mid-seventies, Dorothy started referring to the Catholic Worker as a school. "People come and people go." The people who come here are your family. You get to love a lot of them like your brothers and sisters. After a while it's . . . really, it takes so much out of you. Dorothy has seen all these people come and go, too, and I can't help but think that she started thinking of this term *school* to kind of make her feel better.

Even when Dorothy aged, she did so with a difference. When Jane Sammon met her in 1972, she noticed that "nothing about her voice was vulnerable." And in my own brief meeting with Dorothy, I felt she had become more concentrated in age, instead of diminished, as many of us do.

Dorothy Day was complex. To speak of one part of her personality without taking the others into account can give a distorted or plasticized picture. She was witty yet sometimes wistful; forceful yet often insecure; loved conversation but also sought privacy for prayer, music, reading, and writing; believed in freedom and autonomy yet nevertheless knew she had to lead a movement; in short a complex person—vital, engaged, and engaging.

6.

Later Years

A ROOM OF HER OWN

You know, we die as we live. Dorothy didn't die in an institutionalized, sterilized, intensive care unit but chose to live her final days at home. She had lived with a great deal of integrity and dignity, and so she also was able to die with it.

—MICHAEL HARANK

Until her health called for a sedentary life, Dorothy enjoyed visiting Tivoli or staying at the beach houses she owned in Spanish Camp on Staten Island. Her daughter, Tamar, was finally free of child-rearing and could spend portions of every summer with her. As Tamar said, "She knew she was failing, but she wasn't giving up. She fought it every inch of the way." After Dorothy moved into the city and was no longer able to travel, even to Tivoli or Staten Island, Tamar would visit often. A scene New York Catholic Workers hold dear is Dorothy chatting and watching television with her family—Tamar and Tamar's father, Forster, who frequently joined them. As Tamar said, "Forster was always partial to Dorothy."

Jane Sammon came to the Worker in 1972 and was a member of the community during Dorothy's last years, when she was confined to her room at Maryhouse. Frank Donovan and the young people living at the Worker were very protective of Dorothy. Jane relates:

I would say that my biggest fear [was that she would] see any kind of violence. I couldn't bear that. If she were in a room and there was going to be an eruption, I would be . . . You could hear her the next day talking about hearing windows being broken. She'd say, "Nobody tells me anything." You wanted to protect her because you grew in love for her.

But there were precious times, too. I remember once I was up in her room. (It was the night after my birthday.) I got up to leave, and I took Dorothy's hand. She said, "Oh, it's your birthday! Now, what can I give you?" I said, "Nothing. You've given me enough over the years." With that, she smiled at me and drew her arms up toward me, pulled my face down and kissed me. My birthday treasure. After that we watched "Little Miss Marker" with Shirley Temple.

Some of us would do her medicines. We took turns going up to weigh her, take her pulse, make sure she had her medicine, listen to her complain about all of the above, you know. You always thought, "Not on my watch, dear God."

I'm the person that took her pulse the day [she went to the hospital the last time]. I called [Dr.] Marion Moses to say that her pulse was some ungodly low number, and Dorothy was so annoyed with me for telling on her! Well, off she went to the hospital, and my image of Dorothy, just three weeks before she died, was coming down in one of those scooper seats that the ambulance brings around. She kind of raises her cane to the ensemble gathered on the stairs to say goodbye. Looks right at me as she's passing and says, "It's all her fault!"

Jeannette Noel would be called up almost every day to visit Dorothy. She remembers Dorothy's giggle, "like a little school kid's," even in old age:

We weren't allowed to just walk in on her any time. Frank [Donovan] kept it very close. He was her cop. But out of love, I mean. You couldn't get in without a key, but she would ask for people, and she was still connected.

Frank Donovan began volunteering at the Catholic Worker in the early 1970s. A man of cultivated tastes and exquisite manners, he became the general office manager. When Dorothy, in her later years, settled at Maryhouse, he also became her most zealous supporter and protector. Jane Sammon remembers that Dorothy said of Frank, "God gave me a son in my old age."

People from across the country came to say goodbye to a woman who had been friend, mentor, guide. Joe Zarrella remembers that Dorothy joked with him on his goodbye visit, when he came accompanied by his old pal, Gerry Griffin. "Before I left, she gave me a pamphlet. And I think she wrote on it, 'You always treated me nicer than Gerry!'"

Even in old age, Dorothy Day was the person she needed to be for her many friends who visited her. For instance, the late Dorothy Gauchat of our Lady of the Wayside in Cleveland liked to do things for Dorothy, and Dorothy let her. Dorothy Gauchat told me:

> Once I gave her a nightgown with long sleeves, and you would have thought I had given her a pot of gold. I'd do things for her when I'd visit. She had a shawl, I think, that Tamar had made for her. (Tamar is so gifted.) It was dirty, so I washed it in the bathtub up in her apartment there. Once I went all over looking for lisle stockings because she liked them. Little things like that. What a daughter would do for a mother.
>
> The last time I saw her, I brought her a medallion of the Sacred Heart, and she was thrilled with that. She said to me, "Keep praying to the Holy Angels that the work will continue." She was very worried that it was all going to fall apart. That was the August before she died.

Yet Chuck Matthei remembers that Dorothy seemed unconcerned about what would happen after she was gone:

> What she said was, "If God wills the work to go on, it will continue. If it should take a different form, it will change, and if our task is done, it will end." And she didn't seem to care which of these scenarios would unfold.

Her old friend Sister Peter Claver was also able to make a goodbye visit with Dorothy:

> It was then that we sealed our friendship for eternity. She was sitting in the corner of her room and reached out with both hands. I clasped them and sat on the edge of her bed. For a few minutes we talked about the "Great Retreat" and then, still holding hands, we prayed the Our Father together. I hugged her and made the Sign of the Cross on her forehead and kissed her goodbye. She was just as calm as could be. And strong. There was no talk about death, and you could tell she was just very secure and at peace. It was a final farewell to a long and enduring friendship.

Like most people as they age, Dorothy lived more and more in the past. Los Angeles Catholic Workers Catherine Morris and her husband, Jeff Dietrich, had visited Dorothy at Tivoli in 1975:

> We'd sit with her for hours. She talked constantly—just told stories. Pulled all kinds of skeletons out of the closet. We were amazed. "Whoa . . . She is saying this?" You know, all kinds of relationships, who ran

off with who and all that kind of stuff. She was very reminiscent. We don't know if she was trying to convey some message to us through the stories or what. But she just seemed to feel like going over these things in her head. It didn't seem to bother her. Some of the stuff she was telling was rather scandalous.

Betty Bartelme says she spoke more openly about her pre-conversion life than when they used to chat in earlier days and that Dorothy told her the abortion was the worst thing she'd ever done in her life.

Tina Sipula met Dorothy for the one and only time when she visited New York in 1978, just before opening Clare House in Bloomington, Illinois:

I was pretty shaken by the fact that Dorothy was literally locked in her room. I asked why, and they said it was because so many people wanted to come and see her and if they got into the house, then they'd come into her room. So she had to be locked away. Not that she seemed to mind.

Stanley [Vishnewski] had a key, so he'd take me up to her room almost every night and I'd have dinner with her. First we'd watch the news. The new pope was being elected, and she thought it was fabulous that they had a pope from the Eastern Bloc.

After the news, she talked. She'd talk about Peter, how he always had stuff in his pockets—lists of books he wanted to read—and was unkempt and not very clean, but she said some very endearing things about him and seemed to remember those times with pleasure.

She'd talk about the house in the beginning, and then she'd look at me and ask me what my house was like. I'd tell her and she'd remember for a while and then ask me again the next night. But she'd say, "Keep it simple. Keep it simple." She'd just lie there for a while and then she'd say, "It's too big here. It's not personable." She had her green oxygen tank, and books all over the walls.

When I told her I was from Illinois, she talked about going to the U. of I. and what it was like in those days in Champaign [where Dorothy studied briefly before moving to New York]. They were very radical times, and she felt that those were some of the best years of her life.

I remember one night she came down to the dining room. We were sitting together, and they served her a greasy chicken back and some wilted lettuce and a piece of squash. Everything was way overcooked. She took about two bites and pushed the plate away. "I don't know how they expect me to eat this!"

And then we had a discussion about the bandana or scarf she always wore on her head. I had a student with me, Chris Enserra, and it didn't take us very long to figure out that it was worn because there was so many cases of lice in the house and so many cockroaches. I mean, there were a million cockroaches! So I immediately found a bandana and wore it the whole time I was there. *(Laughter.)*

Stanley just adored her, of course. There was a lot of bantering back and forth. We'd be watching TV and a commercial would come on—she hated commercials—and she'd say "Stanley! Shut that damn thing off! You know I can't stand commercials." It was obvious that they'd been together for a long time, and she could say just about anything to him.

Stanley died in November of 1979. Dr. Marion Moses accompanied Dorothy so she could go to his funeral. It was the last time she left Maryhouse on her own.

BIG QUESTIONS

Robert Ellsberg left Harvard after his sophomore year and came to the Worker in 1975. He edited the paper from 1976 through 1978, then participated in a resistance action at Rocky Flats, Colorado, where he was arrested and spent time in jail for protesting the manufacture of nuclear weapons. He became a Catholic and was received into the church on Holy Thursday of 1980. Shortly after that, he returned to Harvard and completed his degree, writing a senior thesis on Dorothy, which later became the introduction to his anthology of her writings: By Little and by Little. *He now serves as editor-in-chief at Orbis Books.*

I remember the day I met Dorothy. She had been staying up at Tivoli, so I'd been at the Worker maybe a couple of months before I saw her. She came down to the city, and there was a certain excitement, with people whispering, "Dorothy's here!"

There were a lot of very difficult people in the house, but they would just melt at the sight of Dorothy. There was something genteel about her, and her presence had a subtle aura of authority, so it . . . it just put people on their best behavior. They would watch their language and . . . and were just happy to have her around. She was everyone's grandmother.

So this night she came down to have dinner. I think maybe somebody introduced me. She had met my father [Daniel Ellsberg], who had come with Joan Baez to visit her in jail when she was arrested in California for supporting the Farm Workers. Dorothy liked to find some basis for connection with people. So from the beginning she was very friendly with me.

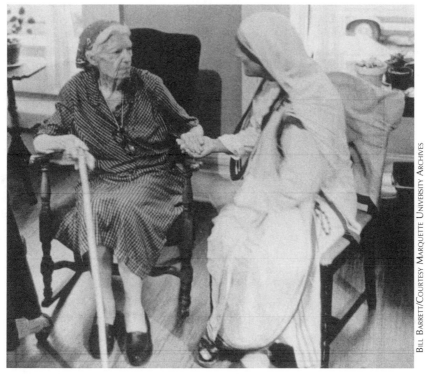

Bill Barrett/Courtesy Marquette University Archives

Dorothy and Mother Teresa in the Maryhouse office, 1979.

Here I was with all these big questions in my life, and here was my big opportunity. I think Dorothy would have been much more interested in how I'd happened to come [to the Worker], but I felt I had to engage her on some higher level, so I said something like, "How do you reconcile the philosophy of anarchism with Catholicism?" She just said, "It's never been a problem with me." For a long time I tried to read all kinds of deep meaning into that statement, but as I got to know her better, I realized that she just didn't have much interest in abstraction.

I remember being awestruck. She was just like the pictures I'd seen—an old lady, with glasses, and a kerchief on her head. Very pretentiously I said that I wanted to share with her some notes that I been putting down about the Catholic Worker. I don't know whether she ever read them or not, but she sent me a little note that said it was a very good thing to keep a journal, and she encouraged me to do that.

I was just soaking her up. And Dorothy began to take an interest in me, too, because I was interested in the political side of things and doing a lot of systematic reading of the stuff Peter Maurin talked about.

Well, after I'd been there a few months, I left for a while. Hitchhiked around the country and visited various Catholic Worker houses. I was in

California when Anne Marie Fraser wrote and asked if I'd take over her job as editor of the paper because she wanted to go to nursing school. Now this didn't reflect the fact that I was brilliant, or even especially qualified to do the job. I was twenty years old, and I was not Catholic, and I'd been at the Worker for less than six months. But Anne Marie had told Dorothy she wanted to retire, and Dorothy had said, "Who do you have in mind to take on the paper?"

Anne Marie apparently said, "Well, I was thinking of young Ellsberg." (Dorothy always used to call me "young Ellsberg." Or "Bob." Sometimes even "Bob Ellsworth.") And Dorothy said, "Well I was thinking of him, too." Whether she really was thinking that or not I don't know, but she had this very agreeable way of . . . of agreeing with you. I even tried this out on her once. She often liked to ask, "What's your favorite novel of Dostoevski?" And if I'd say "*The Brothers Karamazov*," she'd say, "Well, that's mine, too." And if someone would say, "*The Idiot*," she'd say, "Exactly. *The Idiot*." So whether she was actually thinking of me [for the newspaper], I don't know.

My real newspaper debut had been in December of 1975, when I'd been there only a couple of months. Anne Marie had asked me to write about Gandhi. I took it very, very seriously. My first published piece. I wrote about Gandhian politics. The thrust of it was, I guess, that he never saw victory or power or success as the ultimate value. Well, Dorothy loved it. She said something like, "Back in the old days, people would write thought pieces like this, and we used to circulate them and discuss them." She said, "I think you should do more." So for the January issue, I went up to the New York Public Library and read all these obscure books on Gandhi and wrote a bigger piece, on Gandhian economics, which she liked even better. Of course, for the third article, I overreached myself. *(Laughs.)* Decided I'd write on the spirituality of Gandhi, something I had no competence to do. I wrote something very false and pious and that put the Gandhian series to rest pretty fast. But I guess those articles got me the job. That and the fact that no one else was particularly interested in taking it on.

I came back to New York in the spring, and Anne Marie led me through a couple of issues, so I could get an idea of what was involved. The September '76 issue was my first, and that also marked my first anniversary at the Worker. I remember I put this rather dark picture on the front page. And Dorothy said, "People my age don't want to see dark things like that; they want to see cheerful things, like the circus, or flowers, or sunshine."

She would communicate [what] she liked and didn't like, but I began to sense that if there was something she didn't like very much, if I could tell her some story about the author or something or other—that I knew him or that he loved Tolstoy—then she wouldn't veto much. She had idiosyncratic judgments that she . . . that were formed from years in the past. Complicated feelings about some of the heroes of the Catholic peace movement.

Mailing the paper was a big community project, a cottage industry really, and it provided employment for many of the guests and visitors. Dorothy believed that people need to have something, some area they were in charge of, even if it was just sorting socks. You don't criticize those people. They are the masters of that job, whether it's cleaning the grease trap or mopping the floor or cutting the bread. If there's someone who knows how to do something and does it well, that person has authority.

If you criticized someone's job, that sort of implied that you were prepared to step in and do it yourself. If you could do it better, then you could have the job. Editing the paper wasn't, in this respect, any different than cleaning the grease trap. There was a job that had to be done, and someone stepped in or was asked to step in, and then it became his or her job. Editing the paper was my job. It didn't have any special status.

Dorothy tended to define people by their work. She admired hard workers. In the "war between the worker and the scholar," she liked people to be both, and she didn't especially admire people who were just "scholars," who sat around reading all the time. She thought that men were constitutionally prone to this kind of abstraction and that it was responsible for many of the world's problems.

Dorothy had this feeling that the Worker is a kind of school, that people would graduate and move on to all kinds of things. It isn't that the whole world should be at the Catholic Worker, but that it was very important for people to have that formation, that experience, to take into other things. She would very much agree that not everybody should live in a soup kitchen or a house of hospitality. We also need editors, we need journalists, we need teachers. These are all potentially religious vocations, all opportunities to live the beatitudes, to be peacemakers. So she totally admired people like Studs Terkel or Dwight McDonald or Robert Coles, intellectuals or professionals or writers who managed to bring human values to their work. People who were faithful in some way. She loved the respect for human beings that they brought to their writing. Which for her was compassion and a kind of . . . a loyalty to the human scale of things. And they were not all Christian. You didn't have to tip your hat to the Trinity. [It was] just an instinctive kind of sacramentality, a sense of the holiness of the everyday, a sense for community that's inclusive of the saints as well as all the rest of us.

People ask me what Dorothy Day was like, and I know that other people have had other experiences. Of course you have to remember that the Dorothy I knew was in her last five years. It certainly was when she was letting go, when she enjoyed the sense (in a way the fact) that she . . . that not everybody looked to her for the answers for everything. She was very pleased that there was this crop of young people . . . She liked the fact that I was so young.

She still kept a journal. She'd give it to Frank and ask him to type up some notes for her columns, which got to be more and more fragmentary. I'd edit them some, taking out comments that struck me—with all my infinite wisdom—as irrelevant. She pretty much let [her writing] go by that time—was quite detached, actually—but I've heard that she wasn't that way in the past. I kept finding myself wishing that she would write more programmatically, but that's not who she was, and I now appreciate her loyal readership—people who just wanted to see that she was still alive, as she put it. If she mentioned a book she had been looking for, for example, twenty copies would arrive in the next mail. (She said that one of the benefits of getting old was that you could reread all your favorite books with such enjoyment.) Sometimes I'd pick up a book for her from a second-hand bookstore—a novel by Ignazio Silone, or something. And she'd think it was just such a great gift! So many times, she would have read a book and then given it away.

In 1978, after editing the paper for two years, I gave up that job and flew out to Colorado with some Catholic Worker friends to protest at Rocky Flats, the plant that made plutonium triggers for thermonuclear weapons. We sat on the railroad tracks and got arrested. I became separated from the rest of the group and ended up spending the whole time in jail by myself. Fasted for sixteen days and was put in solitary confinement. And it was during that time that I found myself reading scripture and reflecting on my experience at the Worker in a different light. And when I got back to New York, I started working at St. Rose's and did a lot more reading and thinking about Catholicism.[1]

Dorothy was very proud of those Workers who got arrested and went to jail. In her perspective, going to jail was relaxing after running the house, and she wrote me a postcard that said she hoped I was enjoying my retreat. Maybe she romanticized it as she got older, but she did see jail as a good time to practice the works of mercy in visiting the prisoner. When I got back from Colorado, she gave me a copy of *The Little Flowers of Saint Francis*, which she inscribed, "For you to enjoy on your next retreat in jail."

---

[1] St. Rose's was a hospice for cancer patients founded by Rose Hawthorne, the daughter of Nathaniel Hawthorne, after she joined the Catholic church and became a nun. Many Catholic Workers found part-time jobs there, often watching the wards at night.

Then I had this idea to get the Catholic Worker FBI file. I had to get Dorothy's signature on some form to do it, along with her birth date, place of birth, and so forth. It took some cajoling to get her to go along with this. Well, I got the FBI file and pored over it. It wasn't a page turner; it was just a pile of reports documenting the Bureau's long and generally bumbling interest in the Worker. I remember one report that described Dorothy as a Russian immigrant. Another one said she was the founder of the "Dorothy Day Art Studio in Chicago." But then somebody in the house said something to Dorothy like, "Oh, we've got your FBI file! Pretty juicy stuff there, Dorothy!" After this she became alarmed that there was something private in there, something embarrassing. And she asked me to give it back to her so she could check it out. She sort of sat on it and it seemed to disappear, and I forgot about it for a while.

Many months later I asked her, "What happened to that FBI File?" And she said, "Oh, here it is." Things would always appear like that, right at Dorothy's fingertips. She gave it back to me, and I spent some weeks studying it and wrote a rather long and somewhat whimsical two-part article about it.

I remember reading it aloud to her. She loved it! Doubled over laughing. It told the story of the Worker and also exposed the idiocy of the FBI and its efforts to comprehend what the Worker was all about, just what kind of category of subversion the Worker was supposed to represent. Anyway, she found it very amusing. I remember reading to her a passage from a profile that J. Edgar Hoover had composed that said something like, "Dorothy Day is a very erratic and irresponsible person who makes every effort to castigate the Bureau whenever she feels inclined."

"That's marvelous!" she said. "Read it again!"

There was really a playful side to Dorothy. She had this kind of girlish giggle and enjoyed teasing. She could laugh at herself, so it was fun to amuse her. She liked to fool around and tell stories. Almost any idea or any story just kind of pulled a plug and she'd remember something. The joy—it was wonderful!

Then I decided to become a Catholic. One day I went up to Dorothy to tell her of my decision. It sounded so dramatic and serious. Like I was going to become a monk or something. I was so sensitive about triumphalism that I almost didn't tell her at all. We were chatting as usual. I said, "There's something I wanted to talk to you about."

"Yes?"

And I said something like, "Well, I've been thinking about . . . well, *thinking* is not the right word, I've been . . . " I was stumbling along like this and she just sat there perplexed.

She finally said, "What is it?"

"I'm thinking of becoming a Catholic."

She was very quiet. I thought she didn't hear me or that she was going to say, "Well why would you do that?" Instead, she finally asked,
"Well, you're an Episcopalian, right?"

"Yes, that's how I was raised."

"I always thought the Episcopalians were a little well-to-do." And she
squinted the way she did when she was saying something a little mischie-
vous. She was pleased with my decision, but she didn't act as if another
sinner had been saved or something. I was glad she didn't make a big deal
out of it.

I went to see her after the deed was done. I had been received into the
church in the chapel of the Little Brothers of the Gospel, the order that
was inspired by Charles de Foucauld. She gave me a big hug and was just
very . . . just very warm. Then she said, "I used to have a book about
Charles de Foucauld. Would you like it if I gave it to you?"

And I said, "Yes, of course." It was on the shelf at her fingertips. She
autographed it. It was a book she'd had for like thirty years and [it] had
all her underlining in it. And a picture of Charles de Foucauld with his
prayer on the back and names of people she was praying for. Eileen Egan
later told me that my becoming a Catholic had meant more to her than
she let on at the time, although there had never been any reproach or
sense of something lacking in me before. She liked to say that I became
a Christian from reading Gandhi, and that was enough for her.

It was one of the last times I saw her.

A GEOGRAPHY OF THE HEART

*Even at the end Dorothy's relationships with people were individual
and personal. One of the young people who worked with Dorothy during her final days was Michael Harank. Michael had first heard of Dorothy through his older brother Andrew, who went to prison for draft
resistance during the Vietnam War. Michael met her himself while he was
a student at Holy Cross College in Worcester, Massachusetts. Influenced
by having been with Dorothy in her final days, he became an R.N. after
he left the Worker and started Bethany Catholic Worker in Oakland,
California, a home for homeless victims of AIDS.*

When I came to the Worker, Dorothy was living upstairs on the second floor with her room facing toward the street, pretty much confined
to her room, although she'd come down for Mass or special occasions.
We took turns taking up her heart medicine and her meals.

When I went up the first time, she was very welcoming. Her short-term
memory was failing at that point, although her long-term memory wasn't,

so she asked me who I was on several visits. I'd been sick, and when she learned that, she became very solicitous and wanted to make sure I took care of myself and offered me something to drink. So it was like a visit to one's grandmother. I come back to that image often because that's what I felt her presence was—very comforting, reaching out, and welcoming.

Now I didn't know the Dorothy who was active and traveling. I knew the Dorothy who developed into a contemplative hermit, with a little room on Third Street in New York, seven doors down from the Hells Angels, sleeping with her deaf ear up so she wouldn't hear the roar of their motorcycles.

At that point she was a frail human being, physically frail. But her spirit was not frail at all. She spent her days talking on the telephone to friends or reading, praying, watching television. And I think at times she was frustrated by that because she was a woman with a winged foot. Loved to travel—spreading the news of the Catholic Worker movement, encouraging people, raising money, traveling to Russia or India or Cuba or other places.

She showed an immense curiosity. Now when people grow older, they necessarily get a little more confined in their geography. Her geography was a geography of the heart, and I don't think she ever stopped traveling in those regions of the heart, whether it was her family or her friends. She would occasionally give me a letter to answer because she couldn't answer all the letters she received.

I remember one day a priest came up to me, after she'd come down to Mass, and said, "Who is taking care of Dorothy these days?"

I said, "Well, as you can see, she was able to come downstairs, and she's pretty much taking care of herself. We give her medicine. We bring her meals. She's pretty much confined to her room, but she's not bedridden, so she's taking care of herself, which is probably what she likes and we enjoy it, too." It never got to the point where Dorothy was bedridden or utterly dependent. We tried to care for her in a way that honored her own space. And she never got to the point that so many elderly people get to, which is utter dependency. She was able to do her "adult daily living activities," as we say in the nursing profession, quite well. Of course, we'd joke and she'd say, "If you're not good to me, then I might die when you're on the house!"

She'd get frustrated when she didn't remember things—names or events. But that's natural, and she'd just giggle or laugh it off. I remember I was reading at the time some of the journals of Kierkegaard, and one day I came across this wonderful line: "The most horrible thing about humans is that they forget. The most wonderful thing about God is that God forgets." It really struck me, and I thought, "I must share this with Dorothy!"

So the next time I delivered her food, I read it to her and I said, "Just think! You're becoming more like God in your forgetfulness."

And she said, "Oh, Michael!" She was just very pleased. Then she said, "I must write that down right now in my diary or else I'll forget it." It was a wonderful moment because that was a way that she could graciously deal with a very difficult thing. Here was a woman with a very sharp mind, whose short-term memory was being lost.

Once she told me a very funny story about a young man who had courted her when she was studying to be a nurse. (I was rather stunned, actually, because I didn't know her intimately, you know.) She had decided that she wasn't going to date him again, and he was so distraught that he hung on the fire escape of her apartment, pleading with her. She laughed and said, "I don't know why that's come back to me, but it was very, very funny."

Sometimes in the early evening, Stanley Vishnewski and Tamar and Dorothy would be in her room enjoying a public television show or concert and having a glass of wine. She'd feel the need to justify the wine as good for her heart, because, as you know, there was no alcohol in Catholic Worker houses. She'd say, "My doctor recommended it. It's good medicine."

Occasionally her grandchildren would come and visit her, and she really enjoyed that. I think Dorothy needed a close connection with family members. But there was a fierceness, I suspect, in having Dorothy Day as your real grandmother.

Those family visits were a comfort to her because in that last year her sister Della died and Stanley died and also one of the grandchildren. So those times with Tamar and Forster and also with her brother John and Tessa, his wife . . . I think she took great comfort in the company of her family and her friends.

One night I asked her if there was anything that she really missed in her life at the Catholic Worker. After almost fifty years, was there anything that she really longed for? She said that what she missed the most was the companionship of an intimate relationship. I don't know if she used the word *intimate,* because this was seventeen years ago and that word wasn't used as much as it is now, but I know she said "the companionship of a relationship." Then she talked about how comforting it was to be with Forster. It was difficult for her, I think, because she did love him, and she always would love him, but she had had to give him up in her journey to God.

Oh, I remember the morning glories! She loved morning glories. I planted them and they grew in flower boxes along the front facade of Maryhouse, with strings tied to the top floor of the house. Bloomed right into the month of December. Lucy, one of the guests, would count the number of blooms every day. Dorothy could see them outside her window, and she'd talk about how much their beauty lifted her spirits. She loved that quote from Dostoevski and never tired of repeating it: "The world will be saved by beauty."

The only time I ever saw Dorothy's hard edge was about a month before she died. She was being brought down the stairs at Maryhouse, going to the hospital, all tied up and strapped into a seated gurney. She was really, really angry. You could see the sternness on her face, and she looked at me as she was being brought down the steps and she said, "I'll be back soon." I said to myself, "I bet you will." She had mellowed, but you knew she was going to do what she wanted to do. And she did that time, too. Came back to Maryhouse within three days and was not brought to the hospital again.

You know, we die as we live, and she certainly did. She didn't die in an institutionalized, sterilized, intensive care unit. She chose to live her final days at home. Dorothy was one of my first teachers when I started my own journey of working with the dying. She had lived with a great deal of integrity and dignity, and so she also was able to die with it.

"IT'S SO NICE TO HAVE A WOMAN DOCTOR"

Dr. Marion Moses, director of the Pesticide Education Center in San Francisco, became acquainted with Dorothy while working as a nurse and organizer with César Chávez and the United Farm Workers. Her friendship continued when she became Dorothy's personal physician.

I became Dorothy's doctor when I began my residency at Mt. Sinai in New York. That was in July of 1977. I wanted board certification from there in occupational medicine—environmental medicine—because it was one of the best occupational medicine programs in the country. One of the first things I did after I got to New York was to take the subway, and then the ferry and the train, to Spanish Camp out in Staten Island, where Dorothy was staying. It was a beautiful, sunny day in July. Dorothy was out in the backyard, sitting on one of those folding chairs. So I just got a chair and sat next to her. She patted me on the knee and said, "It's so nice to have a woman doctor." She didn't ask me to be her doctor; it was by her fiat. "It's so nice to have a woman doctor."

I had met her when I was first in college, but I really got to know her when I lived in New York in 1968, doing fund raising for César Chávez and working on the grape boycott. And then in 1969 I was caring for César in Fresno when Dorothy visited him, and while I was in medical school in Philadelphia, I'd spend every holiday except Christmas in New

PAT JORDAN

On the beach at Staten Island.

York, so I'd always be down at the Worker. That's when Dorothy and I really got to be very close. We'd sit and talk about César, about unions, about Russian authors—we talked about everything!

I'll never forget the first time I examined her, put a stethoscope to her chest. I was astounded! She had really severe mitral and aortic valve disease. Clearly, she'd had rheumatic fever when she was a little girl. I saw her very often after that, usually at Staten Island. Eileen Egan used to say that if it hadn't been for me, Dorothy wouldn't have lived those three extra years. And I think that's probably true. But I don't think it was so much me; it was getting good, medical care. I'm not saying it was easy, though. I mean, she could really be stubborn.

One of my biggest memories—and I'm not sure what year it was, but it was somewhere between 1977 and 1979—I got a call that she was really sick, and so I got myself down there as quickly as I could. She was having trouble breathing. It was clear that she was going to have to go to the hospital. Well, what I remember is going into that room. Her hair was in braids, but hanging down. And she was fuming! She was sitting there, with her arms crossed over her chest, and she glared at me. "I am not going to any hospital!"

Well, three hours later we had her on the way to the hospital. But it took that long. She really didn't want to go. I had found a good cardiologist at Beth Israel—Dr. Goldberg. He was an old lefty, and he knew about her and loved her and took such good care of her, which was great. I always felt very comfortable having him. You know, she could get her EKGs and meds there, and he could tune her medicine, and basically I just kept a close watch on her. Listened to her heart, made sure that . . . I would titrate her dose of medicine and all that kind of stuff. And basically deal with her stubbornness.

Every time she took the pills, she'd ask, "Do I have to take these pills for the rest of my life?" She must have asked me that a thousand times and I would always say, "Well, Dorothy, unless there's a miracle and you get the heart you had when you were seventeen." And she would laugh. But it was like a little routine with us. A ritual.

Anyway, I will never forget that conversation, convincing her to go to the hospital. I knew what her fears were, I think. She grew up at a time . . . now she didn't tell me this, but I worked a lot with older people and, for many of them, the hospital was where you went to die. Not that she was afraid of death, but she was a very self-sufficient person and she just wanted to be . . . talk about César being a control freak! If anybody was a control freak, it was Dorothy. She wanted to be in control. She wanted to be in control of her life, and she didn't like the hospital.

The only other time she went to the hospital was very close to when she died. And I remember being there with her. I was on one side of the bed and Tamar was on the other side and we were combing her hair, and it was falling out like it does, and she looked at me and she said, "Can I go home?" So I talked to the resident. He's talking about her renal functions being this or that. (You know how they are. It's like a cookbook. They want to make sure your numbers are right.) So I talked to her attending [physician] and basically we got her out the next day. She never left Maryhouse again.

I knew when to push her, and I knew when to do what she wanted, and we were friends. She trusted me. I remember telling her that first time when she didn't want to go to the hospital . . . I never like to blackmail or threaten patients. I try never, never to do that, but I felt so strongly. Because her lung was half full of fluid, and she had to have the fluid taken out of her. She wasn't going to live if she didn't go to the hospital. I told her . . . I almost don't like to even tell you this, but what I really let it get down to is that we couldn't be real friends if she wouldn't let me do what I had to do as a person who was responsible. And I said, "You're going to make it really hard, Dorothy. How can I be your doctor if you won't do what I'm telling you has to be done?"

It wasn't ethics but much more. It was friendship. It was important to Dorothy that we be friends. And that's what I said. "As your friend and your doctor." If it were professional ethics, I'd just pull the doctor crap and say, "You do this or . . . " That's why I took so long. It took three hours to [have her] see things differently. It was hard for her because she was afraid. She didn't want to leave. I was always very honest with her about how sick she was. And she knew that. The valves just weren't working, and her heart was really big and not pumping right. She knew and understood all this.

Well, that's what it was like to have Dorothy for a patient! But she was wonderful. I remember I used to call her almost every day, and I'd see her every week toward the end. Frank would call me sometimes and say, "You always cheer Dorothy up. She's so blue, but then you talk to her." I'd never go unless I knew I had two or three hours, though, because that's what she liked. Sometimes we would just sit there. She always wanted to hear about César and the union, but what she talked about even more was the suffragists. The women's vote. She talked a lot about that.

Her life was winding down. The two things that she talked about the most were her family and what it was like growing up. She tended to talk about the same things over and over again, such as their being in San Francisco at the time of the big earthquake. She'd talk about her bed rolling across the floor. She talked about her family, especially her sister Della. She didn't talk as much about her mother as she did about her father, and she talked about traveling in the South. She talked about Chicago more than almost any other place. Just loved living in that city. Told me about sitting around the table with all the kids and listening to opera. Family things.

She used to talk about Mike Gold, too. She told me he really fell for her and wanted to marry her. I guess he was after her for the longest time. And she told me she had the abortion and also that she took an overdose. Tried to kill herself with laudanum. She told me that. *(Pause.)*

I remember one year I was there all of Holy Week. It was probably in 1975, and I remember we were driving to . . . I think it was St. Joseph's Church in the Village. It was Kathleen Jordan, Dorothy, someone else, and I. Dorothy said, "I used to go to this church with Eugene O'Neill's first wife." I said, "Well, now you're stuck with us, Dorothy. You're really coming down in the world." [She and O'Neill] had been very close, and she'd sit up with him all night when he was drunk.

I'll never forget one of the last times I saw her. I can still see her, sitting in that chair in the corner and saying, "Why does it take so long to die?"

LAST DAYS

One can't ask for a wider embrace at the end.
—MICHAEL HARANK

Dorothy Day died on Saturday, November 29, 1980, at approximately 5:36 P.M. Her daughter, Tamar, was with her. Michael Harank talks of her death, the preparations for the funeral, and the celebration itself:

I think she made a very conscious decision. None of us knows when we're going to die, but I think that her own spiritual practice of prayer is what enabled her to maintain a sense of dignity. There was no fear and there was no panic, but instead a real sense of playfulness. Being able to be in her own room and surrounded by the books that she loved so dearly and all the little things that people had given to her over the years. And, of course, surrounded by her friends and family. One can't ask for a wider embrace at the end.

I had worked the day shift as a nursing assistant at St. Rose's Home and was having a cup of tea in the dining room when Kathy Clarkson came in and said, "I think something has happened to Dorothy." So I went upstairs. Dorothy had evidently fallen on the floor of the bathroom, and by the time I got there, the people who had immediately responded had gotten her onto the bed. And she had clearly died.

When I entered the room, there was a Jesuit priest from Nativity, and Tamar and Frank [Donovan] and Peggy [Scherer]. Then there was myself and Kathy Clarkson and Kassie Temple, and I think a few other people. There was a tremendous reverential presence. Just a silence, a holy silence, honoring the fact that Dorothy had taken her last breath on earth. There was a vigil light, and we prayed the Office of the Dead at that point, and said the Our Father, and gathered around the room. But there was just an incredible stillness. I really felt the presence of God in the magnificent way in which Dorothy had died. With such dignity and surrounded by her friends.

She had spoken to me about how grateful she was to be able to be with her own mother when she had died, and I think her only wish, really, was that her daughter could be with her when she herself died. And Tamar was there. That prayer was answered.

We didn't know when it would happen, of course, but we knew it was going to happen soon. And here it was. It had happened. It was a time of sorrow but also of celebration and gratitude, and of the intimate presence of God and friends and family in that room where she had spent the last five years of her life. It was at dusk, and the light from the windows was shining through, and she was on her bed, very still.

After that, we kept vigil. No one ever left her body alone. Of course, all kinds of things happen when someone dies in the house—all the legal things—and that took quite a few hours. During that time various people came to keep vigil with Dorothy's body and also to keep vigil with Tamar. I remember going in a few times after a number of us had gotten together and shared the responsibility of calling various people to tell them that Dorothy had died.

Tamar had known that Dorothy was going to die soon, and that was why she had made commitments to stay at Maryhouse with her. I remember her crying, but they were quiet tears. And in the Irish tradition of mourning, there were moments of silence and there were moments when stories were told. Of course, it was quite busy with preparations, contacting the coroner, the funeral director, and all of that. But it was a very, very intimate moment.

Sister Mary Kimball washed her and prepared her body for the undertaker, and they came around midnight, or it may have been later. That was a hard part—the strapping, the putting into the bag. If I remember correctly, there was somewhat of a candlelight procession. The vigil light that was burning in the room was taken, and I forget who it was who brought her down, but there was a solemn finality. After the funeral directors took her to the funeral home, there was a real sense of emptiness in the house. The women in the house knew at that point that Dorothy had died, and there was a reverential silence among them. Not one problem in the house that night because they were very much aware that Miss Day, as they affectionately called her, had passed on.

Oh, one little funny thing . . . nobody remembered to tell the funeral home that there was to be no makeup. We had a moment of brief levity, and I think it was Jane [Sammon] who said, "Oh, my God! We have to call the funeral director and tell them not to use makeup!" The thought of Dorothy coming back made up like some mannequin was horrendous and yet funny at the same time.

Well, she came back in the pine casket, unvarnished but finished. Modeled after the casket of Orthodox Jews. The casket was carried into the chapel at Maryhouse, where she had spent many an hour praying. I don't think Dorothy ever came downstairs without making a quick stop in the chapel where the Blessed Sacrament was present, so we decided that was where her body would be laid out. The casket was placed upon that gorgeous, cedar altar. The chapel is probably one of the smallest rooms in the house, but it has two doors [so people could go through and out].

Dorothy was dressed in the famous blue-checkered dress, the dress that she loved. And she had her blue kerchief on with her braids in a bun. Because she was not made up, she looked very much as she had in life. Being eighty-three and having lost so much weight over the years, her bone structure was very, very frail. But it was outstanding. There was a kind of sculptured look to her face, a face that had seen the love of God.

People came to say goodbye. Some people spent hours with her; some people spent a few minutes. Many left little things in the casket. The forgotten and the famous—Daniel Berrigan was there and Eileen Egan. There was a whole stream of people—people who lived in the house, people from the street, people who had come from far away. César Chávez came from California with his wife, Helen, and I. F. Stone came all the way up from Washington, riding a bus.

There was only one day and one night of the wake, if I remember correctly. And, as I said, the atmosphere in the house was one of celebration of Dorothy's life, a remembering of the stories, remembering what had really changed the lives of many people. Storytelling takes mourning and turns it into an art form, and I think that's basically what happened for that thirty-six hours from the time she died until the funeral. People floated in and out of the dining room and had tea and told their stories of Dorothy.

Terry Rogers was a chalice bearer at the funeral and remembers especially "people coming home, coming back, being open to one another in sort of subtle but very special ways. Just a time for people to give thanks, to . . . to emphasize forgiveness." Almost everyone who came to the funeral remembers it as very much a family reunion and a uniting of folks from around the country who had been touched by Dorothy.

The late Michael Harrington recalled:

It was the damnedest funeral I've ever seen. I went to the wake the night before and saw lots of people from my "class." (People were sort of grouped by when they were at the Worker.) She was in a box, which I'm sure violated absolutely all the rules of New York, but nobody was going to tell the Worker not to do it. It was announced that the funeral the next morning would be private, that only family could go to the funeral. A bunch of us were standing around, and we all said, "No way!" The next morning about three hundred people showed up, and they didn't know what to do, so they finally said, "Well, we ask you to decide for yourself. Only those people who consider themselves part of the family should fall in behind the coffin." Whereupon, of course, everybody fell in. I also loved the funeral because the recessional was

"A Mighty Fortress Is Our God." I thought, "Leave it to the Catholic Worker! Here is this woman who's going to be a Catholic saint, and the recessional is a hymn by Martin Luther!"

Michael Harank recalls further:

It was also a very busy time of preparations, with lots of different responsibilities for the food at the reception afterward, and for the mechanics of the funeral, which were not that complicated, actually.[2] Choosing the music, that kind of thing. (I was not involved in that at all.) There wasn't a sense of rushing around and chaos, though, but instead a quiet presence, a quiet, reverential presence from the moment she died right up until she was laid to rest. There was a sign on the door that said, "The house is closed today due to a death in the family." Some of the Workers went around the neighborhood and collected candles from people, and they melted them down to represent people from the neighborhood that she had touched and who loved her. Made it into the big candle that I carried in the procession.

I remember getting up the morning of the funeral and being amazed that it was such an unusually warm day for December. The procession began at Maryhouse, and Tamar was there with Forster and with the grandchildren who were the pall bearers. And Dorothy's brother, John Day, and a woman whose name I can't remember. I had the honor of carrying the paschal candle, which led the procession to Nativity Church, just around the corner. The woman who was in charge of the clothing room at Maryhouse found me this wonderful three-piece suit to wear.

As the procession began, following me was a Franciscan friar— Bill—and one of the Little Brothers of Jesus—Brother Peter—and then the six grandchildren carrying the casket with Dorothy and then the family. Everyone else fell in and marched behind Tamar and John and Forster.

I remembered how Dorothy loved the processions that went through the streets of the Lower East Side—the religious processions of the Italian, Polish, and Ukrainian communities. But usually caskets were not

---

[2] Father Hugo had planned to give the homily at Dorothy's funeral, had already written it, in fact. But Tamar was adamant that Dominican priest Geoffrey Gneuhs, a member of the Maryhouse community, should say the Mass. She said to the Workers, "If Father Hugo does it, I won't come." It appears the Chancery wanted Cardinal Cooke to say the Mass and was trying to get the funeral moved up an hour to fit his schedule. But Tamar said, "Well, we can't make it earlier because then the people who work and eat on the soup line won't be able to come." So the family and the Worker got the funeral they wanted. The cardinal later gave Dorothy a memorial Mass at St. Patrick's Cathedral.

carried from the house to the church, so this was a very unusual experience. There was something very earthy about it. She had made that journey so often, going to Mass at Nativity on Sundays and sometimes during the week, when she was still able to get out.

It was a wonderful procession of friends and family, with many people looking out their windows and others stopping in the street. When we were almost right in front of the church, Cardinal Cooke came up to greet the coffin and to bless it.

But oh . . . just as we were turning the corner, this man came running up. He was quite disheveled, and clearly not in his right mind in some ways, and he just dashed up to the casket. Ordinarily, one would think that when something like this would happen, there would be a bit of chaos and panic. But I think the grandchildren who were carrying the casket knew that this man was in many ways symbolic of the friends of Dorothy throughout the years. He was poor and homeless and suffering from mental illness. The grandchildren stopped, which was a very moving thing, and I remember he went right up to the casket and simply touched it. It was over very quickly, but you could see people were nervous about what was happening. But all he did was go up, touch it, and then he left. One of the "ambassadors of Christ," as Peter used to call them. After that, the cardinal blessed the casket and left, and the procession proceeded into the church.

The family was seated to the left in the front. On the right, the benches had been reserved for the people at Maryhouse and Peter Maurin Farm and St. Joseph House. There was no sense of holding special places for the famous and well-known.[3] I remember coming down and putting the paschal candle next to the altar, and I remember seeing, first thing, César Chávez and his wife, Helen, who were in the middle of the church. And Monsignor Egan from Chicago, and the Episcopal Bishop Paul Moore. (Dorothy had been a very close friend of Jenny Moore, his wife, who had passed away from cancer just a few months before.) Paul Moore was the only bishop that I could see at Dorothy Day's funeral. He was dressed in his colorful episcopal robes, but there was no special place reserved for him, as there was no special place for anybody except for the people of the Catholic Worker community and the family.

---

[3] Betty Bartelme told me: "*Everybody* went to the funeral! I was kind of holding back from joining the Catholic Worker procession to the church, but Michael Harrington came up and grabbed me, so I sat with him and Frank Sheed. When the people in our pew went to communion, one of the ladies from Maryhouse lay down in the empty pew and took a nap. So it was a true Catholic Worker funeral."

Mass was celebrated that day with a real sense of gratitude. I could see in my mind's eye images of her kneeling in that church, with that real sense of reverential solitude and quiet. But at the funeral there was also a sense of real celebration. And the Eucharist . . . the Transfiguration for me was actualized, really incarnated, for me when I saw Forster take communion. I remember that. It was really a powerful moment in the love story between . . . God invites everyone to the table, and I think that was a very special moment in Forster's life. I think he . . . it was a way of expressing his love for Dorothy. Those loves don't disappear, and for me at that point, that was just the most tender and intimate act of love that he could have exhibited.

After the closing hymn the procession filed out in a slow, contemplative way. There was nothing rushed about anything at the funeral, which was really quite wonderful. And the New York Police Department had provided the Number One police car to escort the procession to Resurrection Cemetery on Staten Island. It was a way for New York to say "thank you," but kind of an ironic honor because they had imprisoned her so many times.

The cars didn't go over on the ferry; they went out over the Verrazano Narrows Bridge. When we got to the cemetery, it was still this very beautiful, unusually warm day, with a clear sky. You could smell the saltiness in the air, something that Dorothy always loved about Staten Island. Whether it was smelling the sea on the sheets at the bungalow, or taking a walk, she would always say something about the salt air. They'd put some fake grass at the grave site, which was kind of silly, but the casket was laid on top of the grave by the grandchildren. I stood with the paschal candle at the foot of the casket. At that point Geoffrey Gneuhs said the prayers of committal, and then I sang the "Benedictus," which was Dorothy's favorite song and sung every night at Vespers. It goes like this: *(Sings.)*

At last, all powerful Master, you give me to your servant to go
In peace according to your promise
For mine eyes have seen your salvation.
A light to enlighten the Gentiles,
And give glory to your people Israel.

Then they lowered the coffin into the ground. Traditionally, they ask family and friends to leave during that part. But the cemetery workers, whom Dorothy had supported in the famous Catholic cemetery strike of the 1950s, were called over to lower the casket with everybody still watching. There was something very important to that. I could visualize the scenes from Russian novels, you know, the Russian

Dorothy's funeral procession leaving Maryhouse.

burials where people stayed and watched the body going into the ground.

Forster took a rose from one of the floral arrangements and tossed it into the grave. Then people were invited to take a shovel and to place some dirt on her casket. I remember hearing the sound of the dirt hitting the casket, the thud of the dirt.

Marion Moses remembers this stark final committal as well:

At the cemetery, the light was very clear, and the grass really looked green. It was the first time I'd been to a [grave site] where they didn't have everything all covered up. We could see the hole. The workers actually put the coffin down into the hole with a rope, and I thought, "My God, that's deep!" I remember seeing the coffin going all the way down, with the light getting darker.

Geoffrey Gneuhs, at the time a Dominican priest who served as chaplain at the Catholic Worker, gave the eulogy at Dorothy Day's funeral. He was also an associate editor of the *Catholic Worker* for several years. An artist, he lives today in New York City. Here are his memories of the wake and the grave site:

Among so many who came to her wake and funeral, I especially remember Frank Sheed, who with his wife, Maisie Ward, had been dear, dear friends of Dorothy. Frank was as old, if not older, than Dorothy. (Maisie had died about five years earlier.) He arrived in his signature rumpled suit, with his wispy hair and ruddy face. To me, he had a W. C. Fields look about him, although he was a teetotaler. I escorted him to the chapel where the coffin was placed on the altar. He stood before the coffin for the longest time. There was a line of visitors stretching out to Second Avenue, yet I couldn't dare move him on. Tears were streaming down his face, and he was talking quietly to Dorothy. Saying his farewell. Nearly five decades of being pilgrims together.

On the funeral day I was robed in the full Dominican habit with the black cappa. As we were placing the coffin into the ground, three greyhound dogs suddenly appeared, frolicking and dancing around, an almost playful relief to the solemn moment, the final moment. With a trowel I put dirt onto the coffin and turned to a Dominican colleague, Father Regis Ryan. "The greyhounds!" I knew he caught the uncanny symbolism. A greyhound with a torch is a symbol of the Dominican Order, "the dogs of the Lord." It's a play on the Latin words *Domini canes*. Three stands for the Trinity, of course. And Dorothy often recounted how Eugene O'Neill in a drunken stupor could recite to her Francis Thompson's "The Hound of Heaven." In *The Long Loneliness* she wrote that all of her life she had been haunted, hounded by God. At the grave site I thought, she's no longer "hounded." Instead, the hounds were dancing, rejoicing in celebration. Dorothy was home.

EPILOGUE

After Dorothy

It never rubs off. If you've ever lived at the Worker and been under Miss Day's influence, you can't shake it. You're haunted forever.

—Joe Zarrella

When Dorothy Day died in 1980, reporters asked *Catholic Worker* editor Peggy Scherer what would happen. "We may have lost Dorothy, but we still have the gospel." she replied. This sentiment was echoed by many people who reflected on her legacy.

According to Shelley Douglass of Mary House in Baton Rouge:

She believed it was both necessary and possible to live the gospel, to live it now. And in doing that she provided a cradle for the entire movement for peace and justice in the United States, not just the Catholic peace movement. The number of activists who came through the Catholic Worker . . . It's incredible. In fact, maybe that's the most important legacy—all of us. All the people who look to her for guidance and light and try to translate what she was all about into our own lives.

Historian David O'Brien told me wryly that his line in *Commonweal* about her being the most interesting and influential Catholic in the twentieth century has been quoted more than anything he's ever written. He sees as particularly important Dorothy's idea of keeping a critical distance from contemporary American culture instead of the adapting and embracing seen in much of mainstream Roman Catholicism.

Father Mike Baxter, C.S.C., a theologian at the University of Notre Dame, would agree. He told me in 1987:

The beauty of Dorothy Day was that she took seriously what everyone *says* they believe in Catholicism. She and Peter Maurin weren't starting anything; they handed on a tradition.

BILL BARRETT

Her response was always practical and concrete, always very clear that you try to love that person because he or she is Christ here and now. The "realists" and all the "big picture" people who say the Catholic Worker just does a band-aid operation don't comprehend that the purpose will be vindicated in the kingdom of God.

You know, it used to drive Dorothy Day crazy when people would give that band-aid analogy. And the reason, I think, is because a lot of the people who were criticizing weren't doing anything concrete for the poor. And also, there was just this incredible lack of faith—that what we do now to hand this person a piece of bread would have any eternal meaning.

The people I interviewed realize that since Vatican II, the Catholic Worker is not the only peace and justice movement in the United States. As Nina Polcyn Moore points out:

It is the age of the laity, when people are taking personal responsibility, something which the Worker emphasizes. Dorothy always said we didn't need to ask a priest if we could do something, we just did it. This healthy independence has paved the way for so many creative things in the church. The quest for peace, the work with the poor—all this has been made respectable by the Catholic Worker being the forerunner. Labor unions and all the work to nourish these little sprouts of goodness. This to me has been . . . I don't think we would have gotten as far in our social conscience without Dorothy and the Catholic Worker.

Julian Pleasants, a pioneer Catholic Worker who taught chemistry at Notre Dame and co-founded the first Catholic Worker house in South Bend, compares Dorothy's presence at Notre Dame in his early years with today:

Years ago, when Dorothy used to talk at Notre Dame, the university didn't want outside people to know she was here. They were willing to have their students exposed to her, but they . . . I think they were afraid of losing contributors.

Now students read *The Long Loneliness* as part of their core curriculum, and I come in to talk about it with them. Many of them don't see the point at all. They figure everything's been taken care of. Ha!

As a counterpoint to Julian's experiences, Johannah Hughes Turner remembers:

When I was young, there was a feeling that Catholic Worker was the same as communist or something. People didn't comprehend, and they thought that it must be something horrible. So I was very surprised to discover that it has become so mainstreamed. I mean, people half my age will say, "Oh, Dorothy Day! They told us about her in high school." And if people find out I grew up in the Worker, they want to hear more and more. They think it's pretty special.

Dorothy's old friend Joe Zarrella points out:

Even though Dorothy is respected, she's still controversial. She'd be a hero to everyone if she'd just practiced the works of mercy. And that's the difference between Dorothy and Mother Teresa. Mother Teresa helped the people who are hurt in society, but she didn't attack the institutions that hurt the people she's helping. Dorothy helped the people and also attacked the system.

It seems clear, however, that more people are learning of Dorothy Day and the movement she and Peter Maurin founded. In fact, some practicing Catholic Workers worry that the relative mainstreaming of Dorothy's message has made the Catholic Worker too respectable. Mark White, whom I interviewed in 1987 when he was a member of the Los Angeles Catholic Worker community, is typical of these young people. He comments:

All the conferences, all the books being written about Dorothy, all the people with her picture on the walls of their condominiums. There's a danger that the tradition will be ossified, even within the movement. Now, I'm not saying I have the Catholic Worker orthodox party line, but you see houses now that are nonprofit, tax-exempt corporations. They've made very pragmatic decisions, saying they can serve more people better if they take state money.

The late Eileen Egan also worried that Dorothy's message would be applied by those who would stray from the teachings of the Roman Catholic Church and said she prayed that the fruits of Dorothy's work "wouldn't be imperiled by people in the Worker who have an agenda that differs from that of the church in general."

Would the Worker movement have been different if Dorothy had appointed another strong leader to take her place? Robert Steed, once a member of the New York community, commented that she didn't set it up that way and that she relied on Providence, saying, "These things happen of their own accord." Mary Lathrop, also a member of the New York community, remembers:

People would always ask what was going to happen when Dorothy left us. Everybody seemed to want someone just like her, and the fact of the matter is (that's a phrase she used to say), there is only one Dorothy.

However, John Williams of the Seattle Family Kitchen, Seattle, says:

You know, when Dorothy died, people were quick to say, "Poof! That's the end of the Catholic Worker!" But today, houses are just mushrooming all over the place. That's great because it means it really wasn't [just] Dorothy.

The New York community inevitably feels Dorothy's influence more than the other houses in the movement. Jane Sammon, who lived and traveled with Dorothy during her final years, discusses the "Dorothy says" syndrome:

Whether it's St. Ignatius, or Dorothy, or St. Francis, or our fathers, we can't freeze them into some kind of . . . "Well, that's what they said." But we also have to realize that for some reason, these souls were chosen and given this gift. It doesn't mean that they were gods, but they had a wisdom we need to be aware of. For instance, no one will ever convince me that usury is something the Catholic Worker ought to dismiss as irrelevant now that Dorothy and Peter are dead. I don't think that means, though, that there aren't going to be problems with that. Or that we may use only the founding voice and dismiss other good voices.

Nina Moore concludes:

The people in the Catholic Worker houses will have to live with each other, grow with each other, suffer each other, help each other out of whatever confusions they have because a person like Dorothy is almost impossible to duplicate. Maybe nobody will ever want those boots.

SAINTHOOD

Whether she ever becomes a saint or not, she'll always be St. Dorothy to me.

—FELICIA CARRANO CARL

Even during her lifetime, people would talk about Dorothy's becoming an official saint in the church, a discussion Dorothy heard with consternation. Joe Hughes used to tease her: "When you die, they'll be selling relics before you're cold!" One of her most oft-quoted lines was "Don't call me a saint; I don't want to be dismissed that easily." Pat Jordan tells us:

She knew that some people wanted to call her a saint while she was still living, and she thought that was a way of letting themselves off the hook: "Dorothy can do these things, because she's a saint."

She had little patience with people who came only to worship. Brian Terrell explains:

Nobody hurt Dorothy more than people who would hold her hand and look into her eyes and say, "Dorothy Day, I've always wanted to meet you; I've admired you my whole life." And she'd say, "I'm not feeling well. I'm going upstairs." What she'd often do in those situations is tell people, "Join the work." She'd say to us, "If they were really interested, they wouldn't want to talk to me, an old lady who lives upstairs; they'd want to talk to the people who were doing the work."

Dorothy made me understand the gospel story of the rich young man who comes to Jesus and says, "Good Master." And Jesus says, "Why are you calling me good?" I've heard all kinds of commentaries on that, but Dorothy taught me something that I've never seen in any book—that this person thought that he was doing something for Jesus by saying, "You're so good." Jesus didn't want that. So Jesus puts it on the line: "Give away everything you have and come follow me." Put your money where your mouth is. You're not doing me any good, and you're not doing yourself any good if you're saying "Good Master" when you're not planning on changing anything in your life.

That's how Dorothy reacted to the people who would canonize her before her time, who really felt like they were doing something special for her by admiring her, and that Dorothy must be getting kicks out of this but was too humble to show it. And of course this made her even higher in their estimation. But there's something dehumanizing and violent in that. I would see her recoil. It wasn't just humility; I think she really understood that this personality cult wasn't going to help the movement and wasn't going to help these people in their own spiritual lives. It certainly wasn't doing her any good.

Yet such veneration *did* occur, and Mary Farren reports that at the funeral people would surreptitiously press their rosaries against the casket. People visit her grave on Staten Island, some coming in remembrance of someone they loved, some making what we could call a pilgrimage.

As a small child, Felicia Carrano Carl knew Dorothy when they lived in the same building on Mott Street:

There's a small headstone, just the way she would want it. (She wasn't one for a big show.) I always put flowers on her grave. In fact, I put a small statue of St. Joseph the Worker there, too, and it stayed for about two years. Then the lawn mower came along and broke it, and I felt so bad because I haven't been able to replace it. But she knows my thoughts and prayers are with her.

Pat Jordan told me: "She took seriously the idea that we are all called to be saints, and she wasn't embarrassed about saying that. She'd often quote Leon Bloy: 'There is only one sadness—not to be a saint.'" It isn't the concept of sainthood that bothers her friends; it's what Margaret Magee calls "the riga-ma-roll" surrounding the process and the tendency toward trivialization that often accompanies official status. Jane Sammon says that Dorothy wanted to subvert the notion that "sanctity was plastic that could melt in front of the fire" and worries that canonization might become revisionism, with memories of her life "sanitized." John Magee referred to this tendency toward hagiography in a 1988 interview: "When you read the lives of the saints, they never did anything wrong. And yet one knows the life was a struggle all the way through." Jeanette Noel, long-time Worker, both in Massachusetts and at Maryhouse, dismisses these worries: "Sure, Dorothy will be sanitized and changed. It happens to everyone who's done a lot of good. Look at poor St. Francis—he'd never recognize his place!"

Some worry that a canonization would be used politically in ways inimical to her wishes. In 1998 the late John Cardinal O'Connor decided to officially begin the cause of canonization after meeting several times with people who had been close to Dorothy. In March 2000 her cause was officially accepted by the Vatican and she was declared "a servant of God," the first stage in the process of canonization. The official pronouncement by the U.S. bishops seemed to characterize her as a penitent sinner, perhaps giving the idea that she could be used to persuade people who had left the church because of divorce or abortion to "come home."

Shortly before his death Michael Harrington told me, "Sure, she'll be canonized. As a matter of fact, I'm sort of terrified that this pope might figure out that she's a perfect saint from his point of view. Because she's a political and social radical and a totally conservative, orthodox, and obedient daughter of the church."

Saint-making is a long and complex procedure and can require a great deal of money. Mary Lathrop has an interesting story about Dorothy's attitude toward the process:

Now I'm the only one who would know this, because it was just Dorothy and me alone in her room. But anyway, this was in 1975, in the fall. I'd been down to Baltimore for the canonization of Mother Seton. And after I came back, I was visiting with Dorothy, and she had, I think, a copy of the *Wall Street Journal*, with a front-page story about how much it had cost the Sisters of Charity for the canonization process. And it was $7 million! I asked Dorothy . . . and I don't know how exactly I put the question, but I said, "Well, when the time comes, how much should we put into the kitty?" It was a little bit of a joke, but at the same time . . . Well, she gave a little smile and said, "Oh, about fifteen thousand." Fifteen thousand total from the Catholic Worker. Total. But I think she was smiling because, you know, the church can do things without all that.

Notwithstanding the logistics, many who were close to her speak in favor of official sainthood. Robert Ellsberg points out universal reasons:

Dorothy is a real saint of what Cardinal Bernardin called the "common ground." She challenges the reformers and social activists to maintain their love for the church and the gospel. She challenges conservatives to be attentive to the radical social dimensions of the gospel. She challenges both sides to resolve differences with mutual respect and love, for the benefit of the world.

I think Dorothy had a strong sense of her own sins, her weaknesses and failures. Her standards were so high that her failures stood out all the more sharply. But she had all the more sense of God's grace, of what it meant to be forgiven. Her gravestone has the words "Deo Gratias," as she had requested. She had such a sense of gratitude, a sense that what she had done was because of grace. This was one reason she didn't like to be called a saint, which implied that she deserved all the credit for what she had done. She believed she was responsible for her failures; everything else was due to God.

Jim Forest also speaks in favor of Dorothy's canonization, while addressing some of her worries:

She should be canonized precisely because Dorothy makes sanctity accessible to people. Her canonization would change our idea of what we understand by the word *saint*. If Dorothy can be a saint, probably anybody can be a saint. She wasn't copying anybody. Little by little, she just became free to be Dorothy Day. And she did that out of a lot of wreckage. She never felt good about that herself, in some ways, but she did it.

I think Dorothy felt ashamed that in *The Long Loneliness* she had not been able to reveal some important events in her life that she felt remorse about, as was also the case with Merton in *The Seven Storey Mountain*. Both of them had hidden very important facts, probably both for similar reasons—partly out of shame but also partly because it was clear at the time that, had they written about those things, those aspects of their past would have dominated the perceptions in such a way that people would have just said, "Look, this is Dorothy Day who had an abortion," or, "Look, this is the Thomas Merton who fathered an out-of-wedlock child when he was a college student." But whatever the reasons were, Dorothy certainly felt ashamed and guilty about her omissions in that book, felt she had created an image of herself that was misleading, so that very few people knew the truth about some of this past that she found terribly important—and that if they did know, perhaps they wouldn't be so quick to throw a halo on her.

Dorothy would speak of her worries about the self she presented. Michael Boover met Dorothy while he was a student at Worcester State College. He told her he had read her autobiography, *The Long Loneliness*, and she said in reply, "You know, when you write a book you put yourself down [on paper] and you can't change it. Sometimes you want to, but you can't." Mary Durnin, who knew Dorothy well, says she's glad she knows the whole Dorothy, even the parts omitted from the autobiography, and says, "Knowing Dorothy's dark side, I can live with my own."

People who identify strongly with the movement Dorothy and Peter Maurin founded may feel they have the most at stake in the canonization question. Jim Forest:

I think it's important for the Catholic Worker not to treat Dorothy as private property. She belongs to the human race. It's not for us to say yes or no or try to act as policemen of the process; we only have to be truthful about who she was and not attached to the consequences. All the religious orders have survived the canonization of their founders. Maybe the Catholic Worker can, too. In point of fact, the Catholic Worker is more . . . is better defended against the problems of institutionalization than most movements.

Some think the sins of her pre-conversion life would militate against canonization, but Tom Cornell reminds us to the contrary:

Nothing matters about the pre-conversion life. Absolutely nothing. Her pre-conversion history will not color the church's judgment of her. [William] Miller in his biography indicated that there was a period of some real turmoil that manifested itself in a possible suicide attempt, and also, uh . . . involvement with a lot of men. And the abortion. Dorothy did not want to have those elements of her past made known, not because they were embarrassing for her, but because she felt it would give license to other people.

In that she is like all the saints. St. Francis of Assisi used to say, "Francis is the worst sinner in the world." Now we might think he was being hypocritical, but he wasn't. The closer that you get to God, the more you see your failures to be what God wants you to be. And of course, pride is always a danger. You can lose yourself in thinking that you're holy or thinking that you're saved. None of the saints were without sin.

The miracles required by the church to put the stamp of authenticity on holiness seem superfluous to those I interviewed and no one mentioned them, except in jest.[1] It was almost as if they're ashamed that the church would require such outmoded evidence. Agnes Bird McCormack speaks for many when she writes that Dorothy wouldn't even have wanted people to speculate about it: "She might be [canonized] and she might not be, but it doesn't make a whit of difference." Chuck Matthei also said she wouldn't have been concerned or wanting us to waste our time "arguing for or against the process. She would have let it take its course." Father Richard McSorley told me years ago:

If we had canonizations like they used to, through the will of the people or the voice of the people, we'd already have it. I'm sure if Dorothy had anything to say about miracles being attributed to her, she'd be against it. There might already be miracles from her intercession,

---

[1] Brian Terrell: "You've heard the story about the first Dorothy miracle, haven't you? A whole lot of people from Catholic Worker houses around the country came in for her funeral, of course. The night before the Mass, a bunch of us went out to one of those old Ukrainian bars and got really, really smashed. Not just tipsy but fraternity party drunk. Stomping on tables, that kind of thing. Well, nobody was hung over the next morning. Nobody! A couple of hours after we left the bar, we were all up, surprised to see each other around the coffee pot. Everyone was feeling fine! And somebody said it was Dorothy's first miracle."

but given the kind of person she was, she'd hide them from the public.[2]

Donna Conroy of New York City may have spoken for many when she wrote the following in April 2002 on a Catholic Worker website forum regarding whether Dorothy Day should be canonized:

When I look at her life, it gives me great hope and encouragement and I say, "Yes! Of course Dorothy Day is a saint!" But I find the process of canonization distasteful, with all the miracles and the money needed to verify them. It seems so far removed from the witness of her life.

So instead, I find myself wishing that these "official miracles" could be about justice and peace and reconciliation and food for all. Wouldn't it be a miracle if through her [intercession), we ceased the Cuban embargo or forgave all nations' debts or all governors declared a moratorium on the death penalty, or racial hatred and killing would cease? I think Dorothy Day wouldn't mind at all being associated with these miracles!

Two people have told me they asked Dorothy specifically to pray for someone who was in need of prayers—Robert Coles and Anne Perkins, who is a deacon in the Episcopal church. Anne says, "When you think about it, how many people do you know of whom you'd say, 'My prayers aren't good enough, but yours would be?'" Hers would get through, so to speak.

Tom Cornell concludes in a definitive voice:

Our kids will go to Rome and see Dorothy canonized, and the church will be in a position to make the gospel creditable again because of Dorothy. People will read her because of this recognition. Her writings will be widely available, and the meaning of her life—the meaning of her message—won't be obscured. Her writing is too clear for that. Her wit is too clear for that.

She's an instrument in God's plan. There's no doubt about it. She's not going to be neutered by a bunch of ecclesiastics. They couldn't do it, even if they wanted to, because the record is there. She will be canonized, and she will continue to be a thorn in the side of church and state. But she'll be the glory of the church, too.

---

[2] Michael Harrington said to me in 1988, "It crossed my mind when I got my second cancer, and I thought it would wreck my ideological life, but if Dorothy wanted to cure my cancer . . . " Note that Michael didn't say he prayed to her. And I didn't ask those I interviewed if they did.

Selected Biographies

Betty Bartelme was formerly a senior editor at Doubleday and the Macmillan Company. She was also an adjunct full professor at Hofstra University and has produced many paintings in an abstract mode.

Dan Berrigan, S.J., is a poet and activist priest who counts Dorothy Day as one of his most potent influences. He was interviewed for this book by Jim Loney of Toronto.

Ade Bethune (1914–2002) was a liturgical artist and art director who designed the masthead for the *Catholic Worker* and contributed many graphics to the paper. Broadly skilled as a sculptor, painter, mosaic artist, wood carver, and metal worker, she worked from her studio in Newport, Rhode Island, until her recent death.

Michael Boover lived and worked for a decade at the Mustard Seed Catholic Worker in Worcester and also spent some time at the Worker farm in Sheep Ranch, California. He now lives out the vision on the edge of Worcester where he and his wife Diane raise children, cabbages, tomatoes, and chickens.

Felicia Carrano Carl spent her childhood on Mott Street in the same building that housed the Catholic Worker. In recent years her son David was a Worker at Maryhouse.

Vivian Cherry is a photographer whose work on Dorothy Day was published in *Jubilee* and in the French edition of *The Long Loneliness*. In 2000 she was featured in a one-woman show at the Brooklyn Museum of Art. Her photographs in this book add richness to the memories of Dorothy Day.

Walt Chura ran Simple Gifts, a Catholic Worker bookstore and community center in Albany, New York, from 1976 to 1987. He now teaches, writes, and directs retreats on the Worker, Thomas Merton, and the Shakers.

Sister Peter Claver, a member of the Mission Servants of the Most Blessed Trinity, is a centenarian-plus who has always worked for justice, particularly for African Americans. Dorothy Day has written that Sister Peter contributed the first dollar to the Catholic Worker.

Richard Cleaver arrived at St. Joseph's in New York in 1976, "unexpectedly, reluctantly, and in a defensive mood; served a postulancy that now appears to have been the time of his life; and went on in 1978 to further spiritual formation, still uncompleted." He is the author of *New Heaven, New Earth: Practical Essays on the Catholic Worker Program* and *Know My Name: A Gay Liberation Theology.*

Robert Coles is a writer, psychiatrist, and Harvard professor. Among his many books are *Dorothy Day: A Radical Devotion* and *A Spectacle unto the World: The Catholic Worker Movement*.

Tom Cornell has been a Catholic Worker activist since 1953. An ordained deacon, he lives with his wife, Monica, and son, Thomas Christopher, at Peter Maurin Farm in Marlboro, New York. He is the co-editor of *A Penny a Copy: Readings from* The Catholic Worker.

John Cort was a Catholic Worker in Manhattan until 1938. Since then he has been "a recovered TB patient, journalist, union activist, official in the Peace Corps, Catholic socialist, troublemaker, fortunate husband, and the father of ten." Active in the Association of Catholic Trade Unionists, he is the author of *Christian Socialism* and founder of the periodical *Religious Socialism*.

Michael Cullen, founder of Casa Maria Catholic Worker in Milwaukee, was deported to his native Ireland in 1973 for his participation in a draft-board raid during the Vietnam War. He and his wife, Annette, and their large family were allowed to reenter the United States in the nineties. He currently serves as a deacon in rural Wisconsin, where he is active in the charismatic movement.

Clare Danielsson converted to Christianity as an adult, and Dorothy Day was her godmother. Clare's experiences in community at Tivoli from 1968 to 1974 became the basis for her doctorate and for Boughton Place, the educational community where she now lives.

Rachel de Aragon has worked at Good Shepherd Services for the last thirty years, providing academic and vocational guidance services for adolescent girls in foster care. Dorothy's younger brother John was married to Rachel's Aunt Tessa.

Jim Douglass is a co-founder of Mary's House in Birmingham, Alabama, and is the author of four books on the theology of nonviolence, most recently *The Nonviolent Coming of God*.

Shelley Douglass was with the Catholic Worker at Casa Maria in Milwaukee in 1970. In 1992 she co-founded Mary's House in Birmingham, Alabama, where she has lived and worked ever since.

Sheila Dugan lived at Peter Maurin farm for about six months until her marriage in 1958 to *Catholic Worker* editor Kieran Dugan. She is a mother, grandmother, and lawyer who defends civil rights demonstrators.

Mary Durnin discovered the Catholic Worker and found its theology "reminiscent of my peasant forbears." She went first to Holy Family House in Milwaukee and then to New York, where she became a friend and follower of Dorothy Day.

Eileen Egan (1911–2000) was the first lay person to work for Catholic Relief Services, serving for over thirty years. In 1962 she co-founded the American Pax Association, the harbinger of Pax Christi, USA. She was Dorothy

Day's frequent traveling companion and served as an associate editor of the *Catholic Worker* until her death. Her last book was *Peace Be with You*.

Father Harvey Egan spent time at the Worker in 1937 and 1938, when he was in the seminary. An ardent supporter of the Hugo retreats, he remained a correspondent of Dorothy's for many years as he revitalized St. Joan of Arc parish in Minneapolis.

Robert Ellsberg edited the *Catholic Worker* from 1976 to 1978. He is the author and editor of several books on saints and spiritual masters, including *Dorothy Day: Selected Writings*. He is editor-in-chief of Orbis Books.

Edgar Forand came to the Worker in 1960 and retired recently after many years of faithful service. He counts the times when Dorothy was there as "by far the most vital and happiest."

Jean Forest was associated with the Catholic Worker in the early sixties. She is currently working as a therapist in a New Jersey psychiatric hospital and involved in Hoboken politics as well as the human rights movement in Northern Ireland.

Jim Forest joined the Catholic Worker in Manhattan in 1961 after being discharged from the U.S. Navy as a conscientious objector. A writer, his books include a biography of Dorothy Day, *Love Is the Measure*. He is secretary of the Orthodox Peace Fellowship and editor of its journal, *In Communion*.

Margaret Quigley Garvey started the Davenport Catholic Worker and later married **Michael Garvey**. They "grandparented" the Catholic Worker house in South Bend, Indiana, where Michael writes for Notre Dame.

Dorothy Gauchat (1921–2000) founded Our Lady of the Wayside with her husband, Bill. This home "for children no one wanted" grew out of Bill's leadership of the Cleveland Catholic Worker.

Father Bernard Gilgun was ordained on Pentecost Sunday in 1954 and, as one of his admirers writes, he "has always been on fire with the flame of Pentecost." Noted for working for peace and racial harmony, he has celebrated weekly Mass at a Worker house for over thirty years, either at the House of Ammon in Hubbardston, Massachusetts, which he founded, or at the Mustard Seed in Worcester.

Geoffrey B. Gneuhs volunteered at the New York Catholic Worker in the summer of 1974, when he was in the Dominican seminary. He returned in 1978 and served as chaplain. An artist and writer, he lives in New York City.

Eleanor Corrigan Gosselin (1921–1990) was a pioneer Catholic Worker, attracted by Peter Maurin's ideas. Her contribution to this text is by way of a paper written by Bronwyn O'Neill, daughter of long-time Worker Roger O'Neill.

Judith Gregory lived at the Catholic Worker in New York for two years around 1960. She "never wanted to be a professional" and now lives on a small farm where she "gardens, writes, paints, spins, and sits around talking in the true Catholic Worker tradition."

Michael Harank, a registered nurse, has been involved with the Catholic Worker movement since 1977. He is the founder of Bethany House in Oakland, California, a Catholic Worker house for homeless people with AIDS, and he organized the first gay-lesbian-bisexual-transgendered meeting of Catholic Workers in 1996.

Michael Harrington (1928–1989) spent time with Dorothy at the Catholic Worker in the fifties and later became a leading socialist and writer. His book *The Other America* is credited with inspiring Lyndon Johnson's War on Poverty.

Ruth Boylston Heaney, O.S.B., is the widow of Larry Heaney, a Catholic Worker pioneer who helped to begin Milwaukee's Holy Family House in the late 1930s. In 1975 she entered Our Lady of Peace Benedictine Monastery. As a Benedictine, she has worked in the Missouri prisons for over twenty-five years, counseling prisoners and helping them to achieve justice.

Tamar Hennessy is Dorothy Day's daughter. She lives in Vermont, close to some of her nine children.

Kate Hennessy is Dorothy's youngest granddaughter. She has inherited her "granny's" writing talent as well as her winged feet.

Marjorie Crowe Hughes (1920–2000) came to the Worker in 1939. She served as Dorothy's secretary and is remembered for the nurturing role she played in the Catholic Worker communities of Newburgh, Staten Island, and Tivoli.

Harry Isbell was teaching English at Notre Dame when he met Dorothy Day in the early sixties. Now retired, he lives in San Francisco.

Pat and Kathleen Jordan met and married at the Worker in the early 1970s. After their marriage they lived in one of the Catholic Worker Staten Island bungalows, so they were able to spend time with Dorothy near the end of her life. Pat is an editor of *Commonweal* and recently published a collection of Dorothy's writing published in that magazine.

James Joyce, S.J., folded papers and took part in discussions at the Worker on Chrystie Street while still a teenager. As a priest he was stationed at nearby Nativity Church and would sometimes celebrate liturgies at Maryhouse and St. Joseph House.

Janet Kalven, a long-time member of the Grail and a founding member of Grailville, is an educator, conference coordinator, and community activist. She is the author of a number of books, the most recent being *Women Breaking Boundaries, A Grail Journey, 1940–1995*.

Mary Lathrop first arrived as a volunteer at the New York Catholic Worker in 1959 and remains a devoted member of the Catholic Worker family.

Tom Lewis-Borbely is an artist who lives with his wife across the street from the Mustard Seed Catholic Worker in Worcester, Massachusetts. He was a member of the Catonsville Nine and Baltimore Four, two draft-file-burning actions during the Vietnam War.

Peter Lumsden met Karl Meyer in 1961 as a member of the British Team for the Moscow Peace March. Subsequently, he came to the United States and spent time at the New York house and in Tivoli. A resident of London, he is associated with Simon House and other activities in the Catholic Worker style.

Rosemary Lynch, O.F.S., of Las Vegas, Nevada, has worked for peace and justice for over fifty years, co-founding the Pace e Bene Center for Nonviolence in 1989. She was on the leadership team of the Franciscan Sisters from 1960 to 1977 and has served as a staff member of the Franciscan Center since that time.

Judith Malina, an anarchist, co-founded The Living Theatre in 1947 with her husband, Julian Beck, and she continues to direct and to act on both stage and screen. She was jailed with Dorothy during the civil defense protests.

Ed Marciniak was co-founder of the first Catholic Worker in Chicago. Author of five books, he continues his "vocation as a troublemaker" as president of the Institute of Urban Life in Chicago.

Chuck Matthei (1948–2002) was jailed for resistance during the Vietnam War and later lived at Tivoli. Until his recent death, he served as director of Equity Trust, Inc., an organization that "helps individuals, institutions, and government officials explore the web of relationships inherent in property."

Vincent Ferrer McAloon was host at the Notre Dame University Hospitality Center in Rome for many years. He provided lodging and other assistance to Dorothy during her several trips to Italy.

Agnes Bird McCormack has vivid memories of meeting Dorothy and becoming part of the early Worker. She served as Dorothy's secretary from 1938 to 1944 and continued to be close to the community until her 1958 marriage to fellow Worker Charles McCormack.

Kathleen McKenna and her husband, John, met Dorothy around 1965, when they visited her in New York just before founding Haley House in Boston. "Providence in the form of a working husband and generous children" has enabled Kathe to stay involved as a Worker for thirty-six years and to "grapple with all the daunting Catholic Worker questions about style and mission."

Richard McSorley, S.J. (1914–2002), was director of the Center for Peace Studies at Fordham University. He helped to found several Catholic Worker houses in Washington, D.C.

Katherine Moos Mella learned about the Catholic Worker from her mother, who subscribed to the paper. A fine soprano, she went to the Worker in New York and there met her husband, John. After their marriage in 1938 they returned to Chicago, where they raised eight children.

Karl Meyer has been actively involved with the Catholic Worker since the day in 1957 when he met Dorothy Day and Ammon Hennacy and went to jail with them for thirty days. He was householder of St. Stephen's House of Hospitality in Chicago from 1958 to 1971, and he now practices the "green revolution" at the CW-affiliated Greenlands community in Nashville, Tennessee.

Chris Montesano came to the New York Catholic Worker on First Street in 1968. In 1969 he spent a number of months helping Dorothy edit issues of the *Catholic Worker*. He founded the Catholic Worker Farm in Sheep Ranch, California, with his wife, and there he makes candles and helps to give retreats for persons with AIDS.

Joan Montesano came in 1971 to Martin de Porres House, the Catholic Worker in San Francisco. She and Chris married in 1972, and they have four children. After many years of part-time social work, she now works full time at Sheep Ranch Farm, helping people with developmental disabilities and those with AIDS.

Nina Polcyn Moore met Dorothy while Nina was a student at Marquette University, and the two became lifelong friends, often traveling together. After a summer in New York, Nina helped to start Holy Family House in Milwaukee. For many years she was owner-manager of St. Benet Shop in Chicago, a store specializing in Catholic books and religious art.

Catherine Morris met her husband, Jeff Dietrich, while volunteering at the Los Angeles Catholic Worker soup kitchen. They have been the mainstays of that large house ever since. Catherine shared quarters with Dorothy Day during her last imprisonment.

Rosemary Morse (1923–1999) taught clerical subjects to disadvantaged young women through the University of the Streets on the Lower East Side of New York. In retirement, she helped keep in good repair the Staten Island beach bungalow in which Dorothy Day spent much time in her later years.

Marion Moses, M.D., worked closely with César Chávez and was Dorothy's doctor at the end of her life. Marion is director of the Pesticide Education Center in San Francisco.

Justine L'Esperance Murphy (1917–1989) married Lou Murphy, founder of the first Detroit Catholic Worker. Together they raised six children and operated two houses of hospitality and a soup kitchen.

Pat Murray found the *Catholic Worker* in a public library in Erie, Pennsylvania, when he was fifteen and "a budding socialist." He shared it with Mary, his high-school sweetheart, whom he later married, and they both became part of the Worker and related movements for their entire lives.

Sister Teresa Murray is a Sister of the Good Shepherd in Manhattan. She helped Dorothy to open Maryhouse and was a founder of Cor Maria for homeless women.

Jeannette Noel was the "mother" of the House of Ammon Catholic Worker in Hubbardston, Massachusetts, before coming to Maryhouse in New York. For years she managed the mailing list for the *Catholic Worker*.

David J. O'Brien is director of the Center for Religion, Ethics and Culture and Loyola Professor of Roman Catholic History at the College of the Holy Cross in Worcester, Massachusetts.

Anne Perkins is a "fellow traveler" of the Catholic Worker and a long-term admirer of Dorothy Day.

Julian Pleasants, now professor emeritus of chemistry at Notre Dame, opened the South Bend Catholic Worker in 1941, while still a student at the university. His wife, **Mary Jane,** was one of the early members of the Grail in the United States.

Chuck Quilty is a long-time Catholic Worker/peace activist from Rock Island, Illinois. Most recently he co-founded and is an active member of Voices in the Wilderness: A Campaign to End the UN/US Economic Sanctions against the People of Iraq.

Helen Caldwell Day Riley trained as a nurse at Harlem Hospital and worked with Dorothy Day after becoming a Catholic. She established Blessed Martin House of Hospitality in Memphis, Tennessee, an experience she chronicled in *Not without Tears.*

Nancy Roberts is a professor of journalism at the University of Minnesota. She has published several books on Dorothy Day and the Catholic Worker.

Beth Rogers is a long-time Catholic Worker from Manhattan, using her warm interpersonal skills at Peter Maurin Farm on Staten Island and contributing editorial services and reviews to the *Catholic Worker.*

Terry Rogers is a community health nurse in New York City who was at St. Joseph House from 1971 to 1972. She was a chalice bearer at Dorothy's funeral.

Kathleen Rumpf met Dorothy Day after moving to the Catholic Worker in 1971. She lived for ten years in New York City and Tivoli and then at Viva House in Baltimore. After many years in what Kathleen called "the front lines," she became an active resister and since then has been arrested at the Pentagon, the "Blight House," Griffiss Air Force Base, and the School of the Americas (now WHISC). She is currently in jail ministry with the Catholic Worker in Syracuse.

Patricia Rusk (1928–1999) came to the Worker in the mid-1950s. In her last years she lived in one of the Catholic Worker beach cottages at Spanish Camp on Staten Island and was involved in the campaign to save them from demolition. She is buried in Resurrection Cemetery, close to Dorothy's grave.

Jane Sammon first learned of the Catholic Worker from her father, who was active in the Association of Catholic Trade Unionists (ACTU). She came to Maryhouse in 1972 and stayed.

Ed Sanders was an active poet in the counter-cultural world of the Lower East Side in the 1960s and was sometimes seen around the Catholic Worker. His recent work includes *Chekhov* (1995) and *1968: A History in Verse*, which mixes memoir, anecdote, and factual research.

Dan Shay met Dorothy Day in 1960 through Lou and Justine Murphy of the Detroit Catholic Worker. He, too, opened a Catholic Worker in that city, but for the last thirty years he and his wife, Rosalie, have lived in Santa Rosa, California, where he volunteers at an interfaith homeless shelter and is active in his parish.

Tina Sipula founded Clare House of Hospitality in 1978 in Bloomington, Illinois, and the soup kitchen, Loaves and Fishes, in 1983.

Robert Steed became a Catholic in 1949 and spent some time with the Trappists in Kentucky before "gravitating to the Worker, which seemed the logical thing to do." He now sees himself as nonreligious and slightly conservative, what "Ammon Hennacy would call 'a pipsqueak.'"

Walter Stojanowski was the proprietor of the Beachcomber Hotel, across the street from Dorothy Day's Staten Island cottages on Poillon Avenue. Dorothy would often stop at the hotel for a glass of wine and a chat.

Bob Tavani "wandered into the New York Catholic Worker after the chaos of the sixties. The movement still influences how I see the world." He has worked the last twenty years as a counselor in Minnesota.

Brian Terrell lived at the New York Catholic Worker from 1975 to 1979. He has since "retired to obscurity on a small farm in far-off Maloy, Iowa," where he and his wife, Betsy Keenan, raise children and goats and spread the Catholic Worker message at Strangers and Guests Catholic Worker.

Jack Thornton was at the Catholic Worker from 1938 to 1948, spending a year at the Philadelphia Catholic Worker and then nine on Mott Street in New York. He graduated from Fordham while at the Worker and then farmed in Pennsylvania for fifteen years before moving to Oregon. His granddaughter Ruby Nichols spent two months at the New York house in 1999.

Ed Turner came to the Worker as a volunteer in 1953 and lived at Peter Maurin Farm until leaving to teach in Catholic schools in 1957. He married Johannah Hughes and they have an adult son, Thomas. Both Ed and Johannah contributed many insights that helped my research.

Johannah Hughes Turner is a "birthright" Catholic Worker. Daughter of a CW marriage, she lived at the Worker with her mother, Marge Hughes, when she was a child and also spent time at Tivoli. Now a paralegal, she lives in Charleston, West Virginia.

Louis Vitale, O.F.M., is a social activist and a pastor, a professor of religion, and one of the founders of the Nevada Desert Experience that began the present-day protest of nuclear testing in Nevada. He is now part of the Pace e Bene Center for Nonviolence.

Jean Walsh received her R.N. from Mt. Saint Vincent's College. After she met Dorothy Day, she was spending so much of her time at the Worker that Dorothy asked her to join the community.

Dale Wiehoff met Dorothy Day in 1966 when he was a high school student in St. Cloud, Minnesota. He went on to farm in Wisconsin until 1985, then moved to New York to work for the National Lawyers Guild for ten years before returning to Minnesota. He now works for the Institute for Agriculture and Trade Policy.

Jim Wilson, Catholic Worker, peacemaker, and war resister, currently lives in upstate New York and is the director of an organization providing services to people with disabilities and their families. In 1965 Jim was among the first to burn his draft card in opposition to the war in Vietnam. He served twenty-three months in federal prison for refusing to report for induction.

Gordon Zahn was a conscientious objector during World War II. A cofounder of Pax Christi, he published *The Camp Simon Story* and *In Solitary Witness: The Life and Death of Franz Jagerstatter.*

Joe and Mary Alice Zarrella were pioneer Catholic Workers. After their marriage they moved to Tell City, Indiana, Alice's hometown, where they hosted Dorothy Day on frequent visits, raised a family, and continued their priorities in hospitality, labor, and social justice. Joe is a master storyteller; Mary Alice "keeps him honest."

Index of Names

References in bold face indicate quotations.